The Incredible Internet Guide™ for

TREKKERS

The Complete Guide to Everything Star Trek Online

By James R. Flowers Jr.

Cover Art by Gerry Kissell

©2000 By James R. Flowers Jr. &
Facts on Demand Press
1971 E Fifth Street, Suite 101
Tempe, AZ 85281
(800) 929-3811
www.incredibleguides.com

The Incredible Internet Guide™ for Trekkers
The Complete Guide to Everything Star Trek Online
2000 Revised Reprint Edition

©2000 By James R. Flowers Jr. and Facts on Demand Press
1971 E Fifth Street, Suite 101
Tempe, AZ 85281
(800) 929-3811

ISBN 1-889150-11-8
Graphic Design by Robin Fox & Associates
Cover Art by Gerry Kissell
Edited by James R. Flowers

Cataloging-in-Publication Data

>   Flowers, James R. (James Robert), 1973-
>   The incredible Internet guide for Trekkers :
>   the Complete guide to everything Star Trek online /
>   by James R. Flowers ; cover art by Gerry Kissell. -- 1st ed.
>   p. cm. -- (The incredible internet guide)
>   ISBN: 1-889150-11-8
>
>   1. Star Trek television programs--Computer
>   network resources. 2. Star Trek films--Computer
>   network resources. 3. Web sites--Directories.
>   I. Title.
>
>   PN1992.8.S74F66 1999
>   791.45'75'0973
>
>   QBI99-5000411

Star Trek®, Star Trek: The Next Generation®, Star Trek: Deep Space Nine®, Star Trek: First Contact®, Star Trek: Insurrection®, and Star Trek: Voyager®, et al. are registered trademarks of Paramount Pictures registered in the United States Patent and Trademark Office.

This book was in no way authorized, sanctioned, endorsed, or produced by Paramount Pictures or any of its employees.

To Jim & Virginia Flowers
-- the best parents in the universe.

Contents

Star Trek Fun, Games & Roleplaying 135

Reading About Star Trek 145

Finding More Star Trek Online 167

Building Your Own Star Trek Site 179

Star Trek Science & Technology 183

Star Trek Aliens Online 191

Star Trek Site Profiles 209

Find out more about some of the sites listed in this book, including whether or not they offer graphics, audio, video, chat, and more!

Stardate Listing 277

Want to organize your Star Trek collection? This section presents a list of stardates from the Star Trek novels, comics, series, and films in chronological order.

Introduction

To Boldly Go . . . Online

The Internet has been documented and explored just about as well *as Star Trek: Voyager*'s Delta Quadrant. In other words, very little. Experts estimate that over 50% of the World Wide Web remains uncharted by the major search engines. That's a big black hole.

It is virtually impossible to know the location, content and source of every web page in existence. However, the Incredible Internet Guide series aims to plot a course through the nebulous Web, straight to what you want.

The Incredible Internet Guide for Trekkers collects over 2000 of the best and brightest stars in the Star Trek online universe. Each web page is categorized by its content and what it has to offer.

We've got episode guides, galleries, roleplaying games, aliens, technology, newsgroups, chat rooms, e-zines, software and a cargo bay full of other fun stuff between the covers of this book. All you need is this book, an Internet connection, and a love of Star Trek.

Using your web browser and these pages, you'll visit strange new worlds. You can learn to speak Klingon at the Klingon Language Institute (www.kli.org), review every outfit ever worn by Voyager's Kes at a web site called Style Ocampa (www.geocities.com/Area51/Corridor/6466/Ocampa.html), read the latest Trek news at Trek Today (www.trektoday.com), and much, much more.

You may be asking yourself, "Can't I just use a search engine and find the same stuff?" The answer is "No." Most search engines and webmasters do not register deep links (pages beneath the main or entry page of a site) with search engines, making them "unsearchable." With the *Incredible Internet Guide to Trekkers*, we've logged these pages separately, so that you can go straight to the John Doe's Screensavers page without having to click your way through John Doe's Star Trek Home Page.

In addition, there are thousands of search engines, and no webmaster registers his or her site with every single engine. In compiling the data for this book, we did not rely on a single search engine. Rather, we used *many* search engines, link lists, directories, webrings, word-of-mouth, news articles and more to find what we thought were the best Trek sites in the galaxy.

We don't want you to have to spend your Internet time searching -- we want you to spend your time online having fun. Rather than clicking on the "Untitled Star Trek Page" links you might find at a search engine, with this book in your hands, you can spend the day chatting with other Trek fans, learning how to speak Klingon, playing Trek games, and checking out the latest Trek news. We're organized so that you don't have to be.

Using this Book is as Easy as 1 - 2 - 3

1

First, decide who or what you are looking for. Then, search the Quick Find on the inside front cover. Or simply browse the chapters.

> ➢ *If you're looking for a web site for a person in a particular movie, look in the first chapter -- Cast & Characters.*

> ➢ *If you're looking for activities, check out the Lifestyle chapter.*

> ➢ *If you want to talk online about your interests, see the chapter called Discussion.*

2

Once you find the page number for a section that interests you, turn to that section and read through the list of sites and their descriptions. Or simply browse them all.

3

To get more information on a site, look it up in the back half of the book (where web sites are listed in alphabetical order, like a dictionary)
                              ~Or~
Go online and type in the URL of the site you want to see.

A big question is: are web sites listed under more than one chapter and category? The answer is: do tribbles multiply? Of course! There are many sites that are listed under more than one category. For instance, the Doctor Bashir Newsgroup appears in the Cast & Characters chapter, underneath the heading "Julian Bashir/Siddig El Faddil," but it also appears in the Discussion Chapter as part of the "Newsgroups" list.

If you are new on the Web, you'll soon discover that there's one basic truth about the Internet clickstream: there are a lot of different things that can be found on a Star Trek web site. So, in **the second half** of the *Incredible Internet Guide for Trekkers* you'll find an alphabetical listing of sites that merit additional description – over 260 of them. Here, each site has its URL, a description of what's on that site, and icons to show you at a glance what the site has to offer. So, if you want to know ahead of time what to expect at a site, read the site's profile.

In this book, there are images that are clearly screen captures. Other images were plucked from fans' web sites. These are presented as examples of what you'll see on your computer screen in order to help you find your way around the Internet and show you what you might come across online.

I can't find a page -- what's wrong?

There are a number of things you should be aware of, which this book has no control over. First, some web sites simply "die" off – disappear. Also, web sites do change addresses – they move around. Generally, the page's webmaster will set up a link that takes you to the new location, but not always.

Some sites are only accessible through their main page. One way to try to find a site that won't open is to "truncate" the URL. This is done by deleting the last section of the address. For example, if www.brbpub.com/iig/startrek would not open for you, then try using only www.brbpub.com/iig as the address. Once you are at the "main page" or an "index page," you should then be able to use links to navigate to the specific page you need.

Keeping the Star Trek universe safe for children.

When we found a site that we felt had slightly objectionable material, we marked it in as having "adult content" in the profiles. In order to protect your children from objectionable material, you may wish to visit and use a "child protection" software site, such as popular and effective NetNanny (www.netnanny.com) and CYBERsitter (www.cybersitter.com).

How to save something off a web site onto your computer

There are a number of ways to do this – downloading, screen capture, etc.

To download an item, simply right click (using your right mouse button) on the link to the file. Then choose "Save target as. . ."

To capture a screen, simply press the Alt key simultaneously with the Print Screen button. Then, you must open a word processing document (or something comparable) and paste your capture, and then save the file.

To use an image as wallpaper, right click on it and choose "Set as wallpaper."

To copy/paste text, use your mouse to simply highlight the area you want. Then, choose copy from the Edit menu of your browser, and then choose paste from the Edit menu of your word processing program.

To save a web page's text and/or links, choose "Save file as . . ." from your browser's File menu. You can save the page as plain text (which will eliminate all graphics and links), or you can save it as HTML (which will retain the links if you open it in a program capable of viewing HTML files).

Remember, too, that when you find a site you like and you want to return to it later, use the "Bookmarks" (on Netscape Navigator) or "Favorites" (on Internet Explorer) to remember the site location for you. We suggest that you create an exclusive Star Trek folder in your Bookmarks or Favorites just for your Star Trek sites.

How do you write to us?

We'd certainly like to hear from you, and we'd be especially interested in hearing about anything new or original regarding Star Trek on the Internet. We're not too excited about new web pages that consist mainly of links to other sites. There are plenty of these already. Star Trek fan fiction sites are especially interesting as are sites that have original or derivative artwork, or even rare pictures or merchandise. Sites with sound or video clips are also of interest to us.

Additionally, if you find an error in this edition of the *Incredible Internet Guide for Trekkers,* feel free to e-mail us a correction.

Our e-mail address is `Trek_Changes@klingons.zzn.com`

Sorry, we cannot respond to all e-mail, but we especially like to hear good ideas and good words about Star Trek and our book.

Visit the *Incredible Internet Guide for Trekkers* online

Visit the web site for the *Incredible Internet Guide for Trekkers* at www.incredbielquides.com. You will find interesting Star Trek stuff, including a place to sign up for your own Klingons E-mail address and a message board. Our web site also links to the *Incredible Internet Guide to Star Wars* and other titles in the Incredible Internet Guide Series.

STAR TREK
Cast &
Characters

Whether you want to find out more about Majel Barrett-Roddenberry, Marc Alaimo, Jeri Ryan, George Takei, Patrick Stewart or some other Star Trek star there is a site out there for you. Use this chapter to uncover the acting credits of your favorite Trek cast member, join his or her official fan club, or simply profess your love for him or her. Follow these links to the stars!

Star Trek (The Original Series)

Chekov/Walter Koenig

Walter Koenig is no stranger to the sci-fi world. Though he started as a Russian on the original Star Trek series (amidst the Cold War no less!), he has gone on to write comic books and play the popular Agent Bester on Babylon 5.

All-Movie Guide: Walter Koenig
http://allmovie.com/cg/x.dll?UID=10:49:42|PM&p=avg&sql=B38937

Chekov's Log
www.sentinelguide.com/chekov/index.shtml

Computer Core Dump: Chekov
www.ccdump.org/chekov.html

Good Things Come in Small Packages: A Pavel Chekov Page
www.angelfire.com/fl/pavchekov

Internet Movie Database: Walter Koenig
http://us.imdb.com/M/person-exact?+Koenig,+Walter

Mr. Chekov Drinking Game
www.geocities.com/Hollywood/Hills/6132/drink.htm

Mr. Chekov Page
www.geocities.com/Hollywood/Hills/6132

Official Walter Koenig Web Site, The
www.walterkoenig.com

Russian Inventions: An Ensign Chekov Page
www.fortunecity.com/tattooine/blish/0

Star Trek Character Gallery: Chekov
http://members.easyspace.com/stcg/chekov.html

Teegar Taylor's Mr. Chekov Page
www.geocities.com/Hollywood/Hills/6132

WalterKoenig.Com - The Official Walter Koenig Web Site
www.walterkoenig.com

Warped Factors: A Neurotic's Guide to the Universe
http://hometown.aol.com/Assimiltr/warped.html

Yahoo! Clubs: Chekov's Fan Club!
http://clubs.yahoo.com/clubs/chekovsfanclub

James T. Kirk/William Shatner

One of the most often imitated actors, William Shatner has extended his career beyond that of Captain Kirk. He's hosted Rescue 911, starred in TJ Hooker and written a series of TekWar novels. Thus, it's not surprising that Shatner has quite a few web sites devoted to him.

All-Movie Guide: William Shatner
http://allmovie.com/cg/x.dll?UID=10:51:20|PM&p=avg&sql=B111030

Bring Back Kirk!
www.bringbackkirk.com

Captain Kirk Page, The
www.geocities.com/Area51/Rampart/4537/kirk.html

Computer Core Dump: Kirk
www.ccdump.org/Kirk.html

Hollywood Online - Movie People Database: William Shatner
http://moviepeople.hollywood.com/people.asp?p_id=P111030

Interactive Kirk Novels, The
http://books.dreambook.com/phineasbog/kirkbook.html

Internet Movie Database: William Shatner
http://us.imdb.com/M/person-exact?+Shatner,+William

Kirk Mail (@kirk.zzn.com)
http://kirk.zzn.com

KirkChat Live Chat
www.geocities.com/Area51/Rampart/4537/live.htm

Lycos Celebrity Guide: William Shatner
www.lycos.com/entertainment/celebrities/celebs/Shatner_William.html

Official William Shatner Web Site
www.williamshatner.com

Punch Captain Kirk
www.well.com/user/vanya/kirk.html

ScienceFiction.Com: William Shatner
www.sciencefiction.com/stars/sws.htm

Shatner.Com: The Official Worldwide Fan Club
www.shatner.com

Six Degrees of William Shatner!
www.geocities.com/Area51/Rampart/4537/6degree.html

Star Trek Character Gallery: Kirk
http://members.easyspace.com/stcg/kirk.html

Star Trek Continuum: Kirk
www.startrekcontinuum.com/tos/quadrant.asp?ssector=personnel.asp&ID=23446

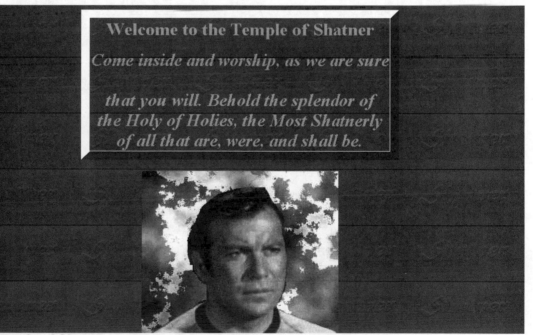

Welcome to the Temple of Shatner

Come inside and worship, as we are sure

that you will. Behold the splendor of the Holy of Holies, the Most Shatnerly of all that are, were, and shall be.

Temple of Shatner
http://comp.uark.edu/~breed/shatner.html

Top Infinite Reasons Kirk is Better Than Picard, The
www.geocities.com/Area51/Rampart/4537/krkbest.html

TV Now: William Shatner TV Schedule
www.tv-now.com/stars/shatner.html

William Shatner Fan Club
http://users.aol.com/maxnova/shatner.htm

Janice Rand/Grace Lee Whitney

As Janice Rand, Grace Lee Whitney appeared in quite a few episodes of the original Trek television series, Star Trek III: The Search for Spock, and in an episode of Star Trek: Voyager. Now, the actress has created her own Trek-inspired musical recordings. To find out more about Grace Lee Whitney and Yeoman Rand, visit these sites.

All-Movie Guide: Grace Lee Whitney
http://allmovie.com/cg/x.dll?UID=10:49:42|PM&p=avg&sql=B76039

Curt Danhauser's Guide to Star Trek Excelsior: Janice Rand
http://www1.ridgecrest.ca.us/~curtdan/Excelsior/SuluPages.cgi?FILE=Rand

Grace Lee Whitney Official Autograph Site
www.graceleewhitney.tf

Grace Lee Whitney Page (Official)
http://members.aol.com/starparty/glw_index.html

International Federation of Trekkers: Excelsior Campaign
http://excelsior.iftcommand.com

Internet Movie Database: Grace Lee Whitney
http://us.imdb.com/M/person-exact?Whitney%2C+Grace+Lee

Star Trek Character Gallery: Yeoman Rand
http://members.easyspace.com/stcg/rand.html

Star Trek Excelsior
http://www1.ridgecrest.ca.us/~curtdan/Excelsior/SuluPages.cgi?FILE=Main

McCoy/DeForest Kelly

Affectionately referred to as "Bones," DeForest Kelley's Dr. McCoy made up one third of the principal trio of the original Star Trek series (Kirk, Spock, and McCoy). Though the talented and charismatic Kelly has passed away, his memory lives on the World Wide Web.

All-Movie Guide: DeForest Kelley
http://allmovie.com/cg/x.dll?UID=10:49:42|PM&p=avg&sql=B37451

Computer Core Dump: McCoy
www.ccdump.org/McCoy.html

Deforest Kelley - Just An Old Country Doctor
http://members.tripod.com/~Nimoy_Kelley/kelley.html

DeForest Kelley Mailing List
www.kilroywashere.com/sarah/list.htm

Deforest Kelley Page, The
www.tu-berlin.de/~gruhlke/forum/deforest

FAQ: DeForest Kelley
www.kilroywashere.com/sarah/faq.htm

Internet Movie Database: DeForest Kelly
http://us.imdb.com/M/person-exact?+Kelley,+DeForest

Official DeForest Kelley Web Site, The
www.deforestkelley.org

Official DeForest Kelley Web Site, The: Sounds
www.kilroywashere.com/sarah/sounds.htm

Star Trek Character Gallery: Dr. McCoy
http://members.easyspace.com/stcg/mccoy.html

William Shatner Connection: DeForest Kelley
www.shatner.com/connection/kelley99.shtml

Montgomery Scott/James Doohan

James Doohan's character, Chief Engineer Montgomery Scott has become forever a part of US pop culture lingo with the phrase, "Beam me up, Scotty." You can "transport" to sites devoted to the lovable Scotty and his alter ego James Doohan by visiting the sites listed here.

All-Movie Guide: James Doohan
http://allmovie.com/cg/x.dll?UID=10:49:42|PM&p=avg&sql=B19684

Computer Core Dump: Montgomery Scott
www.ccdump.org/scotty.html

Internet Movie Database: James Doohan
http://us.imdb.com/Name?Doohan,+James

Rice Chemical Engineering - Faculty & Staff: Montgomery Scott
www.ruf.rice.edu/~che/fun/doohan.html

Star Trek Character Gallery: Montgomery Scott
http://members.easyspace.com/stcg/scott.html

Star Trek: TNG: Cast Photographs: James Doohan
www.daviestrek.com/trek/tng/jamesdoohan.htm

Nurse Chapel/Majel Barrett Roddenberry

See the Lwaxana Troi list in the Other Characters section of this chapter.

Spock/Leonard Nimoy

As Spock, Leonard Nimoy became almost synonymous with pointy ears. His phrase "Live long and prosper" and his trademark hand signal have infiltrated American culture. But Leonard Nimoy is more than Spock. He's directed feature films, written books and recorded albums. To find out more about this multi-talented star, check out these web sites.

A Quote from Mr. Spock
www.cs.ubc.ca/cgi-bin/nph-spock

Alien Voices (I)
http://alienvoices.com

Alien Voices (II)
http://members.tripod.com/~JohndeLancie/jdlav.html

All-Movie Guide: Leonard Nimoy
http://allmovie.com/cg/x.dll?UID=10:49:42|PM&p=avg&sql=B104553

All-Music Guide: Leonard Nimoy
http://allmusic.com/cg/x.dll?UID=10:49:42|PM&p=amg&sql=BP||||24
674

Ambassador Spock's Logical Sci-Fi Picks Ring: Sites List
www.webring.org/cgi-bin/webring?ring=logic;list

Computer Core Dump: Spock
www.ccdump.org/spock.html

Illogical Spock
http://izan.simplenet.com/illspock.htm

In Search of Middle C: The Music of Leonard Nimoy
www.calweb.com/~ejr/spock_sings.html

Internet Movie Database: Leonard Nimoy
http://us.imdb.com/M/person-exact?+Nimoy,+Leonard

Leonard Nimoy Albums Page
www.geocities.com/Hollywood/Set/1931/records.html

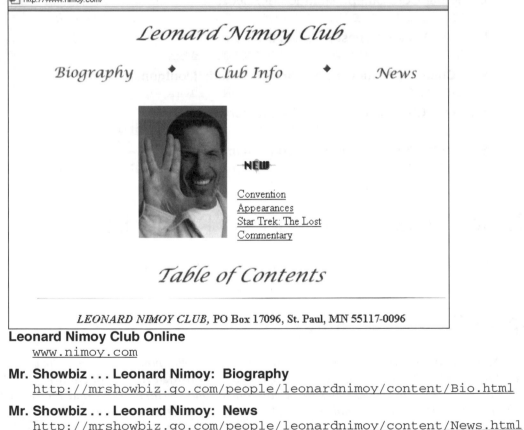

Leonard Nimoy Club Online
www.nimoy.com

Mr. Showbiz . . . Leonard Nimoy: Biography
http://mrshowbiz.go.com/people/leonardnimoy/content/Bio.html

Mr. Showbiz . . . Leonard Nimoy: News
http://mrshowbiz.go.com/people/leonardnimoy/content/News.html

ScienceFiction.Com: Leonard Nimoy
www.sciencefiction.com/stars/sln.htm

Spock Mail (@spock.zzn.com)
http://spock.zzn.com

Spock Webring: Sites List
www.webring.org/cgi-bin/webring?ring=spock;list

Spock's Pages
http://ourworld.compuserve.com/homepages/SpocksPages

Star Trek Character Gallery: Spock
http://members.easyspace.com/stcg/spock.html

Star Trek: TNG: Cast Photographs: Leonard Nimoy
www.daviestrek.com/trek/tng/leonardnimoy.htm

T'Pring's Spock Page
http://members.tripod.com/~tpring

TV Now: Leonard Nimoy TV Schedule
www.tv-now.com/stars/nimoy.html

Sulu/George Takei

In addition to being a part of the Enterprise's crew, Hikaru Sulu went on to command the USS Excelsior, as seen in an episode of Voyager. Fans on the Web are campaigning for Takei to captain his own Trek series. For more on the actor, his role, and his ship visit these sites.

All-Movie Guide: George Takei
http://allmovie.com/cg/x.dll?UID=10:49:42|PM&p=avg&sql=B69644

Computer Core Dump: Sulu
www.ccdump.org/sulu.html

GeorgeTakei.Com - Official George Takei Web Site
www.georgetakei.com

George Takei
www.geocities.com/Area51/Labyrinth/8303/gt.html

George Takei Mailing List
www.onelist.com/subscribe/Takei

International Federation of Trekkers: Excelsior Campaign
http://excelsior.iftcommand.com

Internet Movie Database: George Takei
http://us.imdb.com/M/person-exact?Takei%2C+George

Star Trek Character Gallery: Sulu
http://members.easyspace.com/stcg/sulu.html

Star Trek Excelsior
http://www1.ridgecrest.ca.us/~curtdan/Excelsior/SuluPages.cgi?FILE=Main

Star Trek Excelsior: Excelsior Bridge
http://www1.ridgecrest.ca.us/~curtdan/Excelsior/SuluPages.cgi?FILE=Bridge

Star Trek Excelsior: Timeline
http://www1.ridgecrest.ca.us/~curtdan/Excelsior/SuluPages.cgi?FILE=Timeline

Yahoo! Clubs: Takei - A George Takei Fan Club
http://clubs.yahoo.com/clubs/takei

Uhura/Nichelle Nichols

As an African-American, the presence of Uhura on the original series' bridge was controversial. Nonetheless, Nichelle Nichols persevered as Uhura inspiring others, such as Whoopi Goldberg, to get into the entertainment business. These are some of the best sites devoted to Nichols and Uhura.

All-Movie Guide: Nichelle Nichols
http://allmovie.com/cg/x.dll?UID=10:49:42|PM&p=avg&sql=B52569

Computer Core Dump: Uhura
www.ccdump.org/uhura.html

Internet Movie Database: Nichelle Nichols
http://us.imdb.com/M/person-exact?+Nichols,+Nichell

Star Trek Character Gallery: Uhura
http://members.easyspace.com/stcg/uhura.html

Uhura - Star Trek Page
http://users.aol.com/jabron/uhura.htm

Uhura.Com
www.uhura.com

Star Trek: The Next Generation

Beverly Crusher/Gates McFadden

Gates McFadden's Dr. Crusher appeared in only six of the seven seasons of Star Trek: The Next Generation. The producers dropped her from the second season in favor of Diana Muldaur. Nonetheless, the fans demanded that Gates return, and her character's suggested relationship with Captain Picard has been the source of much fan discussion.

AAA Star Trek: Gates McFadden
http://eonmagazine.com/startrek/gates%20main.html

All-Movie Guide: Gates McFadden
http://allmovie.com/cg/x.dll?UID=10:51:20|PM&p=avg&sql=B47356

Andrew Tong's Gates McFadden
www.ugcs.caltech.edu/st-tng/cast/mcfadden.html

Bay's Picard/Crusher Stories
www.geocities.com/TelevisionCity/Stage/8486/Stories.html

Beverly Crusher WAV Files
www.geocities.com/Area51/Zone/7932

Chief Medical Officer Beverly H Crusher
www.geocities.com/Area51/Corridor/4891

Computer Core Dump: Crusher
www.ccdump.org/crusher.html

Dancing Doctor's Domain, The
www.lustchip.com/dancingdoctor

Federation Sound Archive: Crusher
www.domaindlx.com/timbo/crusher.html

Internet Movie Database: Gates McFadden
http://us.imdb.com/Name?McFadden,+Gates

Star Trek Character Gallery: Dr. Beverly Crusher
http://members.easyspace.com/stcg/crusher.html

Star Trek: TNG: Cast Photographs: Gates McFadden
www.daviestrek.com/trek/tng/gatesmcfadden.htm

Tales by Wolfen (Fan Fiction)
http://members.tripod.com/~wolf_fen/wolftales.htm

The Gallery (of Gates McFadden & Patrick Stewart)
www.geocities.com/Broadway/Wing/1796/index.html

Data/Brent Spiner

Taking the difficult role of an emotionless android, Brent Spiner captivated fans.   His character's constant efforts to understand humanity as well as Spiner's periodic appearances as other characters (Data's brother Lore and his maker -- Dr. Soong), stand out as an integral part of Star Trek: The Next Generation's success.   To read more about this fine actor, his character Data, and even his own album, visit the sites listed here.

All-Movie Guide: Brent Spiner
http://allmovie.com/cg/x.dll?UID=10:51:20|PM&p=avg&sql=B67254

All-Music Guide: Brent Spiner
http://allmusic.com/cg/x.dll?UID=10:51:20|PM&p=amg&sql=BP||||14885

Andrew Tong's Brent Spiner
www.ugcs.caltech.edu/st-tng/cast/spiner.html

AnneDroidz' Brent Page
http://members.aol.com/AnneDroidz/brent.html

Brent Spiner by Ozq
http://members.xoom.com/ozq2/main.htm

Brent Spiner Central
http://members.aol.com/soongme/index.htm

Brent Spiner Fan Page: Picture Collections
www.asahi-net.or.jp/~ti3y-itu/pictures.html

Brent Spiner Fan Page: Same Old BS - A Biography
http://members.aol.com/soongme/bio.htm

Brent Spiner Fanzine Information
http://world.std.com/~jhlee/bdft/fanzine.html

Brent Spiner Info Page
http://members.aol.com/BrentFemme/index.html

Brent Spiner Info Page: Lore Pics
http://members.aol.com/BrentFemme/lorepix.htm

Brent Spiner Newsgroup
alt.fan.brent-spiner

Brent Spiner Page
www.millennianet.com/lee/brentpage.html

Brent Spiner Page: Photos
www.millennianet.com/lee/brentphotos.html

Brentwatch
http://members.aol.com/Katherina1/brentwatch1.html

Computer Core Dump: Data
www.ccdump.org/data.html

Data & Tasha Fanfic Page, The
www.geocities.com/Area51/Stargate/1206

DataGurl's Brent Spiner
http://members.tripod.com/~datasgurl/spinerframe.html

Federation Sound Archive: Data
www.domaindlx.com/timbo/data.html

Friends of Brent Spiner (FOBS) Mailing List
www.spiner.org/community/maillist.htm

Friends of Brent Spiner (FOBS) Webring
http://members.xoom.com/ozq2/fobs.htm

Friends of Brent Spiner Webring: Sites List
www.webring.org/cgi-bin/webring?ring=fobs;list

Hollywood Online - Movie People Database: Brent Spiner
http://moviepeople.hollywood.com/people.asp?p_id=P|67254

Insufficient Data - A Brent Spiner Tribute Page
http://hometown.aol.com/marieutah/Brent-index.html

Internet Movie Database: Brent Spiner
http://us.imdb.com/Name?Spiner,+Brent

Ismaela's Unauthorized Brent Spiner Fan Page
www.geocities.co.jp/Broadway/1776

Ismaela's Unauthorized Brent Spiner Fan Page: Brent's Voice Files
www.geocities.co.jp/Broadway/1776/vozcarpe.html

Ismaela's Unauthorized Brent Spiner Fan Page: Fan Art
www.geocities.co.jp/Broadway/1776/cumple.html

Jaysha27's Brent Spiner & Star Trek Club Page
http://hometown.aol.com/jaysha27/club/index.htm

Laura's Brent Spiner Site
www.lustchip.com

Lieutenant Commander Data Ring: Sites List
www.webring.org/cgi-bin/webring?ring=ltcommdata;list

Mr. Showbiz . . . Brent Spiner
http://mrshowbiz.go.com/people/brentspiner

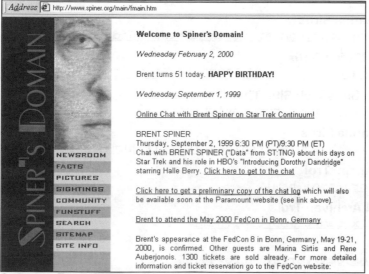

Spiner's Domain
www.spiner.org

Spiner's Domain: Brent Spiner Forum
http://apps.vantagenet.com/aforums/thread.asp?id=19971211163257

Spiner's Domain: Virtual Post Office
http://www3.all-yours.net/program/start20?write17400607

Spiners' Domain: Brent Spiner Techno Mixes
www.spiner.org/funstuff/techno.htm

Spiners' Doman: Brent Spiner FAQ
www.spiner.org/facts/stats.htm

Star Trek Character Gallery: Data
http://members.easyspace.com/stcg/data.html

Star Trek: TNG: Cast Photographs: Brent Spiner
www.daviestrek.com/trek/tng/brentspiner.htm

TV Now: Brent Spiner TV Schedule
www.tv-now.com/stars/spiner.html

Welcome, Brent Spiner Fans!
http://world.std.com/~jhlee/bdft/bdft.html

Worf's Star Trek Site: Ode to Spot
www.bazza.com/sj/trek/ode.html

Yahoo! Internet Life - Star Trek Special: The Dope on Data
www.zdnet.com/yil/content/mag/startrek/datanew.html

Yahoo! Internet Life: Star Trek Special: Spiner Speaks
www.zdnet.com/yil/content/mag/startrek/spiner9612a.html

Deanna Troi/Marina Sirtis

Marina Sirtis has the distinction of playing the first "ship's counselor" on Star Trek. Not only that, her character, Deanna Troi, was the first Betazoid ever seen in the Star Trek universe. Sirtis' emotionally moving performance along with Deanna's love triangles with other cast members (Riker and Worf), are two of the reasons Star Trek: The Next Generation is so much fun to watch.

AAA Star Trek: Marina Sirtis
http://eonmagazine.com/startrek/marina%20address.html

All-Movie Guide: Marina Sirtis
http://allmovie.com/cg/x.dll?UID=10:51:20|PM&p=avg&sql=B66014

Alternative Marina Sirtis Web Site, The
http://members.tripod.com/~msirtis

Andrew Tong's Marina Sirtis
www.ugcs.caltech.edu/st-tng/cast/sirtis.html

Computer Core Dump: Troi
www.ccdump.org/troi.html

Federation Sound Archive: Troi
www.domaindlx.com/timbo/troi.html

Forever Imzadi
www.geocities.com/Paris/Metro/4010

Hollywood Online - Movie People Database: Marina Sirtis
http://moviepeople.hollywood.com/people.asp?p_id=P|66014

Imzadi - Their Hearts Beat As One
http://members.xoom.com/invilil

Imzadi International Webring
http://people.delphi.com/dpj/ii_ra.htm

Imzadi International Webring: Sites List
www.webring.org/cgi-bin/webring?ring=imzadi;list

Imzadi Pictures
www.freespeech.org/feydreams/galle1.html

Infinitely Imzadi
www.geocities.com/Area51/Hollow/2955

Infinitely Imzadi: Fan Fiction
www.geocities.com/Area51/Hollow/2955/fanfic.htm

Infinitely Imzadi: Images of Imzadi
www.fortunecity.com/tattooine/pratchett/66/imzadicards.htm

Infinitely Imzadl: Images of Marina
www.geocities.com/Area51/Hollow/2955/marinag.htm

Infinitely Imzadi: Interviews
www.geocities.com/Area51/Hollow/2955/interviews.htm

Infinitely Imzadi: Marina Sirtis
www.geocities.com/Area51/Hollow/2955/marinasirtis.htm

Internet Movie Database: Marina Sirtis
http://us.imdb.com/Name?Sirtis,+Marina

Marina Sirtis Tribute Page
http://over.to/troilover

Riker/Troi Webring: Sites List
www.webring.org/cgi-bin/webring?ring=rtring;list

Star Trek Character Gallery: Troi
http://members.easyspace.com/stcg/troi.html

Star Trek: TNG: Cast Photographs: Marina Sirtis
www.daviestrek.com/trek/tng/marinasirtis.htm

Worf/Troi Domain, The
http://members.aol.com/reid756/wtdomain.html

Worf/Troi Homepage
www.geocities.com/Hollywood/Academy/4310

Worf/Troi Webring: Sites List
www.webring.org/cgi-bin/webring?ring=worftroi;list

Geordi Laforge/Levar Burton

Levar Burton's Geordi Laforge was the first Trek regular character to be handicapped. Besides being an excellent role model as Geordi, Levar's developed a fan following for his performances in Roots and Reading Rainbow. Discover more about this talented actor and Geordi using the sites listed here.

All-Movie Guide: LeVar Burton
http://allmovie.com/cg/x.dll?UID=10:51:20|PM&p=avg&sql=B9812

Andrew Tong's Levar Burton
www.ugcs.caltech.edu/st-tng/cast/burton.html

Computer Core Dump: LaForge
www.ccdump.org/laforge.html

Federation Sound Archive: LaForge
www.domaindlx.com/timbo/laforge.html

Internet Movie Database: Levar Burton
http://us.imdb.com/M/person-exact?+Burton,+LeVar

Star Trek Character Gallery: LaForge
http://members.easyspace.com/stcg/laforge.html

Star Trek: TNG: Cast Photographs: Levar Burton
www.daviestrek.com/trek/tng/levarburton.htm

Guinan/Whoopi Goldberg

Academy Award-winning actress Whoopi Goldberg was inspired by Nichelle Nichols, who played Uhura on the original Star Trek. As such, she was thrilled to play Guinan on Star Trek: The Next Generation. As part of a mysterious race, Guinan and her connection to Picard fascinated fans for many seasons. For more on this enjoyable character and actress, visit these sites.

All-Movie Guide: Whoopi Goldberg
http://allmovie.com/cg/x.dll?UID=10:51:20|PM&p=avg&sql=B27431

Federation Sound Archive: Guinan
www.domaindlx.com/timbo/guinan.html

History of Guinan, The
www.geocities.com/Area51/Chamber/2541/gstory.html

Internet Movie Database: Whoopi Goldberg
http://us.imdb.com/M/person-exact?+Goldberg,+Whoopi

Star Trek Character Gallery: Guinan
http://members.easyspace.com/stcg/guinan.html

Star Trek: TNG: Cast Photographs: Whoopi Goldberg
www.daviestrek.com/trek/tng/whoopigoldberg.htm

Whoopi Page, The
www.tu-berlin.de/~gruhlke/forum/whoopi

Jean-Luc Picard/Patrick Stewart

Boldly going where no man had gone before, Patrick Stewart played the first captain of the "next generation" of Star Trek series. Confronted with die-hard Kirk fans, Stewart forged ahead and created his own captain, aboard his own enterprise. In fact, the classically trained actor had no trouble garnering fans. His penchant for Shakespeare made Star Trek popular in academic circles as well. His popularity shows no signs of slowing down -- he's even been cast to play the telepathic mutant, Professor X in the upcoming X-Men film based on the comic book of the same name.

A Man I Call Friend - Patrick Stewart
http://members.tripod.com/~daisy1701dy/dyp.html

All-Movie Guide: Patrick Stewart
http://allmovie.com/cg/x.dll?UID=10:51:20|PM&p=avg&sql=B68265

Andrew Tong's Patrick Stewart
www.ugcs.caltech.edu/st-tng/cast/stewart.html

Bay's Picard/Crusher Stories
www.geocities.com/TelevisionCity/Stage/8486/Stories.html

CNN Showbiz: Let Picard be your guide to the universe
www.cnn.com/SHOWBIZ/9606/20/tech.guide/index.html

Complete Patrick Stewart Filmography, The
www.tu-berlin.de/~stewart-page/ps-film.html

Address 🅔 http://www.ccdump.org/picard.html

JEAN-LUC PICARD

Pictures:

STARFLEET PERSONNEL FILE -- Picard, Jean-Luc

Rank: Captain
Current assignment: Commander, U.S.S. Enterprise NCC-1701/E **Full Name:** Jean-Luc Picard
Date of birth: July 13, 2305
Place of birth: Labarre, France, Earth
Parents: Maurice and Yvette Picard
Education: Starfleet Academy, 2323-27
Marital status: Single
Children: None
Quarters: Formerly, Enterprise: Deck 9, Room 3601
Office: Enterprise: Deck 1 Ready Room, adjoining Main Bridge

Starfleet Career Summary

2333   Assigned as commander and first officer on USS Stargazer, later promoted to captain after death of his superior in battle

2355 -- Forced to abandon Stargazer after encounter with then-unknown Ferengi, with few casualties

Computer Core Dump: Picard
www.ccdump.org/picard.html

E! Online: Q&A with Patrick Stewart
www.eonline.com/Hot/Qa/Stewart

French Captain/Borg Newsgroup
alt.french.captain.borg.borg.borg

Hollywood Online - Movie People Database: Patrick Stewart
http://moviepeople.hollywood.com/people.asp?p_id=P|68265

Internet Movie Database: Patrick Stewart
http://us.imdb.com/Name?Stewart,+Patrick

Lycos Celebrity Guide: Patrick Stewart
www.lycos.com/entertainment/celebrities/celebs/Stewart_Patrick.html

Mr. Showbiz . . . Patrick Stewart
http://mrshowbiz.go.com/people/patrickstewart

Patrick & His Women!
http://members.easyspace.com/mejensen/patrick/patwomen.html

Patrick Stewart Online
www.tu-berlin.de/~stewart-page

Patrick Stewart Online: Interviews
www.tu-berlin.de/~stewart-page/interviews.html

Patrick Stewart Ring, The: Sites List
www.webring.org/cgi-bin/webring?ring=patrick_stewart;list

Patrick Stewart Tribute Page
http://members.tripod.com/~PatrickStewart/index.html

Pinch Captain Picard
www.geocities.com/Area51/Rampart/4537/pinch.html

Sexy Bald Captain Newsgroup
alt.sexy.bald.captain

Star Trek Character Gallery: Picard
http://members.easyspace.com/stcg/picard.html

Star Trek: TNG: Cast Photographs: Patrick Stewart
www.daviestrek.com/trek/tng/patrickstewart.htm

Tales by Wolfen (Fan Fiction)
http://members.tripod.com/~wolf_fen/wolftales.htm

The Gallery (of Gates McFadden & Patrick Stewart)
www.geocities.com/Broadway/Wing/1796/index.html

Top Infinite Reasons Kirk is Better Than Picard, The
www.geocities.com/Area51/Rampart/4537/krkbest.html

TV Now: Patrick Stewart TV Schedule
www.tv-now.com/stars/pstew.html

Kathryn Pulaski/Diana Muldaur

Diana Muldaur's Dr. Pulaski was a regular cast member for only one season of Star Trek: The Next Generation. Though her time in the Star Trek universe was brief, she was around long enough to develop a following. Visit these sites to learn more about Muldaur and Pulaski.

Internet Movie Database: Diana Muldaur
http://us.imdb.com/M/person-exact?+Muldaur,+Diana

Star Trek Character Gallery: Dr. Pulaski
http://members.easyspace.com/stcg/pulaski.html

Reginald Barclay/Dwight Schultz

As Reginald Barclay, Dwight Schultz showed us that although Starfleet's standards are high, not everyone who joins the crew of a starship performs like a well-oiled machine. Rather, Barclay's bumbling efforts to do a good job serving on the Enterprise made many an episode of Star Trek: The Next Generation worth watching.

All-Movie Guide: Dwight Schultz
http://allmovie.com/cg/x.dll?UID=10:51:20|PM&p=avg&sql=B63894

Internet Movie Database: Dwight Schultz
http://us.imdb.com/M/person-exact?+Schultz,+Dwight

Star Trek Character Gallery: Reginald Barclay
http://members.easyspace.com/stcg/barclay.html

Ro Laren/Michelle Forbes

As Ro Laren, Michelle Forbes joined the cast of Star Trek: The Next Generation as a recurring character. Forbes' Bajoran character was so popular that she was asked to become a regular on Deep Space Nine when it was being created, but she declined. Forbes has gone on to appear in films such as Kalifornia and series such as Homicide: Life on the Street. The following sites are devoted to Forbes and/or Ro Laren.

CJ Tassilo Michelle Forbes Home Page
www.physik.uni-regensburg.de/~krt04517/Forbes

Filk Tunes & Parodies
www.physik.uni-regensburg.de/~krt04517/Forbes/rofilk.html

Homicide: Michelle Forbes
www.nbc.com/homicide/presskit/pk_cox.html

Internet Movie Database: Michelle Forbes
http://us.imdb.com/M/person-exact?+Forbes,+Michelle

Michelle Forbes
www.kristoffer.com/forbes2.shtml

Michelle Forbes Central
www.jsp.umontreal.ca/~chabotma/Michelle.html

Star Trek Character Gallery: Ro Laren
http://members.easyspace.com/stcg/ro.html

Tasha Yar/Denise Crosby

Denise Crosby was one of the original cast members of Star Trek: The Next Generation. Killed off in the second season, she returned later as another character -- the first blonde Romulan! The new character was not popular with fans, and therefore did not return. Nonetheless, Crosby is still involved in the Trek universe -- she narrated the documentary Trekkies.

Bomis: Denise Crosby Ring
www.bomis.com/rings/denisecrosby

Celebrity Central: Denise Crosby
www.jalmon2.com/%7Edecrpg1.html

Data & Tasha Fanfic Page, The
www.geocities.com/Area51/Stargate/1206

Denise Crosby
www.geocities.com/Hollywood/9365/DeniseC.html

Denise Crosby Repository, The
www.stack.nl/~boris/Denise/denise.html

Denise Crosby Unofficial Fan Club
www.laughingstar.com/Denise_Crosby

Denise Crosby: Spanish Tribute
http://moviepeople.hollywood.com/people.asp?p_id=P|17807

E! Online: Denise Crosby
www.eonline.com/Facts/People/0,12,245,00.html

Federation Sound Archive: Tasha
www.domaindlx.com/timbo/tasha.html

Hollywood Online - Movie People Database: Denise Crosby
http://moviepeople.hollywood.com/people.asp?p_id=P|15880

Internet Movie Database: Denise Crosby
http://us.imdb.com/Name?Crosby,+Denise

Lieutenant Tasha Yar / Denise Crosby
http://physik.kfunigraz.ac.at/%7Ejom/yar/yar.htm

Star Trek Character Gallery: Denise Crosby
http://us.imdb.com/M/person-exact?Crosby%2C+Denise

Star Trek Character Gallery: Natasha Yar
http://members.easyspace.com/stcg/yar.html

Star Trek: TNG: Cast Photographs: Denise Crosby
www.daviestrek.com/trek/tng/DeniseCrosby.htm

Wesley Crusher/Wil Wheaton

Wil Wheaton became a teen idol after appearing on Star Trek: The Next Generation. However, the response to his character, Wesley Crusher, was a divided one. Some fans liked the character, others hated it. Nonetheless, Wil Wheaton was part of the Next Generation cast for over half of its run.

Anti-Wesley Crusher Newsgroup
alt.wesley.crusher.die.die.die

Cinnae's Wil Wheaton Page
http://meltingpot.fortunecity.com/belgium/49/wil.htm

Computer Core Dump: Wesley
www.ccdump.org/wcrusher.html

Die, Wesley Crusher, Die!
http://freespace.virgin.net/chris.robson/wes.htm

Federation Sound Archive: Wesley
www.domaindlx.com/timbo/wesley.html

Internet Movie Database: Wil Wheaton
http://us.imdb.com/M/person-exact?Wheaton,%20Wil

Kenny's Wil Wheaton Page
www.ndirect.co.uk/~kennymac

Star Trek Character Gallery: Wesley Crusher
http://members.easyspace.com/stcg/wesley.html

Star Trek: TNG: Cast Photographs: Wil Wheaton
www.daviestrek.com/trek/tng/wilwheaton.htm

Wil Wheaton
www.ymshomepage.com/yesterday/wheaton.html

Wil Wheaton Discussion Board, The
www.insidetheweb.com/mbs.cgi/mb129977

Wil Wheaton Photo Collection
www.geocities.com/Area51/5306

Wil Wheaton Picture Gallery
http://pics.teencelebsplus.com/wheaton/wheaton.html

Wil Wheaton Webring, The
http://meltingpot.fortunecity.com/belgium/49/wwwr.htm

William Riker/Jonathan Frakes

Jonathan Frakes' involvement with Star Trek is tremendous. Not only did he play the popular William Riker, second-in-command of the Enterprise on Star Trek: The Next Generation, he also directed two of the Star Trek feature films (First Contact and Insurrection). Plus, he got the opportunity to play a transporter-created duplicate of himself dubbed Thomas Riker on both Next Generation and Deep Space Nine. And, thanks to Q, he popped up on Voyager. Frakes loves Star Trek, and it shows. His involvement with the franchise will no doubt continue for a long time to come.

All-Movie Guide: Jonathan Frakes
http://allmovie.com/cg/x.dll?UID=10:51:20|PM&p=avg&sql=B24630

Andrew Tong's Jonathan Frakes
www.ugcs.caltech.edu/st-tng/cast/frakes.html

Computer Core Dump: Riker
www.ccdump.org/riker.html

Federation Sound Archive: Riker
www.domaindlx.com/timbo/riker.html

Forever Imzadi
www.geocities.com/Paris/Metro/4010

Hollywood Online - Movie People Database: Jonathan Frakes
http://moviepeople.hollywood.com/people.asp?p_id=P|24630

Imzadi - Their Hearts Beat As One
http://members.xoom.com/invilil

Imzadi International Webring
http://people.delphi.com/dpj/ii_ra.htm

Imzadi International Webring: Sites List
www.webring.org/cgi-bin/webring?ring=imzadi;list

Imzadi Pictures
www.freespeech.org/feydreams/galle1.html

Infinitely Imzadi
www.geocities.com/Area51/Hollow/2955

Infinitely Imzadi: Fan Fiction
www.geocities.com/Area51/Hollow/2955/fanfic.htm

Infinitely Imzadi: Images of Imzadi
www.fortunecity.com/tattooine/pratchett/66/imzadicards.htm

Infinitely Imzadi: Images of Jon
www.geocities.com/Area51/Hollow/2955/jong.htm

Infinitely Imzadi: Interviews
www.geocities.com/Area51/Hollow/2955/interviews.htm

Infinitely Imzadi: Jonathan Frakes
www.geocities.com/Area51/Hollow/2955/jonfrakes.htm

Infinitely Imzadi: William Thomas Riker
www.geocities.com/Area51/Hollow/2955/willriker.htm

Mr. Showbiz . . . Jonathan Frakes
http://mrshowbiz.go.com/people/jonathanfrakes

Riker/Troi Webring: Sites List
www.webring.org/cgi-bin/webring?ring=rtring;list

Star Trek Character Gallery: Riker
http://members.easyspace.com/stcg/riker.html

Star Trek: TNG: Cast Photographs: Jonathan Frakes
www.daviestrek.com/trek/tng/jonathanfrakes.htm

Worf/Michael Dorn

Michael Dorn's character Worf was promoted to Security Chief after the death of the character Tasha Yar. Along with this promotion, Dorn's visibility in Star Trek: The Next Generation increased, and soon, he became an incredibly popular character. His Klingon sense of humor and struggle to retain his honor has delighted fans of both the Next Generation and Deep Space Nine. In fact, Dorn has the distinction of being the only actor to be a regular cast member of more than one Star Trek series.

All-Movie Guide: Michael Dorn
http://allmovie.com/cg/x.dll?UID=10:51:20|PM&p=avg&sql=B19753

Andrew Tong's Michael Dorn
www.ugcs.caltech.edu/st-tng/cast/dorn.html

Computer Core Dump: Worf
www.ccdump.org/worf.html

Federation Sound Archive: Worf
www.domaindlx.com/timbo/worf.html

Hollywood Online - Movie People Database: Michael Dorn
http://moviepeople.hollywood.com/people.asp?p_id=P|19753

Internet Movie Database: Michael Dorn
http://us.imdb.com/Name?Dorn,+Michael

Star Trek Character Gallery: Worf
http://members.easyspace.com/stcg/worf.html

Worf & Jadzia - A Change of Heart
www.geocities.com/Area51/Vault/3063

Worf Mail (@worf.zzn.com)
http://worf.zzn.com

Worf's Different Looks
http://members.tripod.com/~ds9promenade/worf.html

Worf/Troi Domain, The
http://members.aol.com/reid756/wtdomain.html

Worf/Troi Homepage
www.geocities.com/Hollywood/Academy/4310

Worf/Troi Webring: Sites List
www.webring.org/cgi-bin/webring?ring=worftroi;list

Star Trek: Deep Space Nine

Benjamin Sisko/Avery Brooks

Avery Brooks has the distinction of being the first African-American captain of a Star Trek series. As Benjamin Sisko, he also became the Bajoran "emissary." Throughout the course of Deep Space Nine, Avery Brooks played both roles well and as such, his fans have developed some excellent sites to honor him.

Computer Core Dump: Sisko
www.ccdump.org/sisko.html

Star Trek Character Gallery: Captain Benjamin Sisko
http://members.easyspace.com/stcg/sisko.html

TV Now: Avery Brooks TV Schedule
www.tv-now.com/stars/avbrook.html

Dax (Jadzia & Ezri)/Terry Farell & Nicole de Boer

As a Trill, the character of Dax has lived through many lifetimes and with each came a new "host." During the course of Deep Space Nine, viewers got to know two of those hosts, played by Terry Farell (Jadzia) and Nicole de Boer (Ezri). Sites devoted to either and both of these lovely ladies are all over the 'Net.

AAA Star Trek: Terry Farrell
http://eonmagazine.com/startrek/terry%20Farrell%20Main.html

Computer Core Dump: Ezri Dax
www.ccdump.org/ezridax.html

Computer Core Dump: Jadzia Dax
www.ccdump.org/dax.html

Counselor's Personal Log (Ezri Dax Message Board)
www.insidetheweb.com/mbs.cgi/mb445254

Ezri Dax/Nicole deBouer Message Board
www.insidetheweb.com/mbs.cgi/mb146847

FedNet: Pictures: Deep Space Nine
www.geocities.com/Area51/Rampart/3219/FedNet/pics/3.html

Internet Movie Database: Nicole de Boer
http://us.imdb.com/Name?de+Boer,+Nicole

Internet Movie Database: Terry Farrell
http://us.imdb.com/Name?Farrell,+Terry

Jadzia Dax Memorial Ring
www.jdmemorial.tsx.org

Jadzia Dax Newsgroup
alt.fan.jadzia.dax.slug.slug.slug

Julian & Ezri Multimedia
http://members.tripod.com/~chrys42

Julian/Ezri Relationshippers
http://beam.to/julianezri

Julian/Ezri Relationshippers: Ezri Bio
www.geocities.com/Area51/Nova/2872/ezbio.html

Nicole deBoer - Spellbound
www.nikkideboer.com

Nicole deBoer - Spellbound: Articles & Interviews
www.nikkideboer.com/interviews.htm

Nicole deBoer - Spellbound: Gallery
www.nikkideboer.com/photos.htm

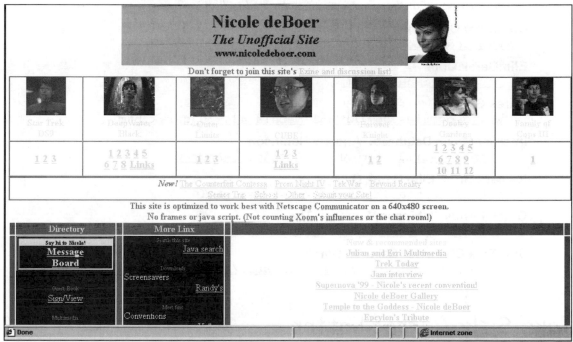

Nicole deBoer - The Unofficial Site
www.nicoledeboer.com

Nicole deBoer Adoration Page
www.geocities.com/Hollywood/Screen/6620/nicole

Nicole deBoer Appreciation Page
www.geocities.com/Hollywood/Mansion/2947

Nicole deBouer Fan Webring
http://members.xoom.com/scifioz/webring.htm

Nicole deBouer Fan Webrlng: Sites List
www.webring.org/cgi-bin/webring?ring=nicolering;list

Star Trek Character Gallery: Jadzia Dax
http://members.easyspace.com/stcg/dax.html

Starfleet Supply: Jadzia Dax
www.geocities.com/Area51/Stargate/7952/dax.html

Temple to the Goddess Nicole deBoer
www.geocities.com/Hollywood/Palace/7432

Trill - Through the Eyes of Dax
www.geocities.com/Area51/Quadrant/2919/index.html

Ultimate J & J (Julian & Jadzia) Webring, The
www.geocities.com/Hollywood/4498

Ultimate Star Trek Collection: Trill
http://startrek.fns.net.fsn.net/aliens/8472.html

Garak/Andrew Robinson

As Garak, Andrew Robinson intrigued fans with his complicated past and intrigue-filled present. He was one of the most popular recurring characters on Deep Space Nine, and as such, it's no surprise that there are web sites devoted to him.

Computer Core Dump: Elim Garak
www.ccdump.org/garak.html

ElimGarak.Com
http://elimgarak.com

Garek Gallery
www.geocities.com/Area51/Nebula/4349/g_garak.html

Internet Movie Database: Andrew Robinson
http://us.imdb.com/AName?Robinson,+Andrew

Kamar Sutra: Elim Garak Gallery
http://elimgarak.com/art/garakart.html

Official Andy Robinson Web Site, The
http://members.aol.com/primeview/andysclub.html

Star Trek Character Gallery: Garak
http://members.easyspace.com/stcg/garak.html

Jake Sisko/Cirroc Lofton

Long time viewers of Deep Space Nine had the opportunity to watch Cirroc Lofton and his character, Jake Sisko, grow up. Playing the son of the station's captain, Cirroc was the first "human civilian" cast member that did not join Starfleet before the end of the series.

Computer Core Dump: Jake Sisko
www.ccdump.org/jsisko.html

Internet Movie Database: Cirroc Lofton
http://us.imdb.com/M/person-exact?+Lofton,+Cirroc

Star Trek Character Gallery: Jake Sisko
http://members.easyspace.com/stcg/jake.html

Julian Bashir/Siddig El Faddil

Siddig El Faddil played Dr. Julian Bashir on Star Trek: Deep Space Nine. For a time, he went by an easier to remember name -- Alexander. As Dr. Bashir he won the hearts of fans and his fellow cast member and wife, Nana Visitor who played Kira Nerys.

Computer Core Dump: Bashir
www.ccdump.org/bashir.html

Doctor Bashir Newsgroup
alt.fan.doctor.bashir.grind.thrust.drool

Internet Movie Database: Alexander Siddig
http://us.imdb.com/Name?Siddig,+Alexander

Julian & Ezri Multimedia
http://members.tripod.com/~chrys42

Julian & Ezri Multimedia: Sound Clips
http://members.tripod.com/~chrys42/sound.htm

Julian/Ezri Relationshippers
http://beam.to/julianezri

Julian/Ezri Relationshippers: Bashir Bio
www.geocities.com/Area51/Nova/2872/jubio.html

Real Life Love - Alex & Nana
http://members.tripod.com/~LdyAmarige/index.html

Address   http://www.sidcity.com/

Welcome to Sid City
The Official Website of Alexander Siddig/Siddig El Fadil
You are visitor 0 0 3 5 0 7 1 to visit Sid City since 5 December 1996.

Sid City is devoted to Alexander Siddig/Siddig El Fadil, the actor and director currently co-starring in *Star Trek: Deep Space Nine* as Dr. Julian Bashir. In March 1998, Sid named this site his "official" representative on the web. Sid City works in cooperation with Sid's official fan club, The Doctor's Exchange. In addition to new, exclusive information posted regularly, this site is in continuous upgrades and revisions, so be sure to bookmark us! The bar at the right will help you navigate the site, and don't forget to scroll down this page for Important Stuff and the Current Poll.

Lunch with the Doctor III
Photo by JoBeth Taylor

SID CITY
(listed in alphabetical order)

Awards/Credits
What we've won, who's helped us improve

Bashir's Bio
The good Doctor's life story

Convention Appearances
Confirmed appearances only!

Doctor's Exchange

IMPORTANT STUFF

Sid City - The Official Web Site of Alexander Siddig/Siddig El Fadil
www.sidcity.com

Star Trek Character Gallery: Bashir
http://members.easyspace.com/stcg/bashir.html

Ultimate J & J (Julian & Jadzia) Webring, The
www.geocities.com/Hollywood/4498

Kira Nerys/Nana Visitor

One of the most talented actresses ever to appear in the Star Trek universe, Nana Visitor hypnotized Deep Space Nine audiences as the rebellious and strong-willed Kira Nerys. It's not surprising that this beautiful Bajoran has a following on the 'Net.

Bajoran Consulate
http://users.dx.com.au/wormhole/mainpage.html

Celebarama: Nana Visitor
http://celebarama.speedhost.com/nanavisitor/index.html

Deep Space Love
www.geocities.com/Area51/Shire/5920/index2.html

Internet Movie Database: Nana Visitor
http://us.imdb.com/Name?Visitor,+Nana

Kira Nerys Newsgroup
alt.fan.major.kira.pant.pant.pant

NANITES: The Official Nana Visitor Fan Club
www.nanites.com

Odo/Kira FAQ
http://members.tripod.com/~OdoGoddess/OdoGoddess/okfaq.txt

Real Life Love - Alex & Nana
http://members.tripod.com/~LdyAmarige/index.html

Star Trek Character Gallery: Kira
http://members.easyspace.com/stcg/kira.html

The Observatory
http://ourworld.compuserve.com/homepages/nanafan

Leeta/Chase Masterson

Chase Masterson's Leeta started out as a dabo girl and ended up as the wife of a Ferengi named Rom. Read more about Leeta and Chase at these sites.

AAA Star Trek: Chase Masterson
http://eonmagazine.com/startrek/bio%20janeway.html

Internet Movie Database: Chase Masterson
http://us.imdb.com/M/person-exact?+Masterson,+Chase

Official Chase Masterson Fan Club, The
www.chaseclub.com

Star Trek Character Gallery: Leeta
http://members.easyspace.com/stcg/leeta.html

Miles O'Brien/Colm Meaney

Colm Meaney's character Miles O'Brien began as merely a recurring character as the transporter chief on Star Trek: The Next Generation. But when the producers of Star Trek decided to create Deep Space Nine, they transported Miles from the transporter room to Deep Space Nine.

Chief O'Brien Page, A
www.astro.umd.edu/~sgeier/obrien.html

Colm Meaney's Virtual Irish Pub
http://hometown.aol.com/hheyer2003/colm/colm.html

Computer Core Dump: O'Brien
www.ccdump.org/obrien.html

Federation Sound Archive: O'Brien
www.domaindlx.com/timbo/obrien.html

Internet Movie Database: Colm Meaney
http://us.imdb.com/Name?Meaney,+Colm

Miles O'Brien's Homepage (German)
http://home.t-online.de/home/MilesOBrien/space.htm

Star Trek Character Gallery: O'Brien
http://members.easyspace.com/stcg/obrien.html

Nog/Aron Eisenberg

As Nog, Aron Eisenberg has entertained many a Trekker. His ability to create such a memorable Ferengi has made him a favorite recurring character. He even has his own fan club. Visit these sites for more information on Aron and Nog

Aron Eisenberg Fan Club
http://hometown.aol.com/SoupTime/Aron_Eisenberg-Nog_FanClub.htm

Internet Movie Database: Aron Eisenberg (Nog)
http://us.imdb.com/Name?Eisenberg,+Aron

Maximum Defiant: Ensign Nog
www.maximumdefiant.com/crew/nog.html

Odo/Rene Auberjonois

Odo, Deep Space Nine's shapeshifting security officer, was the first "changeling" to appear in the Trek universe. Making use of emerging "morphing" technology, Auberjonois' Odo was the perfect "outsider" of humanity. Through the eyes of this non-solid, audiences learned more about what it means to be human. Deep Space Nine may be over, but Odo is still shapeshifting his way through the 'Net.

An Odo Page for Odo-Lovers
http://hometown.aol.com/luvds9/OdoLoversODO.html

Computer Core Dump: Odo
www.ccdump.org/odo.html

Deep Space Love
www.geocities.com/Area51/Shire/5920/index2.html

Odo Mail (@odo.zzn.com)
http://odo.zzn.com

Odo's Bucket Page
www.mindspring.com/~blittle/odosbucket/trek.html

Odo's Top Ten Pet Peeves About Being Solid
http://www2.uic.edu/~rcasti1/odo_t10.html

Odo-Chat
www.renefiles.com/comlink7.html

Odo/Kira FAQ
http://members.tripod.com/~OdoGoddess/OdoGoddess/okfaq.txt

Rene Auberjonois Internet Link
www.renefiles.com/index.html

Send E-Mail to Rene Auberjonois
www.renefiles.com/comlink2.html

Star Trek Character Gallery: Odo
http://members.easyspace.com/stcg/odo.html

Quark/Armin Shimmerman

As Deep Space Nine bar owner Quark, Armin Shimmerman has made audiences laugh over. His never-ending quest for fortune is the source of much comic relief. As such, it's no wonder that Quark and his ears have found their way onto many a web page.

Armin Shimmerman Articles
www.walrus.com/~quark/armin/articles.html

Armin Shimmerman Chat Transcripts
www.walrus.com/~quark/armin/chats.html

Armin Shimmerman Mailing List
www.walrus.com/~quark/armin/armin_shimerman.html

Computer Core Dump: Quark
www.ccdump.org/quark.html

Internet Movie Database: Armin Shimmerman
http://us.imdb.com/M/person-exact?+Shimerman,+Armin

Official Armin Shimmerman Web Site, The
www.walrus.com/~quark/armin/index.html

Quark's Place: Gallery
www.orlinter.com/users/grandnag/cast.htm

Star Trek Character Gallery: Quark
http://members.easyspace.com/stcg/quark.html

Wayoun/Jeffrey Combs

Wayoun is perhaps the most well-known of the Vorta characters. His character has even been cloned. For more information on this popular bad guy, visit the sites listed below.

Internet Movie Database: Jeffrey Combs (Wayoun)
http://us.imdb.com/Name?Combs,+Jeffrey

Wayoun Gallery
www.geocities.com/Area51/Nebula/4349/g_weyoun.html

Star Trek: Voyager

B'Elanna Torres/Roxanne Biggs Dawson

As B'Elanna Torres, Roxanne Biggs Dawson has the distinction of being the first half-human/half-Klingon/female regular character on a Trek series. With a forehead less prominent than most Klingons, B'Elanna and her relationship with Tom Paris are the subject of much fan discussion.

B'Elanna Sound Files
www.angelfire.com/az/chadtrek/soundfiles.html

B'Elanna Torres Chat
www.angelfire.com/az/chadtrek/chat2.html

Cascade's B'Elanna Torres Archive
www.fortunecity.com/tattooine/mothership/231/index1.html

Chad's B'Elanna Torres Page
www.angelfire.com/az/chadtrek

Computer Core Dump: Torres
www.ccdump.org/torres.html

KoaliTion Headquaters
http://user.aol.com/jyorraku/ktmain.html

KoaliTion Message Board (Kim/Torres)
www.netbabbler.com/goto/?forumid=6337

Kommunity ChaTter (Kim/Torres)
http://user.aol.com/jyorraku/chat.html

Kret Rats P/T Home Page
http://members.tripod.com/~Maihe

Kret Rats: P/T Fan Fiction
http://members.tripod.com/~Maihe/stories.html

Kret Rats: P/T Fan Poetry
http://members.tripod.com/~Maihe/poems.html

Kret Rats: P/T Pictures
http://members.tripod.com/~Maihe/pictures.html

Lanna's P/T Picks
www.geocities.com/TelevisionCity/Set/6627

Paris/Torres (P/T) Fan Ring
www.geocities.com/EnchantedForest/2931/PTRing.htm

Promising Times - A Paris/Torres Page
www.geocities.com/Area51/Nebula/4145/paristorres.html

Star Trek Character Gallery: Torres
http://members.easyspace.com/stcg/torres.html

Star Trek Continuum: Roxanne Biggs Dawson Bio
www.startrekcontinuum.com/earth/quadrant.asp?ssector=castad.asp
&ID=69081

Star Trek News (II): Paris/Torres Central
www.geocities.com/Area51/Dimension/9268/paris-torres.html

Star Trek Pages - M' My Torres (In German)
www.homestead.com/MaTorres/index.html

Chakotay/Robert Beltran

Robert Beltran has the distinction of playing the first regular native American character on Star Trek. As Voyager's Commander Chakotay, Beltran has developed a tremendous fan following, especially with those who would like to see a relationship between his character and Captain Janeway.

Chakotay/Paris Slash Ring: Sites List
www.webring.org/cgi-bin/webring?ring=cpslash;list

Computer Core Dump: Chakotay
www.ccdump.org/chakotay.html

JetC14 Fan Fiction Archive
http://web.ukonline.co.uk/sammi.w2/jetc/jetc14fanfic.htm

RABBLE - Robert Adame Beltran who are Bi-lingual Lovers of Español
www.geocities.com/Hollywood/Studio/8221/index.html

Robert Beltran is Commander Chakotay
http://freespace.virgin.net/julie.ingrey

Robert Beltran Newsgroup
alt.fan.robert-beltran

Robert Beltran Webring: Sites List
www.webring.org/cgi-bin/webring?ring=beltran;list

Running Horse's Voyager Page
http://members.tripod.com/~dianerhsmith/index.html

Star Trek Character Gallery: Chakotay
http://members.easyspace.com/stcg/chakotay.html

TV Now: Robert Beltran TV Schedule
www.tv-now.com/stars/beltran.html

Harry Kim/Garret Wang

As Harry Kim, Garret Wang has developed quite a following. His position as merely a human ensign have made him the source of constant speculation that his character would be killed off. Nonetheless, his appeal with the ladies has made Wang quite popular.

All Garret Things: Gallery
http://members.tripod.com/~TrekkerH/GW2.html

Computer Core Dump: Harry Kim
www.ccdump.org/kim.html

GWAPES - The Garret Wang Appreciation Society
http://members.tripod.com/~GWAPES/gwapes.html

Kim/Seven Webring
www.geocities.com/TelevisionCity/Studio/2869/code.html

KoaliTion Headquaters
http://user.aol.com/jyorraku/ktmain.html

KoaliTion Message Board (Kim/Torres)
www.netbabbler.com/goto/?forumid=6337

Kommunity ChaTter (Kim/Torres)
http://user.aol.com/jyorraku/chat.html

Seven of Nine & Harry Kim Webring: Sites List
www.webring.org/cgi-bin/webring?ring=7kim&list

Star Trek Character Gallery: Kim
http://members.easyspace.com/stcg/kim.html

Star Trek Continuum: Garret Wang Blo
www.startrekcontinuum.com/earth/quadrant.asp?ssector=castad.asp&ID=69087

Kathryn Janeway/Kate Mulgrew

Replacing Genevive Bujold on short notice, Kate Mulgrew became the first female to captain a Star Trek series. As Captain Kathryn Janeway, Mulgrew has exhibited extraordinary range and talent attempting to bring her crew home.

AAA Star Trek: Kate Mulgrew
http://eonmagazine.com/startrek/bio%20janeway.html

A Touch of Kate
http://members.tripod.com/~sofa_spud/km/kate.html

A Touch of Kate: Kate Mulgrew Transcripts
http://members.tripod.com/~sofa_spud/km/kmtrans.html

A Woman In Command
http://members.tripod.com/~TrekLover/index-KM.html

Captain Janeway Mailing List
www.onelist.com/subscribe.cgi/CaptainJaneway

Captain Janeway's Webring
www.geocities.com/Area51/Stargate/4761/webringjane.htm

Captain Janeway's Webring: Sites List
www.webring.org/cgi-bin/webring?ring=kjaneway18;list

Captain Kathryn Janeway's Web Site
www.geocities.com/Area51/Stargate/4761

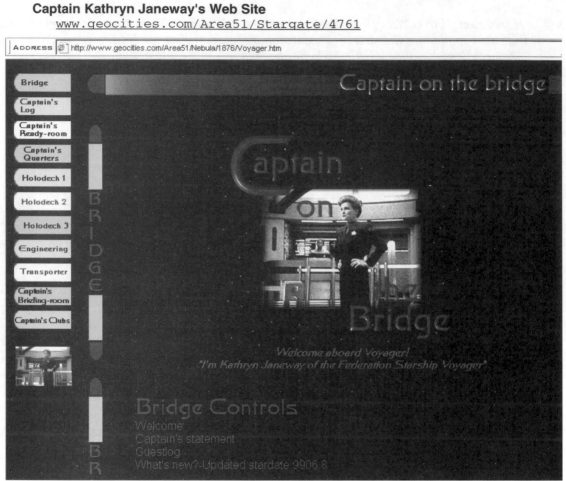

ADDRESS http://www.geocities.com/Area51/Nebula/1876/Voyager.htm

Captain on the Bridge
http://warp9.to/captainonthebridge

Captain's Quarters - Typically Janeway
www.geocities.com/Area51/Nebula/1876/CaptainsQuarters.htm

Computer Core Dump: Janeway
www.ccdump.org/janeway.html

Hollywood Online - Movie People Database: Kate Mulgrew
http://moviepeople.hollywood.com/people.asp?p_id=P|51214

Holodeck 2 - The Complete Janeway Picture Collection
www.geocities.com/Area51/Nebula/1876/JanewayCollection.htm

Janeway Mail (@janeway.zzn.com)
http://janeway.zzn.com

JetC14 Fan Fiction Archive
http://web.ukonline.co.uk/sammi.w2/jetc/jetc14fanfic.htm

JuPiter Station (II)
www.geocities.com/~jupiterstation

JuPiter Station (II): J/P Picture Gallery
www.geocities.com/~jupiterstation/JuPgallery.htm

JuPiter Station (II): J/P Sounds
www.geocities.com/~jupiterstation/JuPSounds.htm

Kate Mulgrew Nexus, The
http://members.tripod.com/~SailorMoose/kmnexus/entrance.html

Kate Mulgrew Webring
www.geocities.com/Area51/Starship/1131/webrings.html

Kate Mulgrew Webring: Sites List
www.webring.org/cgi-bin/webring?ring=kmring;list

Kate Speaks Out - Interviews with Kate Mulgrew
www.geocities.com/Area51/Nebula/1876/Kate2.htm

Mr. Showbiz . . . Kate Mulgrew
http://mrshowbiz.go.com/people/katemulgrew

Nuts About Kate
www.geocities.com/Area51/Nebula/8845/NAK_Main.htm

So why finally a woman captain?
www.trekplanet.com/janeway.html

Star Trek Character Gallery: Janeway
http://members.easyspace.com/stcg/janeway.html

Totally Kate! - The Kate Mulgrew Page
http://members.tripod.com/~marcia_2/Index.htm

Totally Kate!: Mulgrew Articles
http://members.tripod.com/~marcia_2/articles.htm

Totally Kate!: Mulgrew Bio
http://members.tripod.com/~marcia_2/bio.htm

Totally Kate!: Mulgrew Photos
http://members.tripod.com/~marcia_2/photos.htm

Totally Kate!: Mulgrew Television, Radio & Online Interviews
http://members.tripod.com/~marcia_2/intervew.htm

TV Now: Kate Mulgrew TV Schedule
www.tv-now.com/stars/mulgrew.html

Yahoo! Clubs: Captain Janeway's Crew
http://clubs.yahoo.com/clubs/captainjanewayscrew

Kes/Jennifer Lien

Jennifer Lien played Kes for two full seasons of Star Trek: Voyager. Although her character was killed off to make room for Jeri Lynn Ryan's Seven of Nine, Lien did garner a lot of fans as the first Ocampan character.

Great Seven/Kes Debate, The
www.geocities.com/Area51/Rampart/3448/poll.html

Hollywood Online - Movie People Database: Jennifer Lien
http://moviepeople.hollywood.com/people.asp?p_id=P264193

Internet Movie Database: Jennifer Lien
http://us.imdb.com/M/person-exact?+Lien,+Jennifer

Jennifer Lien Webring
www.geocities.com/Area51/Rampart/4311/voyager.html

Jennifer Lien Webring: Sites List
www.webring.org/cgi-bin/webring?ring=jenlien1&list

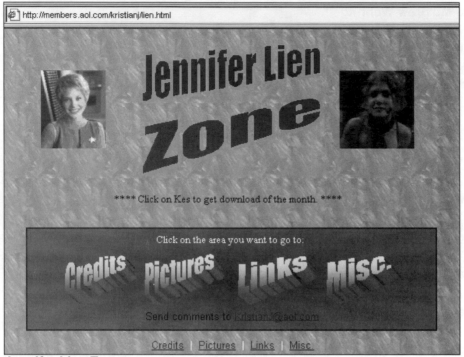

Jennifer Lien Zone
http://members.aol.com/kristianj/lien.html

Kes FAQ
www.vliet.org/jl/kesfaq.html

Star Trek Character Gallery: Kes
http://members.easyspace.com/stcg/kes.html

Star Trek Continuum: Jennifer Lien Bio
www.startrekcontinuum.com/earth/quadrant.asp?ssector=castad.asp
&ID=69082

Star Trek Voyager Women: Kes
www.sherylfranklin.com/trekwomen_kes.html

Star Trek Voyager Women: Kes: Pictures
www.sherylfranklin.com/trekwomen_kes_sites.html

Style Ocampa: The Clothes & Times of Kes
www.geocities.com/Area51/Corridor/6466/Ocampa.html

SVKS - Star Trek Voyager Kes Site
www.vliet.org/jl

Ultimate Star Trek Collection: Ocampa
http://startrek.fns.net.fsn.net/aliens/ocampa.html

USS Prometheus: A Tribute to Kes
www.geocities.com/Area51/Shadowlands/7129/tribute.html

Neelix/Ethan Phillips

Ethan Phillips was one of the first actors to play a Ferengi on Star Trek: The Next Generation. Little did he know that years later he would become the first Talaxian by playing Neelix, Voyager's chef.

Computer Core Dump: Neelix
www.ccdump.org/neelix.html

Internet Movie Database: Ethan Phillips
http://us.imdb.com/M/person-exact?+Phillips,+Ethan

THE NEELIX DEATH SQUAD
(slightly defunct) HOMEPAGE

Enter if you dare...

Welcome to the Neelix Death Squad (NDS) Homepage! This team is comprised of highly trained, highly motivated, and highly aggressive knights, who happen to not like a certain knave in Star Trek Voyager. As you can see, this scurvy knave is Neelix.

NDS - Neelix Death Squad
www.geocities.com/Area51/Rampart/1470

Star Trek Character Gallery: Neelix
http://members.easyspace.com/stcg/neelix.html

Talxian Trader's Corner
www.geocities.com/Area51/Shire/3691/index.html

Ultimate Star Trek Collection: Talaxians
http://startrek.fns.net.fsn.net/aliens/talaxian.html

Seska/Martha Hackett

Martha Hackett developed quite a following as the malicious Seska on Star Trek: Voyager. Although, her character was killed off, her fans remain loyal. Find out more about Martha and Seska by visiting these sites.

Internet Movie Database: Martha Hackett
http://us.imdb.com/M/person-exact?Hackett%2C+Martha

The Official Martha Hackett Fan Club

Official Martha Hackett Fan Club
www.marthahackett.com

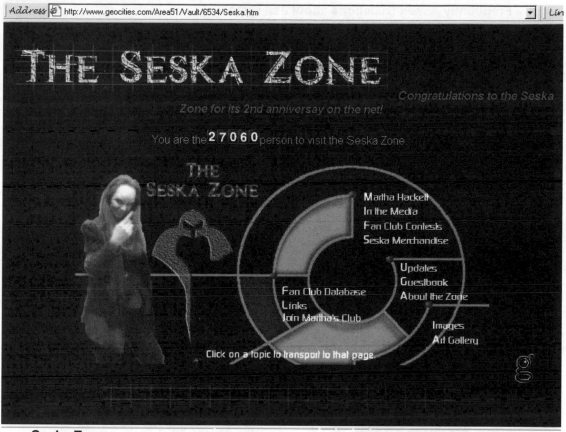

Address | http://www.geocities.com/Area51/Vault/6534/Seska.htm

Seska Zone
www.geocities.com/Area51/Vault/6534/Seska.htm

Star Trek Character Gallery: Seska
http://members.easyspace.com/stcg/seska.html

Seven of Nine/Jeri Lynn Ryan

Jeri Lynn Ryan did not join the cast of Star Trek: Voyager until its third season, but much like Heather Locklear did for Melrose Place, Ryan increased the show's ratings. With her bombshell looks and connection to the overwhelmingly popular Borg, Jeri Lynn Ryan and her character, Seven of Nine, have become mainstays in the Star Trek universe and on the Internet.

AAA Star Trek: Jeri Ryan
http://eonmagazine.com/startrek/jeri%20page%201.html

Celebarama: Jeri Ryan
http://celebarama.speedhost.com/jeriryan/index.html

Computer Core Dump: Seven of Nine
www.ccdump.org/7of9.html

Designation: Seven of Nine Webring: Sites List
http://nav.webring.com/cgi-bin/navcgi?ring=7of9;list

Etheria's Realm: Seven of Nine
www.geocities.com/Area51/Realm/3995/seven.html

Frequently Asked Questions about Jeri Ryan
www.jerilynn.com/faq.htm

Great Seven/Kes Debate, The
www.geocities.com/Area51/Rampart/3448/poll.html

Internet Movie Database: Jeri Lynn Ryan
http://us.imdb.com/M/person-exact?Ryan%2C+Jeri+Lynn

Jeri Ryan Newsgroup
alt.fan.jeri-ryan

Kim/Seven Webring
www.geocities.com/TelevisionCity/Studio/2869/code.html

Lycos Celebrity Guide: Jeri Ryan
www.lycos.com/entertainment/celebrities/celebs/RyanJeri.html

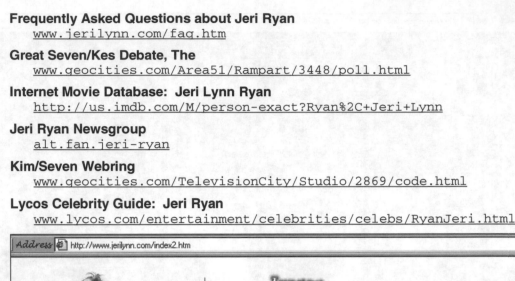

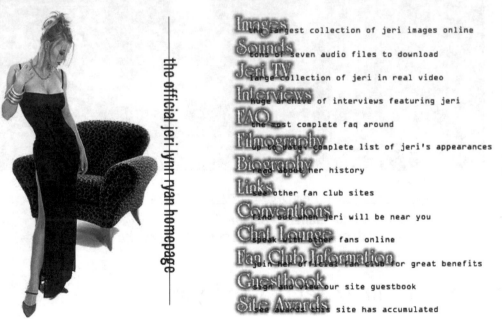

Official Jeri Lynn Ryan Homepage, The
www.jerilynn.com

Official Jeri Lynn Ryan Homepage, The: Biography
www.jerilynn.com/bio.htm

Official Jeri Lynn Ryan Homepage, The: Fan Art
www.jerilynn.com/fanart.htm

Official Jeri Lynn Ryan Homepage, The: FAQ
www.jerilynn.com/faq.htm

Official Jeri Lynn Ryan Homepage, The: Filmography
www.jerilynn.com/film.htm

Official Jeri Lynn Ryan Homepage, The: Interviews
www.jerilynn.com/interv.htm

Official Jeri Lynn Ryan Homepage, The: Pictures
www.jerilynn.com/pics.htm

Seven of Nine & Harry Kim Webring: Sites List
www.webring.org/cgi-bin/webring?ring=7kim&list

Seven of Nine E-Mail Postcards
www.fine-art-gallery.com/postcard.html

Seven of Nine's Collective
www.SevenofNineB.org

Star Trek Character Gallery: Seven of Nine
http://members.easyspace.com/stcg/sevenofnine.html

Yahoo! Clubs: Jeri Ryan's Net
http://welcome.to/jerilynn

The Holographic Doctor/Robert Picardo

Robert Picardo's holographic doctor is one of the most popular characters in Star Trek today. His difficulty grasping the concepts of human interaction and his never-ending wisecracks have kept the audience in stitches. To activate the Web's offerings for Picardo's Emergency Medical Hologram, simply visit the sites listed below.

All-Movie Guide: Robert Picardo
http://allmovie.com/cg/x.dll?UID=10:51:20|PM&p=avg&sql=B56658

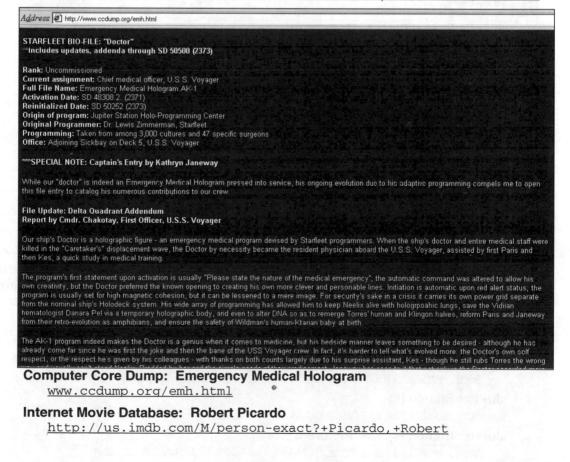

Address http://www.ccdump.org/emh.html

STARFLEET BIO-FILE: "Doctor"
Includes updates, addenda through SD 50500 (2373)

Rank: Uncommissioned
Current assignment: Chief medical officer, U.S.S. Voyager
Full File Name: Emergency Medical Hologram AK-1
Activation Date: SD 48308.2. (2371)
Reinitialized Date: SD 50252 (2373)
Origin of program: Jupiter Station Holo-Programming Center
Original Programmer: Dr. Lewis Zimmerman, Starfleet
Programming: Taken from among 3,000 cultures and 47 specific surgeons
Office: Adjoining Sickbay on Deck 5, U.S.S. Voyager

SPECIAL NOTE: Captain's Entry by Kathryn Janeway

While our "doctor" is indeed an Emergency Medical Hologram pressed into service, his ongoing evolution due to his adaptive programming compels me to open this file entry to catalog his numerous contributions to our crew.

File Update: Delta Quadrant Addendum
Report by Cmdr. Chakotay, First Officer, U.S.S. Voyager

Our ship's Doctor is a holographic figure - an emergency medical program devised by Starfleet programmers. When the ship's doctor and entire medical staff were killed in the "Caretaker's" displacement wave, the Doctor by necessity became the resident physician aboard the U.S.S. Voyager, assisted by first Paris and then Kes, a quick study in medical training.

The program's first statement upon activation is usually "Please state the nature of the medical emergency"; the automatic command was altered to allow his own creativity, but the Doctor preferred the known opening to creating his own more clever and personable lines. Initiation is automatic upon red alert status; the program is usually set for high magnetic cohesion, but it can be lessened to a mere image. For security's sake in a crisis it carries its own power grid separate from the nominal ship's Holodeck system. His wide array of programming has allowed him to keep Neelix alive with hologrpoahic lungs, save the Vidiian hematologist Danara Pel via a temporary holographic body, and even to alter DNA so as to remerge Torres' human and Klingon halves, reform Paris and Janeway from their retro-evolution as amphibians, and ensure the safety of Wildman's human-Ktarian baby at birth.

The AK-1 program indeed makes the Doctor is a genius when it comes to medicine, but his bedside manner leaves something to be desired - although he has already come far since he was first the joke and then the bane of the USS Voyager crew. In fact, it's harder to tell what's evolved more: the Doctor's own self respect, or the respect he's given by his colleagues - with thanks on both counts largely due to his surprise assistant, Kes - though he still rubs Torres the wrong

Computer Core Dump: Emergency Medical Hologram
www.ccdump.org/emh.html

Internet Movie Database: Robert Picardo
http://us.imdb.com/M/person-exact?+Picardo,+Robert

NEWS

BIOGRAPHY

PICTURES

STAGE CREDITS

FILMOGRAPHY

SEEN & HEARD

THE HOLODOC

THE FAN CLUB

INTERVIEWS

CON REPORTS

FANFICTION

GUESTBOOK

OTHER SITES

© ECR

Welcome! The Emergency Medical Holographic Program is **ACTIVE!** This is the official site of CARPE, the **Central Alliance of Robert Picardo Enthusiasts.** This site is dedicated to actor Robert Picardo and his **Star Trek: Voyager** character, the Holographic Doctor.

In these pages you will find the latest news for Picardo-philes, including listings of Bob's upcoming TV and convention appearances; biographical information; a wide variety of pictures; a listing of Bob's stage credits; an annotated, illustrated filmography (with pictures and with stories from behind-the-scenes); a section featuring one of Bob's past roles, with a picture and a sound bite; a section devoted to the Holographic Doctor; **CARPE** news and information; interviews; convention reports; Voyager/Holodoc fanfiction; a Guestbook for you to sign and fill with your

Official Robert Picardo Homepage, The
http://members.aol.com/rpicardo/index.html

Official Robert Picardo Homepage, The: Interviews
http://members.aol.com/rpicardo/intervie.html

Star Trek Character Gallery: The Holographic Doctor
http://members.easyspace.com/stcg/doctor.html

TV Now: Robert Picardo TV Schedule
www.tv-now.com/stars/picardo.html

Tom Paris/Robert Duncan McNeill

As Tom Paris, Robert Duncan McNeill strives to bring Voyager back to earth. Along the way, he's found time to strike up a romance with B'Elanna Torres. This relationship is the source of much 'Net discussion. Find out more about this tumultuous relationship and Paris by visiting the sites listed here.

Chakotay/Paris Slash Ring: Sites List
www.webring.org/cgi-bin/webring?ring=cpslash;list

Janeway's Tom Yum Page
www.geocities.com/Area51/Rampart/1470/tomyum.html

JuPiter Station (II)
www.geocities.com/~jupiterstation

JuPiter Station (II): J/P Picture Gallery
www.geocities.com/~jupiterstation/JuPgallery.htm

JuPiter Station (II): J/P Sounds
   www.geocities.com/~jupiterstation/JuPSounds.htm

Kret Rats P/T Home Page
   http://members.tripod.com/~Maihe

Kret Rats: P/T Fan Poetry
   http://members.tripod.com/~Maihe/poems.html

Kret Rats: P/T Pictures
   http://members.tripod.com/~Maihe/pictures.html

Lanna's P/T Picks
   www.geocities.com/TelevisionCity/Set/6627

Paris-Philes, The
   www.geocities.com/Area51/Rampart/1812

Paris/Torres (P/T) Fan Ring
   www.geocities.com/EnchantedForest/2931/PTRing.htm

Promising Times - A Paris/Torres Page
   www.geocities.com/Area51/Nebula/4145/paristorres.html

Robert Duncan McNeill Biography
   www.lustchip.com/bios/mcneillbio.htm

Star Trek Character Gallery: Paris
   http://members.easyspace.com/stcg/paris.html

Star Trek Continuum: Robert Duncan McNeill Bio
   www.startrekcontinuum.com/earth/quadrant.asp?ssector=castad.asp
   &ID=69083

Star Trek News (II): Paris/Torres Central
   www.geocities.com/Area51/Dimension/9268/paris-torres.html

The Protonic Pages - The Further Adventures of Captain Proton
   www.geocities.com/Area51/Rampart/1812/ProtonAnimations.html

Tom Paris Ring: Sites List
   www.webring.org/cgi-bin/webring?ring=parisring&list

Tuvok/Tim Russ

As the first African-American actor to play a regular Vulcan cast member, Tim Russ has illustrated that even alien races can come in different colors. In one episode's flashbacks, Russ even worked alongside original series characters Sulu and Rand. For more on Tim and Tuvok, see the sites below.

Computer Core Dump: Tuvok
   www.ccdump.org/tuvok.html

Funky Vulcan Café, The
   www.geocities.com/~teepee47/tim_russ

Star Trek Character Gallery: Tuvok
   http://members.easyspace.com/stcg/tuvok.html

Star Trek Continuum: Tim Russ Bio
   www.startrekcontinuum.com/earth/quadrant.asp?ssector=castad.asp
   &ID=69086

Star Trek Excelsior
http://www1.ridgecrest.ca.us/~curtdan/Excelsior/SuluPages.cgi?FILE=Main

Tim Russ Sings the Voyager Loveboat Theme
www.geocities.com/~teepee47/tim_russ/multimedia.html

Tuvok Appreciation
www.geocities.com/~teepee47/tim_russ/multimedia.html

Tuvok Appreciation: WAVs
www.geocities.com/Hollywood/Studio/4436/tuvokwav.html

Tuvok Secret Agent Man
www.geocities.com/Area51/Lair/4979/disguise.html

Other Trek Personalities

Gene Roddenberry

If it weren't for Gene Roddenberry, this book would not be in your hands. Roddenberry created Star Trek and supervised its production until his death. His dream lives on, and new creations, such as his television series Earth: The Final Conflict, grace the airwaves. Find more about the founding father of the final frontier by visiting these sites.

All-Movie Guide: Gene Roddenberry
http://allmovie.com/cg/x.dll?UID=10:49:42|PM&p=avg&sql=B108615

Andrew Tong's Gene Roddenberry
www.ugcs.caltech.edu/st-tng/roddenberry.html

Earth: The Final Conflict Worldring
www.inforamp.net/~nburgess/echobase/worldring.html

Earth: The Final Conflict Worldring: Sites List
http://nav.webring.com/cgi-bin/navcgi?ring=efcworld;list

EFC (Earth: The Final Conflict) Central Webring
www.geocities.com/Area51/5259/webring.html

EFC (Earth: The Final Conflict) Central Webring: Sites List
http://nav.webring.com/cgi-bin/navcgi?ring=efc;list

Gene Roddenberry's Earth: The Final Conflict
www.roddenberry.com/creations/efc/index.efc.html

Internet Movie Database: Gene Roddenberry
http://us.imdb.com/Name?Roddenberry,+Gene

Roddenberry's Masterpiece: Dedication to Roddenberry
www.geocities.com/Area51/4396/dedication.html

Roddenberry.Com
www.roddenberry.com

Gowron/Robert O'Reilly

As the feisty Chancellor Gowron, Robert O'Reilly drank blood wine and spoke Klingon in episodes of both Next Generation and Deep Space Nine. Killed off in the final episodes of Deep Space Nine, Gowron and O'Reilly still have a following.

AURORA - Appreciation & Unity for the Robert O'Reilly Alliance
www.geocities.com/Area51/1908/aurora.htm

Internet Movie Database: Robert O'Reilly
http://us.imdb.com/M/person-exact?O%27Reilly%2C+Robert

Robert O'Reilly Biography
www.lustchip.com/bios/robertbio.htm

Star Trek Character Gallery: Gowron
http://members.easyspace.com/stcg/gowron.html

Gul Dukat/Marc Alaimo

Marc Alaimo wowed viewers as Gul Dukat on Deep Space Nine. Gifted with the ability to make his character good and bad, Alaimo has developed a loyal following. Therefore, it's not surprising that there are web sites devoted to the actor and the character he plays.

Dukat Photogallery, The
http://members.theglobe.com/RatboyX/photogalleries.html

Dukat Polls
www.kardasi.com/gd/dukat_polls.htm

Dukat's Romantic Fanfiction
www.kardasi.com/gd/contents.htm

Gul Dukat
www.geocities.com/Area51/Labyrinth/8873/dukat.htm

Gul Dukat Gallery
www.geocities.com/Area51/Nebula/4349/g_dukat.html

Gul Dukat's Homepage
http://members.aol.com/malaimo/index.htm

Internet Movie Database: Marc Alaimo
http://us.imdb.com/M/person-exact?+Alaimo,+Marc

Star Trek Character Gallery: Dukat
http://members.easyspace.com/stcg/dukat.html

Lwaxanna Troi/Majel Barrett Roddenberry

Majel Barrett Roddenberry is an extraordinary woman. Not only has she managed to help keep her husband's dream alive, but she has participated in every version of Star Trek. She began as Number One in the pilot episode for the original series, and then, rejoined the cast later as Nurse Chapel. When the series returned with the Next Generation, she appeared as Lwaxanna Troi. Throughout the new series, including Deep Space Nine and Voyager, she has performed as the voice of the computer. Learn more about this multi-faceted actress by accessing these sites.

Deep Space Nine Bible
gopher://wiretap.spies.com/00/Library/Media/Trek/deep9.bib%09%09%2B

Internet Movie Database: Majel Barrett
http://us.imdb.com/M/person-exact?Barrett%2C+Majel

Roddenberry.Com
www.roddenberry.com

Star Trek Character Gallery: Nurse Chapel
http://members.easyspace.com/stcg/chapel.html

Other Characters

The actors who've guest-starred on the various Star Trek series are as varied as the names of their characters. Nonetheless, a great deal of them strike a chord with fans so much so that some of them even have their own web sites and fan clubs online.

AAA Star Trek: Actor Birthdays
http://eonmagazine.com/startrek/birthday%20page.html

Alexander Enberg (Ensign Vorik) Fan Page
http://members.aol.com/BrentFemme/enberg.html

All-Movie Guide: Kirstie Alley (Saavik)
http://allmovie.com/cg/x.dll?UID=10:51:20|PM&p=avg&sql=B1093

All-Movie Guide: Ricardo Montalban (Khan)
http://allmovie.com/cg/x.dll?UID=10:51:20|PM&p=avg&sql=B50098

Casey Biggs: The Official Web Site (Damar)
http://members.aol.com/primeview/biggsclub.html

Celeste Yarnell's Celestial Pets Site
www.celestialpets.com

Celeste Yarnell's Home Page
www.celesteyarnell.com

David L Ross - Star Trek Crew Member Lt. Johnson/Galloway
www.startrekltgalloway.com

Eggy's Carey Page (Josh Clark - Lt. Carey on Voyager)
http://members.aol.com/SkizyQueen/Carey.html

Address http://www.wlu.edu/~madams/3rd.of.5.html ▼ Go

Hugh Borg: Jonathan del Arco

"I am Hugh." -Third of Five

This page is devoted to Jonathan del Arco, most notably known for his role as Hugh in Star Trek: The Next Generation. He first appeared in I, Borg (code 223, stardate 45854.2, airdate May 9, 1992) during season five, and his character returned in the seventh, and final, season opener (Descent, Part II, code 253, stardate 47025.4, airdate September 18, 1993). Unfortunately, he did not make a reappearance in the motion picture, Star Trek: First Contact, which prominantly dealt with the Borg. In 1989 Jonathan appeared as "Angel," a member of the 10th street gang in Lost Angels. You kind of have to look for him, but he's there. He played "Young Cesar" in 1992's The Mambo Kings. I also remember seeing him in an episode of Blossom, where he played Six's strange, foreign prom date in "Last Tango" (episode 4.24). He made a guest appearance on CBS's short-lived Pearl as "Carlo" on November 6, 1996. A short four days later Jonathan appeared as Jimmy Porter in an episode of Pacific Blue (thanks Katharine!). More recently, he played Nunzio on an epsode of Boy Meets World.

Hugh Borg: Jonathan del Arco
www.wlu.edu/~madams/3rd.of.5.html

Internet Movie Database: Aron Eisenberg (Nog)
http://us.imdb.com/Name?Eisenberg,+Aron

Internet Movie Database: James Darren (Vic Fontaine)
http://us.imdb.com/Name?Darren,+James

Internet Movie Database: John Hertzler (General Martok)
http://us.imdb.com/Name?Hertzler,+John

Internet Movie Database: Kirstle Alley
http://us.imdb.com/Name?Alley,+Kirstie

Internet Movie Database: Louise Fletcher (Vedek/Kai Winn)
http://us.imdb.com/Name?Fletcher,+Louise

Internet Movie Database: Max Grodenchik (Rom)
http://us.imdb.com/Name?Grod%E9nchik,+Max

Internet Movie Database: Philip Anglim (Vedek Bareil)
http://us.imdb.com/Name?Anglim,+Philip

Internet Movie Database: Roaslind Chao (Keiko O'Brien)
http://us.imdb.com/Name?Chao,+Rosalind

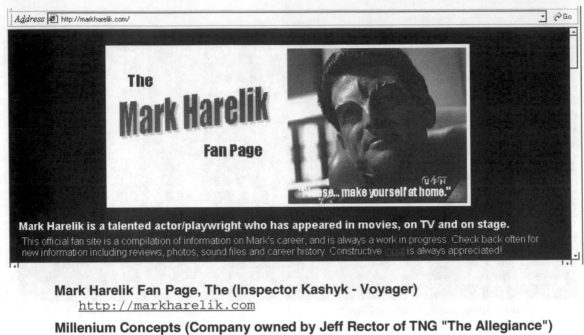

Address 🅔 http://markharelik.com/   ▾   ⟳ Go

Mark Harelik Fan Page, The (Inspector Kashyk - Voyager)
http://markharelik.com

Millenium Concepts (Company owned by Jeff Rector of TNG "The Allegiance")
www.milleniumconcepts.net

Official John Colicos Fan Club (Kor)
www.klingon.org/Colicos/pages

Philip Anglim (Vedek Bareil) - Acting Naturally
www.angelfire.com/mo/gutterduck/ds9.html

Production Crew

To accomplish the special effects, costuming, writing and other technical tasks it takes to make a single episode of Star Trek requires a large crew. Although the crew may not be equal in number to that of the Enterprise, it certainly functions like a well-oiled machine. Learn more about those who remain behind the scenes by visiting these sites.

AAA Star Trek: Behind the Scenes
http://eonmagazine.com/startrek/behind_the_scenes.html

All-Movie Guide: Brannon Braga
http://allmovie.com/cg/x.dll?UID=10:51:20|PM&p=avg&sql=B188731

All-Movie Guide: Jerry Goldsmith
http://allmovie.com/cg/x.dll?UID=10:51:20|PM&p=avg&sql=B91941

All-Movie Guide: Michael Piller
http://allmovie.com/cg/x.dll?UID=10:51:20|PM&p=avg&sql=B149463

All-Movie Guide: Rick Berman
http://allmovie.com/cg/x.dll?UID=10:51:20|PM&p=avg&sql=B212471

All-Movie Guide: Ronald D Moore
http://allmovie.com/cg/x.dll?UID=10:51:20|PM&p=avg&sql=B192252

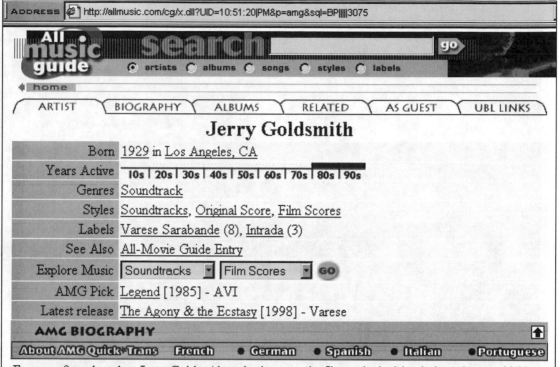

ADDRESS http://allmusic.com/cg/x.dll?UID=10:51:20|PM&p=amg&sql=BP||||3075

All music guide   search   go

○ artists ○ albums ○ songs ○ styles ○ labels

◄ home

ARTIST   BIOGRAPHY   ALBUMS   RELATED   AS GUEST   UBL LINKS

Jerry Goldsmith

Born	1929 in Los Angeles, CA
Years Active	10s	20s	30s	40s	50s	60s	70s	80s	90s
Genres	Soundtrack
Styles	Soundtracks, Original Score, Film Scores
Labels	Varese Sarabande (8), Intrada (3)
See Also	All-Movie Guide Entry
Explore Music	Soundtracks ▼ Film Scores ▼ GO
AMG Pick	Legend [1985] - AVI
Latest release	The Agony & the Ecstasy [1998] - Varese

AMG BIOGRAPHY   ⬆

About AMG Quick*Trans   French   ● German   ● Spanish   ● Italian   ● Portuguese

For over four decades, Jerry Goldsmith ranked among the film and television industry's most highly-regarded and prolific composers; at the peak of his activity during the 1960s, he was estimated to have scored an average of about six films annually. Born in Los Angeles on February 10, 1929, Goldsmith studied music at the University of South Carolina, and after accepting a job as an office clerk at CBS television later graduated to the network's music department in 1950. There he composed themes for series including Gunsmoke, Perry Mason, Have Gun Will Travel, The Twilight Zone and The Man From U.N.C.L.E. before turning to film in 1957, debuting with the score to Black Patch. Under the tutelage of the great Alfred Newman, Goldsmith rose to prominence with 1962's Lonely Are the Brave, and subsequently emerged as one of Hollywood's most prolific composers. Among his credits were such diverse offerings as Patton, Planet of the Apes, Seconds, Chinatown, Poltergeist and Rambo: First Blood Part II; while nominated for over a dozen Academy Awards, Goldsmith won only one, for 1976's The Omen. Additionally, he regularly toured concert halls, performing his music and conducting the likes of the San Diego Symphony and Britain's Royal Philharmonic. -- **Jason Ankeny, All-Music Guide**

All-Music Guide: Jerry Goldsmith
http://allmusic.com/cg/x.dll?UID=10:51:20|PM&p=amg&sql=BP|||||3075

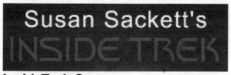

Susan Sackett's
INSIDE TREK

InsideTrek.Com
(Home page of Gene Roddenberry's former executive assistant - Susan Sackett)
www.insidetrek.com

Maximum Defiant: Behind the Scenes: The Real Deal
 www.maximumdefiant.com/bts/reald.html

Maximum Defiant: Ronald Moore Speaks!
 www.maximumdefiant.com/misc/moore.html

Psi Phi's Deep Space Nine Director Credits
 www.psiphi.org/DS9/ep/directors.html?ix

Voyager Director Credits
 www.psiphi.org/voy/ep/directors.html

Voyager Musician Credits
 www.psiphi.org/voy/ep/music.html

Voyager Producer Credits
 www.psiphi.org/voy/ep/producers.html

Voyager Writer Credits
 www.psiphi.org/voy/ep/writers.html

Q/John de Lancie

See the "Q / John de Lancie" entry in the Aliens & Technology chapter.

Saavik/Kirstie Alley & Robin Curtis

Yes, Kirstie Alley was actually a part of the Star Trek universe! She played Saavik in Star Trek II: The Wrath of Kahn. However, she chose not to reprise the role for the sequel, Star Trek III: The Search for Spock. Thus, the talented Robin Curtis took her place for both the third and fourth Trek films. Discover more on Saavik and her two faces by visiting these sites.

ADDRESS | http://allmovie.com/cg/x.dll?UID=10:51:20|PM&p=avg&sql=B1093

Kirstie Alley

Birth	Jan 12, 1955 - Wichita, KS
Occupation	Actor
Years Active	10s	30s	40s	50s	60s	70s	80s	90s
Countries	USA
Genres	Drama, Comedy, Crime, Children's/Family, Science Fiction, Mystery, Feminist Film, Family-Oriented Adventure, Historical Epic, Biography [Feature], Gangster Film, Crime Drama, Alien Invasion Films, Space Adventure, Sci-Fi Action, Detective Film, Docudrama, Screwball Comedy, Farce, Satire, Slapstick
See Also	Add New Link

BIOGRAPHY

About AMG Quick-Trans   French   ● German   ● Spanish   ● Italian   ● Portuguese

Versatile American actress Kirstie Alley has found success in feature films, but is still best known for her portrayal of neurotic Rebecca Howe during the latter years of the television series *Cheers.* Noted for her unusual beauty, thick chestnut-colored hair and whiskey voice, Alley studied drama in her native Kansas and then became an interior decorator. For a while, she went through a wild and crazy phase in which she abused cocaine and hung out with bikers, but when the life-style got old, Alley moved to California, underwent drug rehabilitation and became a devout Scientologist. She made her feature film debut playing Savic, a Vulcan student of Mr. Spock in *Star Trek II: The Wrath of Khan* and then played a major role in the television mini-series *North and South,* but she did not become a real star until she was selected to replace Shelly Long in *Cheers* in the late '80s. Though the role of Rebecca marked Alley as a comedienne, she is also a talented dramatic actress as she demonstrated in the 1988 outdoor thriller *Shoot to Kill.* In 1989, Alley had her first box-office hit with *Look Who's Talking;* that coupled with *Cheers* made her one of the most popular actresses in Hollywood and the winner of Emmys, a People's Choice Award and a Golden Globe for *Look Who's Talking.* With the demise of *Cheers,* Alley's career became more sporadic and the quality of her films has been uneven. In the fall of 1997, Alley stars in a new sitcom, *Veronica's Closet,* scheduled on the NBC Fall primetime lineup. -- Sandra Brennan

All-Movie Guide: Kirstie Alley (Saavik)
http://allmovie.com/cg/x.dll?UID=10:51:20|PM&p=avg&sql=B1093

Internet Movie Database: Kirstie Alley
http://us.imdb.com/Name?Alley,+Kirstie

Internet Movie Database: Robin Curtis
http://us.imdb.com/Name?Curtis,+Robin+(I)

Sarek/Mark Lenard

The vastly-talented Mark Lenard played Spock's father Sarek in the original Trek series, the feature films, and on Star Trek: The Next Generation. Although Sarek passed away, his impact on the fans is still felt on the Internet.

All-Movie Guide: Mark Lenard
http://allmovie.com/cg/x.dll?UID=10:49:42|PM&p=avg&sql=B41778

ADDRESS http://us.imdb.com/Name?Lenard,+Mark

IMDb   SEARCH   INDEX   SNACK BAR   NEWS   BOX OFFICE   AWARD WINNERS   HELP   ABOUT

Search for title/name:

[   ] GO

○ Title ⊙ Name
more search options

Mark Lenard
Filmographies:
filmography only
combined filmography
sorted by ratings
sorted by votes
awards
titles for sale
by genre
power search
worked with

Biographical:
biography
trivia
quotes
other works
publicity
agent

Offsite links:
for sale @ Amazon.com
on tv this week
official-site
miscellaneous
FAQ
photographs

Mark Lenard

Date of birth (location)
15 October 1924,
Chicago, Illinois, USA
Date of death (details)
22 November 1996,
New York, New York, USA. (mulitple myeloma)

Buy related

VHS-videos (22)
DVDs (3)
Soundtracks (3)
Books

amazon.com

Filmography as: Actor, Notable TV guest appearances

Actor filmography
(1990s) (1980s) (1970s) (1960s) (1950s)

1. Star Trek VI: The Undiscovered Country (1991) .... Ambassador Sarek
2. Radicals, The (1990)

3. Star Trek IV: The Voyage Home (1986) .... Sarek
   ... aka Voyage Home: Star Trek IV, The (1986)
4. Star Trek III: The Search for Spock (1984) .... Ambassador Sarek

Internet Movie Database: Mark Lenard
http://us.imdb.com/Name?Lenard,+Mark

Star Trek: TNG: Cast Photographs: Mark Lenard
www.daviestrek.com/trek/tng/marklenard.htm

THE BEST STAR TREK
Film Sites

Which Star Trek film cost the most to make? Which one made the most money? These questions and more can be answered by accessing the sites in this chapter. Using these web addresses, you'll find full production credits, still images, multimedia clips, and detailed information about every one of the Star Trek feature films.

Star Trek: The Motion Picture

Hot on the heels of 2001: A Space Odyssey, Star Trek's first foray into film was a sprawling effort centering on a mysterious craft simply known as V'ger. Successful enough to warrant "sequels," the first Trek film is a must-see.

All-Movie Guide: Star Trek: The Motion Picture
http://allmovie.com/cg/x.dll?UID=10:51:20|PM&p=avg&sql=FStar|Trek|--|The|Motion|Picture

Amazon.Com: Star Trek - The Motion Picture
www.amazon.com/exec/obidos/ASIN/6303201954/remixparadisesho

Movie Review Query Engine: Star Trek Motion Picture - Reviews
www.mrqe.com/lookup?^Star+Trek%3a+The+Motion+Picture+(1979)

Mr. Showbiz . . . Star Trek - The Motion Picture
http://mrshowbiz.go.com/reviews/moviereviews/movies/StarTrektheMotionPicture_1979.html

Outpost 21: The Motion Picture
www.steve.simplenet.com/feature_films/1_center.html

Reel.Com: Star Trek: The Motion Picture
www.reel.com/Content/moviepage.asp?mmid=1696

Star Trek: The Motion Picture Review
http://clgray.simplenet.com/strtrk/stmovie/sti.html

Starbase 6503: Star Trek - The Motion Picture
www.geocities.com/Area51/Corridor/6503/TREKMOV1.HTM

Star Trek II: The Wrath of Khan

Ricardo Montalban reprised his popular role as Khan from the original series to wreak havoc once again. The battles and emotions shown in this film are some of the best the Trek franchise has to offer.

All-Movie Guide: Star Trek II
http://allmovie.com/cg/x.dll?UID=10:51:20|PM&p=avg&sql=A46540

Amazon.Com: Star Trek II - The Wrath of Khan
www.amazon.com/exec/obidos/ASIN/6300213803/remixparadisesho

Movie Review Query Engine: Star Trek II - Reviews
www.mrqe.com/lookup?^Star+Trek%3a+The+Wrath+of+Khan+(1982)

Mr. Showbiz . . . Star Trek II - The Wrath of Khan
http://mrshowbiz.go.com/reviews/moviereviews/movies/StarTrekIIT
heWrathofKhan_1982.html

Outpost 21: The Wrath of Kahn
www.steve.simplenet.com/feature_films/2_center.html

Reel.Com: Star Trek II
www.reel.com/content/moviepage.asp?MMID=1701

Star Trek II: The Wrath of Khan Review
http://clgray.simplenet.com/strtrk/stmovie/stii.html

Starbase 6503: Star Trek II - The Wrath of Khan
www.geocities.com/Area51/Corridor/6503/TREKMOV2.HTM

Star Trek III: The Search for Spock

Terraforming, Robin Curtis' Saavik and the rebirth of Spock make Star Trek III an exciting addition to the Trek feature films. Watch the film and then check out these fine sites.

All-Movie Guide: Star Trek III
http://allmovie.com/cg/x.dll?UID=10:51:20|PM&p=avg&sql=A46540

Amazon.Com: Star Trek III - The Search for Spock
www.amazon.com/exec/obidos/ASIN/6300214400/remixparadisesho

Movie Review Query Engine: Star Trek III - Reviews
www.mrqe.com/lookup?^Star+Trek+III%3a+The+Search+for+Spock+(1984)

Mr. Showbiz . . . Star Trek III - The Search for Spock
http://mrshowbiz.go.com/reviews/moviereviews/movies/StarTrekIII
TheSearchforSpock_1984.html

Outpost 21: Search for Spock
www.steve.simplenet.com/feature_films/3_center.html

Reel.Com: Star Trek III
www.reel.com/content/moviepage.asp?MMID=1702

Star Trek III: The Search for Spock Review
http://clgray.simplenet.com/strtrk/stmovie/stiii.html

Starbase 6503: Star Trek III - The Search for Spock
www.geocities.com/Area51/Corridor/6503/TREKMOV3.HTM

Star Trek IV: The Voyage Home

Star Trek IV gave the Trek characters the opportunity to interact with present day humanity. A Klingon starship, sperm whales, and Spock's reaction to America made the fourth Trek feature a humorous adventure worthy of repeat viewing.

All Movie Guide: Star Trek IV
http://allmovie.com/cg/x.dll?UID=10:51:20|PM&p=avg&sql=A46552

Amazon.Com: Star Trek IV - The Voyage Home
www.amazon.com/exec/obidos/ASIN/6305609721/remixparadisesho

Movie Review Query Engine: Star Trek IV - Reviews
www.mrqe.com/lookup?^Star+Trek+IV%3a+The+Voyage+Home+(1986)

Mr. Showbiz . . . Star Trek IV - The Voyage Home
http://mrshowbiz.go.com/reviews/moviereviews/movies/StarTrekIVT
heVoyageHome_1986.html

Outpost 21: Voyage Home
www.steve.simplenet.com/feature_films/4_center.html

Reel.Com: Star Trek IV
www.reel.com/Content/moviepage.asp?mmid=1411

Star Trek IV: The Voyage Home Review
http://clgray.simplenet.com/strtrk/stmovie/stiv.html

Starbase 6503: Star Trek IV - The Voyage Home
www.geocities.com/Area51/Corridor/6503/TREKMOV4.HTM

Star Trek V: The Final Frontier

Directed by William Shatner, the Final Frontier deals with two touchy subjects -- God and Spock's brother. As a result, it's one of the least popular of the Trek films, but there are still some web sites devoted to it.

All-Movie Guide: Star Trek V
http://allmovie.com/cg/x.dll?UID=10:51:20|PM&p=avg&sql=FStar|Tr
ek|V:|The|Final|Frontier

Amazon.Com: Star Trek V - The Final Frontier
www.amazon.com/exec/obidos/ASIN/6305350205/remixparadisesho

Movie Review Query Engine: Star Trek V - Reviews
www.mrqe.com/lookup?^Star+Trek+V%3a+The+Final+Frontier+(1989)

Mr. Showbiz . . . Star Trek V - The Final Frontier
http://mrshowbiz.go.com/reviews/moviereviews/movies/StarTrekVTh
eFinalFrontier_1989.html

Outpost 21: The Final Frontier
www.steve.simplenet.com/feature_films/5_center.html

Reel.Com: Star Trek V
www.reel.com/Content/moviepage.asp?mmid=1733

Star Trek V: The Final Frontier Review
  http://clgray.simplenet.com/strtrk/stmovie/stv.html

Starbase 6503: Star Trek V - The Final Frontier
  www.geocities.com/Area51/Corridor/6503/TREKMOV5.HTM

Star Trek VI: The Undiscovered Country

Star Trek VI was the last film to focus entirely on the original series cast.   An intriguing mystery complete with Kim Cattrall and Iman, the Undiscovered Country is a fan favorite.

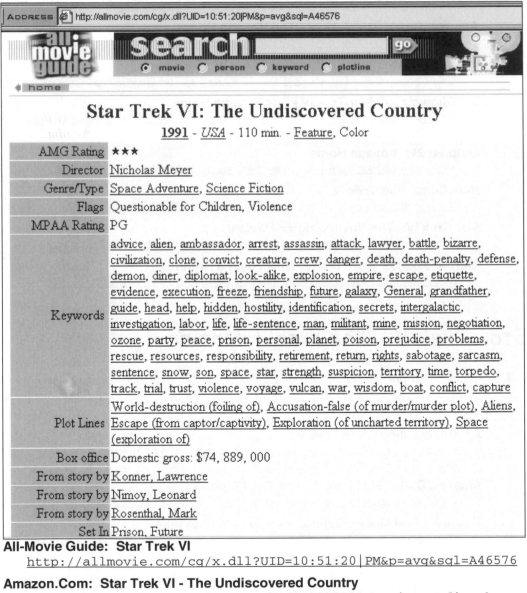

All-Movie Guide: Star Trek VI
  http://allmovie.com/cg/x.dll?UID=10:51:20|PM&p=avg&sql=A46576

Amazon.Com: Star Trek VI - The Undiscovered Country
  www.amazon.com/exec/obidos/ASIN/6305252599/remixparadisesho

Movie Review Query Engine: Star Trek VI - Reviews
  www.mrqe.com/lookup?^Star+Trek+VI%3a+The+Undiscovered+Country+(1991)

Mr. Showbiz . . . Star Trek VI - The Undiscovered Country
http://mrshowbiz.go.com/reviews/moviereviews/movies/StarTrekVITheUndiscoveredCountry_1991.html

Outpost 21: The Undiscovered Country
www.steve.simplenet.com/feature_films/6_center.html

Reel.Com: Star Trek VI
www.reel.com/Content/moviepage.asp?mmid=3040

Star Trek VI: The Undiscovered Country Review
http://clgray.simplenet.com/strtrk/stmovie/stvi.html

Starbase 6503: Star Trek VI - The Undiscoverd Country
www.geocities.com/Area51/Corridor/6503/TREKMOV6.HTM

Star Trek: Generations

Generations was the first Trek film to feature the Next Generation cast. It also featured the first meeting between Kirk and Picard. As such, Generations is frequently the topic of Trek discussions. Visit these sites to learn more about the seventh Trek feature film.

All-Movie Guide: Generations
http://allmovie.com/cg/x.dll?UID=10:51:20|PM&p=avg&sql=A133894

Amazon.Com: Star Trek - Generations
www.amazon.com/exec/obidos/ASIN/6305181721/remixparadisesho

Movie Review Query Engine: Generations - Reviews
www.mrqe.com/lookup?^Star+Trek%3a+Generations+(1994)

My Star Trek Page
http://bearcat.ubly.k12.mi.us/~todd/startrek/sttrek.html

Optical Data Network: Generations Mosaic
www.alphalink.com.au/~til/Mosaics/GenerationsMosaic.jpg

Outpost 21: Generations
www.steve.simplenet.com/feature_films/7_center.html

Reel.Com: Star Trek: Generations
www.reel.com/Content/moviepage.asp?mmid=7697

Star Trek: Generations Review
http://clgray.simplenet.com/strtrk/stmovie/stvii.html

Starbase 6503: Generations
www.geocities.com/Area51/Corridor/6503/TREKMOV7.HTM

United Federation of Planets . . . Generations
www.gh.cs.su.oz.au/~matty/Trek/generations.html

Star Trek: First Contact

First Contact marked the first time the Borg assimilated their way onto the big screen. Tremendously popular with Trek fans, First Contact has some interesting sites devoted to it. Check out the sites below to learn more about First Contact, including the debut of the Borg Queen!

All-Movie Guide: First Contact
http://allmovie.com/cg/x.dll?UID=10:51:20|PM&p=avg&sql=A136562

Amazon.Com: Star Trek - First Contact
www.amazon.com/exec/obidos/ASIN/6305127638/remixparadisesho

CNN Showbiz: New Star Trek film aims for the gut, not just the head
www.cnn.com/SHOWBIZ/9611/22/star.trek/index.html

CNN Showbiz: Patrick Stewart Celebrates His First Decade With First Contact
www.cnn.com/SHOWBIZ/9611/28/patrick.stewart

Hollywood Online: First Contact
www.hollywood.com/movies/startrek/index.html

Hollywood.Com: First Contact
www.hollywood.com/videoguide/movies/startrek

Movie Review Query Engine: First Contact - Reviews
www.mrqe.com/lookup?^Star+Trek%3a+First+Contact+(1996)

Mr. Showbiz . . . First Contact
http://mrshowbiz.go.com/reviews/moviereviews/movies/StarTrekFir
stContact_1996.html

Optical Data Network: First Contact Mosaic
www.alphalink.com.au/~til/Mosaics/FirstContactMosaic.jpg

Outpost 21: First Contact
www.steve.simplenet.com/feature_films/8_center.html

Reel.Com: Star Trek: First Contact
www.reel.com/content/moviepage.asp?MMID=12493

Sector 0-0-1: First Contact Pictures
http://members.aol.com/NCC2364/movie

Spock5774's First Contact Pics
http://hometown.aol.com/spock5774/TNGMOV3.HTM

Star Trek Stuff: First Contact
http://members.xoom.com/Neelix/stfc.html

Star Trek: First Contact Photo Gallery
www.geocities.com/Area51/Vault/5990/photo.htm

Starbase 6503: First Contact
www.geocities.com/Area51/Corridor/6503/TREKMOV8.HTM

Starfleet Command: First Contact
www.geocities.com/Area51/9802/Firstcon.htm

United Federation of Planets . . . First Contact
www.gh.cs.su.oz.au/~matty/Trek/firstcontact.html

Star Trek: Insurrection

Insurrection, the ninth Trek feature film, was the second to be directed by Jonathan Frakes. To find out more about this film and its dazzling special effects, visit the sites listed here.

AAA Star Trek: Insurrection Screenshots
http://eonmagazine.com/startrek/INSURRECTION%20SCREENSHOTS.html

Amazon.Com: Star Trek - Insurrection
www.amazon.com/exec/obidos/ASIN/B00000ILBK/remixparadisesho

Insurrection Supplement
www.geocities.com/Area51/Dimension/9644/sti_addon.html

Joan's Secret Little Star Trek: Insurrection Scrapbook
www.geocities.com/Area51/Crater/9082

Movie Review Query Engine: Insurrection - Reviews
www.mrqe.com/lookup?^Star+Trek%3a+Insurrection+(1998)

Mr. Showbiz . . . Insurrection
http://mrshowbiz.go.com/reviews/moviereviews/movies/StarTrekIns
urrection_1998.html

Spock5774's Star Trek: Insurrection Page
http://hometown.aol.com/spock5774/TNGMOV3.HTM

Star Trek News (II): Insurrection Image Gallery
www.geocities.com/Area51/Dimension/9268/insurrectionimages.html

Yahoo! Internet Life . . . Insurrection Photo Gallery
www.zdnet.com/yil/content/mag/9812/trekpics.html

Yahoo! Internet Life: The Star Trek Universe Online
www.zdnet.com/yil/content/mag/9812/trek.html

Star Trek X

Rumors are already circulating on the 'Net about the tenth Star Trek feature film. Here are some sources for news and rumors about the film.

Countdown to November 23rd 2001 (the premiere date for Star Trek X)
http://www2.wavetech.net/cgi-
bin/rfriedcd.cgi?=2001%2C11%2C23%2C20%2C20%2C00

Star Trek 10 Webring
http://m3.easyspace.com/globaltrek/webring

Star Trek X Information Page, The
www.geocities.com/Area51/Rampart/4537/st10.html

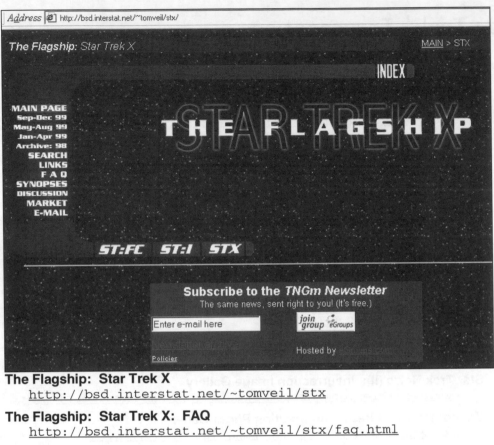

The Flagship: Star Trek X
http://bsd.interstat.net/~tomveil/stx

The Flagship: Star Trek X: FAQ
http://bsd.interstat.net/~tomveil/stx/faq.html

Trek Galaxy: Star Trek 10
http://user.super.net.uk/~nikolas/startrek10.htm

Free Enterprise

William Shatner stars in Free Enterpise -- a reference-filled spoof of the science fiction genre and its fans.

All-Movie Guide: Free Enterprise
http://allmovie.com/cg/x.dll?UID=10:51:20|PM&p=avg&sql=A174172

Internet Movie Database: Free Enterprise
http://us.imdb.com/Title?0141105

TrekToday: Review of Free Enterprise
www.trektoday.com/articles/free_enterprise.shtml

Films - Miscellaneous

From film theme songs to video clips to photographic stills, these sites offer a potpourri of Trek film fun.

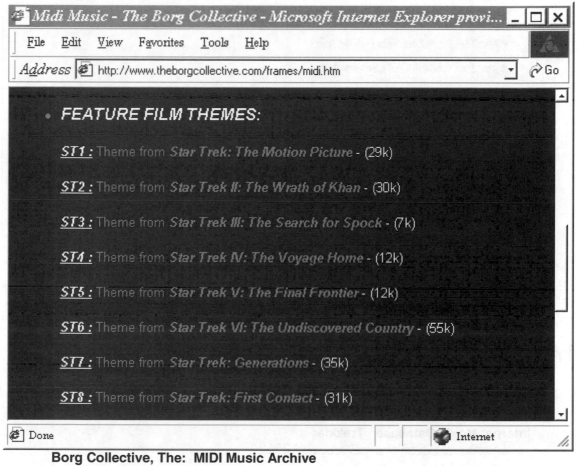

Borg Collective, The: MIDI Music Archive
www.theborgcollective.com/frames/midi.htm

Paramount Pictures
www.paramount.com

Species 8472: Star Trek Movie Clips
http://members.xoom.com/the8472s/movies.html

Star Trek - The Collective: Ready Room
www.excelsior.free-online.co.uk/sttc

ADDRESS http://aia.wu-wien.ac.at/Startrek/Filme/filme.html

Hier finden Sie Informationen (Kurzbeschreibungen und viele Bilder) zu den Star-Trek-Filmen.

- Star Trek 1 - Der Film
- Star Trek 2 - Der Zorn des Khan
- Star Trek 3 - Auf der Suche nach Mr. Spock
- Star Trek 4 - Zurück in die Vergangenheit
- Star Trek 5 - Am Rande des Universums
- Star Trek 6 - Das unentdeckte Land
- Star Trek 7 - Treffen der Generationen
- Star Trek 8 - Erster Kontakt
- Star Trek 9 - Insurrection

E-Mail | Home | Chronologie | DS9 | Filme | Milchstraße | TNG | TOS | Raumschiffe | Voyager |

Star Trek Film Information (in German)
http://aia.wu-wien.ac.at/Startrek/Filme/filme.html

Ultimate Star Trek Collection: The Movies
http://startrek.fns.net.fsn.net/movies/movies.html

Trekkies

Trekkies is a film documentary narrated by Denise Crosby that focuses on Star Trek fans and conventions. These sites are devoted to Trekkies.

Internet Movie Database: Trekkies
http://us.imdb.com/Title?0120370

Star Trek Continuum: Trekkies
www.startrek.com/trekkies

Trekkies
www.trekdoc.com

Trekkies Mail (@trekkies.zzn.com)
http://trekkies.zzn.com

THE BEST STAR TREK
Series Sites

The debate continues -- which Star Trek series is the best? Well, regardless of your answer, there are plenty of web sites devoted to each of them. If you've missed an episode, you'll find episode guides. If you can't get enough of a particular cast, you'll find fan fiction and pictures. All you need to do is pick your favorite series and warp your way to the sites listed here.

Star Trek (The Original Series)

It all started here. The original series premiered in the 1960s, and Star Trek has been a part of American culture ever since. To expand your enjoyment and knowledge of the original series, visit these terrific sites.

AAA Star Trek: Original Series Gallery
http://eonmagazine.com/startrek/1701shipthumbs.html

Being Mark Farinas
www.1pc.net/trotsky

Classic Trek on the 'Net: Novel Reviews by Trekkie Guy
www.geocities.com/Area51/Rampart/9065/review.htm

Double Trouble with Tribbles
www.skotophile.com/StarTrek/Tribbles.html

Eric's Excruciatingly Detailed Star Trek (TOS) Plot Summaries
www.treasure-troves.com/startrek

FanFiction.Net: The Original Series
www.fanfiction.net/text/browse-
listfiles.cfm?category=StarTrek%3A+The+Original+Series

FedNet: Pictures: Original Series
www.geocities.com/Area51/Rampart/3219/FedNet/pics/1.html

Internet Movie Database: Star Trek: The Original Series
http://us.imdb.com/Title?0060028

Lost Races of Star Trek: The Original Series
http://izan.simplenet.com/lostrace.htm

Main Engineering: Pictures: The Original Series
http://mainengineering.simplenet.com/pictures_tos.html

Original Series Newsgroup
alt.tv.star-trek.tos

Outpost 21: The Original Series
www.steve.simplenet.com/tos

Sabarwolf's Star Trek Picture Archive: The Original Series
http://members.tripod.com/~sabarwolf/sttos.html

Sci-Fi Channel Star Trek Episode Search
www.scifi.com/startrek/episodes

Sector 0-0-1: Episode Guides: The Original Series
http://members.aol.com/NCC2364/guide/tos.html

Spock's Mind
http://members.tripod.de/Spock1701

Star Trek (Original Series) Episode Guide
gopher://wiretap.spies.com/00/Library/Media/Trek/startrek.epi%0
9%09%2B

Star Trek Character Gallery: Original Series
http://members.easyspace.com/stcg/tos.html

Star Trek Continuum: Original Series - Images & Videos
www.startrekcontinuum.com/tos/listarchives.html

Star Trek Continuum: Original Series Episode Guide
www.startrekcontinuum.com/tos/quadrant.asp?ssector=log.asp

Star Trek Continuum: Original Series Media Archives
www.startrekcontinuum.com/tos/quadrant.asp?ssector=archives.asp

Star Trek Frontier: The Original Series
www.geocities.com/Area51/Dimension/7551/main_tos.html

Star Trek Journeys
www.fortunecity.com/lavender/hoskins/85/index.html

Star Trek Millenium: Original Series Crew
http://home.bip.net/s_t_m/toscpics.htm

Star Trek Original Series Books
www.geocities.com/Area51/Nebula/6309/QRY-
STARTREK_OriginalSeries_The_1.html

Star Trek Romance/Love List
gopher://wiretap.spies.com/00/Library/Media/Trek/startrek.lov%0
9%09%2B

Star Trek TOS Trivia
www.geocities.com/TelevisionCity/3555/startrivia.html

Star Trek: The Original Series - Trailers
http://members.xoom.com/the8472s/tos/tos.html

Star Trek: The Original Series Bad Guys
http://members.tripod.com/~Tvamp/TOS.html

Starbase 6503: The Original Series Database
www.geocities.com/Area51/Corridor/6503/STTOS.html

The Dysonsphere: Original Series: Picture Gallery
http://home1.swipnet.se/~w-10546/tos/TOSgallery.htm

The Old Star Trek Page
www.odyssey.on.ca/~cbos/TOS/TOS.html

The Site for TOS Stories
www.ludwig.ucl.ac.uk/st/StarTrek/Stories/stories.html

Trekhoo: Original Series Images
www.startrekker.net/cgi-
bin/cgiwrap/startrekker/pictures/viewpictures.cgi

Ultimate Star Trek Collection: Original Series
http://startrek.fns.net.fsn.net/tos/tos.html

USS Quetzalcoatl: The Original Series
http://members.xoom.com/_XOOM/Tona_Q/NCC-20942/tos-e.htm

Wolf 359: Classic Trek 3D Stills
http://wolf359a.anet-stl.com/tos.html

Star Trek: The Animated Series

The animated version of Star Trek featured many of the voices from the original series as well as some new characters, including a feline crew member named M'Ress. The show is rerun on Nick-At-Nite's TV Land, and has numerous web sites devoted to it.

Caitians (Feline species from the Animated Series)
www.geocities.com/Area51/Corridor/6496/caitian.html

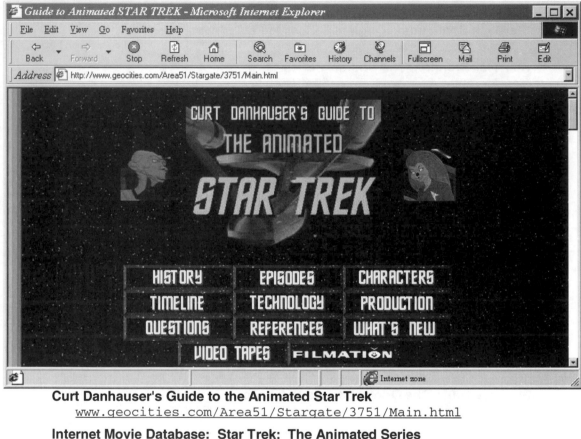

Curt Danhauser's Guide to the Animated Star Trek
www.geocities.com/Area51/Stargate/3751/Main.html

Internet Movie Database: Star Trek: The Animated Series
http://us.imdb.com/Title?0069637

Kzinti in the Star Trek Universe
gopher://wiretap.spies.com/00/Library/Media/Trek/startrek.kzn%09%09%2B

My Caitian World
www.concentric.net/~Psgibbs/index_.htm

Outpost 21: The Animated Series
www.steve.simplenet.com/tas/index_nf.html

Sabarwolf's Star Trek Picture Archive: Animated Series
http://members.tripod.com/~sabarwolf/sttas.html

Sheryl's Animated Star Trek Page
www.sherylfranklin.com/trekanim.html

Star Trek Continuum: The Animated Series
www.startrekcontinuum.com/lcars/quadrant.asp?ssector=animated.asp

Star Trek: The Animated Series
http://mainengineering.simplenet.com/tas_main.html

Star Trek: The Animated Series: Animations
http://mainengineering.simplenet.com/tas_animations.html

Star Trek: The Animated Series: Art
http://mainengineering.simplenet.com/tas_art.html

Star Trek: The Animated Series: Greeting Cards
http://mainengineering.simplenet.com/tas_greetingcards.html

The Dysonsphere: Animated Series: Picture Gallery
http://home1.swipnet.se/~w-10546/tas/TASgallery.htm

Ultimate Star Trek Collection: The Animated Series
http://startrek.fns.net.fsn.net/tas/tas.html

USS Quetzalcoatl: The Animated Series
http://members.xoom.com/_XOOM/Tona_Q/NCC-20942/tas-e.htm

Star Trek: The Next Generation

Gene Roddenberry boldly went where no one had gone before in creating a syndicated sequel to a series that had ended many years prior. Nonetheless, the Next Generation rejuvenated the Trek franchise in that it introduced a whole new "generation" of fans to the Trek universe. Plus, it brought Trek mainstays such as Q and the Borg into the fold. There are many sites devoted to this fine series -- here are some of the best.

"Child's Play" (An Unused Next Generation Script)
www.el-dorado.ca.us/~dmnews/script/childs_play.html

AAA Star Trek: Next Generation Gallery
http://eonmagazine.com/startrek/sttng%20gallery%20page%201.html

Bay's Picard/Crusher Stories
www.geocities.com/TelevisionCity/Stage/8486/Stories.html

Big Bill's Star Trek Stuff
www.kruse.demon.co.uk/index.htm

Data & Tasha Fanfic Page, The
www.geocities.com/Area51/Stargate/1206

Ern Yoka's Star Trek TNG Page
http://ernyoka.somewhere.net

FanFiction.Net: Next Generation
www.fanfiction.net/text/browse-
listfiles.cfm?category=StarTrek%3A+The+Next+Generation

Federation Sound Archive: WAVs
www.domaindlx.com/timbo/thewavs.html

Identity, Paranoia & Technology on the Next Generation
http://eng.hss.cmu.edu/cyber/startrek.html

Imazadi - Their Hearts Beat As One
http://members.xoom.com/invilil

Internet Movie Database: The Next Generation
http://us.imdb.com/Title?0092455

Main Engineering: Pictures: Next Generation
http://mainengineering.simplenet.com/pictures_tng.html

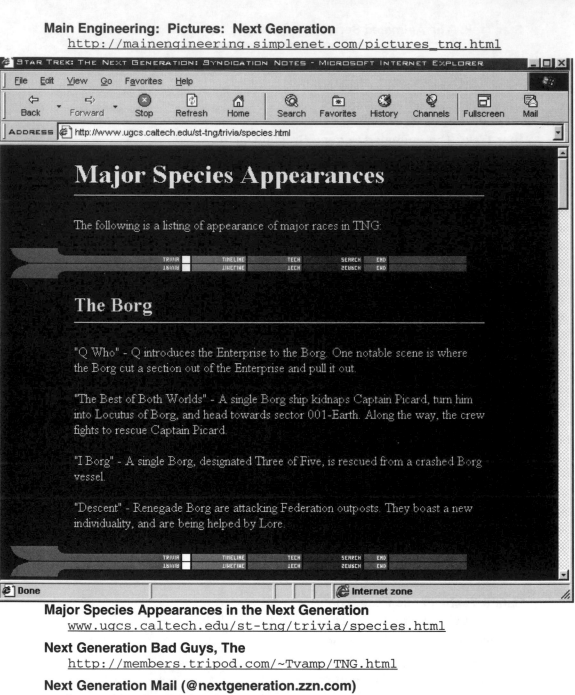

Major Species Appearances in the Next Generation
www.ugcs.caltech.edu/st-tng/trivia/species.html

Next Generation Bad Guys, The
http://members.tripod.com/~Tvamp/TNG.html

Next Generation Mail (@nextgeneration.zzn.com)
http://nextgeneration.zzn.com

Next Generation Newsgroup I
alt.tv.star-trek.tng

Next Generation Newsgroup II
alt.tv.star-trek.next-gen

Operation SNAFU (Blooper & Gaff Information for TNG)
www.ugcs.caltech.edu/st-tng/trivia/snafu.html

Outpost 21: Next Generation
www.steve.simplenet.com/tas/index_nf.html

Outpost 21: Next Generation Episode Guide
www.steve.simplenet.com/episode_guides/tng

Quirks, Quarks & Tribbles: Next Generation
www.geocities.com/Area51/Vault/3203/tng.htm

Ryan's Star Trek Page
http://www2.mmind.net/ryanj

Sabarwolf's Star Trek Picture Archive: Next Generation
http://members.tripod.com/~sabarwolf/sttng.html

Sector 0-0-1: Episode Guides: Next Generation
http://members.aol.com/NCC2364/guide/tng.html

Star Trek - The Collective: Memory Core
www.geocities.com/Area51/Dimension/9644/memcore.html

Star Trek Character Gallery: Next Generation
http://members.easyspace.com/stcg/tng.html

Star Trek Continuum: Next Generation - Images & Videos
www.startrekcontinuum.com/tng/listarchives.html

Star Trek Continuum: Next Generation Episode Guide
www.startrekcontinuum.com/tng/quadrant.asp?ssector=log.asp

Star Trek Continuum: Next Generation Media Archives
www.startrekcontinuum.com/tng/quadrant.asp?ssector=archives.asp

Star Trek Frontier . . . The Next Generation
www.geocities.com/Area51/Dimension/7551/main_tng.html

Star Trek Millenium: Next Generation Crew
http://home.bip.net/s_t_m/tngcpics.htm

Star Trek Next Generation Books
www.geocities.com/Area51/Nebula/6309/QRY-
STARTREK_NextGeneration_The_1.html

Star Trek Relationshippers: TNG Profiles
www.geocities.com/~teepee47/relprof-tng.html

Star Trek TNG List of Lists
www.ugcs.caltech.edu/st-tng/trivia/list.html

Star Trek: The Next Generation - Trailers
http://members.xoom.com/the8472s/tng/tng.html

Star Trek: The Next Generation by Spast
http://www2.vo.lu/Homepages/ahmadzadeh/startrek

Starbase 6503: Next Generation Database
www.geocities.com/Area51/Corridor/6503/STTNG.html

Starfleet Supply: Next Generation Episode Guide
www.geocities.com/Area51/Stargate/7952/sttnge.html

Ten Forward Lounge
www.interlog.com/~pcarr/star_trek/home.html

The Dysonsphere: Next Generation: Picture Gallery
http://home1.swipnet.se/~w-10546/tng/TNGgallery.htm

TNG Mail (@tng.zzn.com)
http://tng.zzn.com

Ultimate Star Trek Collection: Next Generation
http://startrek.fns.net.fsn.net/tng/tng.html

USS Concordant . . . The Next Generation
http://goliat.eik.bme.hu/~wraith/tng/tng.html

USS Quetzalcoatl: Next Generation
http://members.xoom.com/_XOOM/Tona_Q/NCC-20942/tng-ie.htm

Star Trek: Deep Space Nine

Deep Space Nine was the first Star Trek series that was not set on a starship. Rather, it was set on an alien space station. Decidedly darker than either of the two previous Trek series, Deep Space Nine developed its own place in the Star Trek universe. Its wildly popular characters and war with the Dominion made it a fan favorite. Check out these Deep Space Nine-related sites.

AAA Star Trek: Deep Space Nine "Past & Present"
http://eonmagazine.com/startrek/ds9%20look%20past-present.html

AAA Star Trek: Deep Space Nine Gallery
http://eonmagazine.com/startrek/ds9%20gallery%20page%201.html

AllExperts.Com: Ask a Question about Deep Space Nine
www.allexperts.com/tv/ds9.shtml

Crew's Reviews - DS9 & Voyager Episode Reviews
www.geocities.com/Hollywood/Academy/6325/reviews.html

Deep Space Nine Bad Guys
http://members.tripod.com/~Tvamp/DS9.html

Deep Space Nine Bible
gopher://wiretap.spies.com/00/Library/Media/Trek/deep9.bib%09%09%2B

Deep Space Nine Mail (@deepspacenine.zzn.com)
http://deepspacenine.zzn.com

Defiant Mail (@defiant.zzn.com)
http://defiant.zzn.com

Defiant Pictures
www.geocities.com/Area51/Corridor/1364/defiant.html

Double Trouble with Tribbles
www.skotophile.com/StarTrek/Tribbles.html

DS9 Episode Guide 98
www.geocities.com/TimesSquare/4818/ds92.htm

DS9 Personnel Gallery
www.geocities.com/Area51/Nebula/4349/g_ds9.html

DS9 Windows Desktop Theme
http://users.dx.com.au/wormhole/themes.html

Dukat Photogallery, The
http://members.theglobe.com/RatboyX/photogalleries.html

FanFiction.Net: Deep Space Nine
www.fanfiction.net/text/browse-listfiles.cfm?category=StarTrek%3A+Deep+Space+Nine

FedNet: Pictures: Deep Space Nine
www.geocities.com/Area51/Rampart/3219/FedNet/pics/3.html

Garak's Star Trek Tailor Shop: Deep Space Nine Quotes
www.geocities.com/Hollywood/Academy/6325/ds9quote.html

Garak's Star Trek Tailor Shop: Tour Deep Space Nine
www.geocities.com/Hollywood/Academy/6325/tactical/tourds9.html

Internet Movie Database: Deep Space Nine
http://us.imdb.com/Title?0106145

Jade Dixon's Ultimate Deep Space Nine Page
www.geocities.com/Hollywood/Set/8113

Julian & Ezri Multimedia
http://members.tripod.com/~chrys42

Julian/Ezri Relationshippers
http://beam.to/julianezri

Locutus' Hang: Deep Space Nine Pictures
www.geocities.com/Area51/Labyrinth/8852/pic5.htm

Main Engineering: Pictures: Deep Space Nine
http://mainengineering.simplenet.com/pictures_ds9.html

Maximum Defiant
www.maximumdefiant.com

Maximum Defiant: Multimedia: Sounds
www.maximumdefiant.com/multi/sounds/index.html

My Adventure on Star Trek - Deep Space Nine
www.capital.net/~jorel/ds91.htm

Optical Data Network: Deep Space Nine Season 6 Pictures
www.alphalink.com.au/~til/DS9.htm

Optical Data Network: Deep Space Nine Season 7 Pictures
www.alphalink.com.au/~til/DS9-S7.htm

Outpost 21: Deep Space Nine
www.steve.simplenet.com/ds9

Outpost 21: Deep Space Nine Episode Guide
www.steve.simplenet.com/episode_guides/ds9

Psi Phi's Deep Space Nine Archive
www.psiphi.org/DS9/?

Psi Phi's Deep Space Nine Director Credits
www.psiphi.org/DS9/ep/directors.html?ix

Psi Phi's Deep Space Nine Novels
www.psiphi.org/DS9/books.html?ix

Red Dwarf & Star Trek Gallery: Deep Space Nine
www.geocities.com/Hollywood/4196/ds9pg.htm

Sabarwolf's Star Trek Picture Archive: Deep Space Nine
http://members.tripod.com/~sabarwolf/stds9.html

Sector 0-0-1: Episode Guides: Deep Space Nine
http://members.aol.com/NCC2364/guide/ds9.html

Species 8472: Complete Episodes
http://members.xoom.com/the8472s/complete.html

Star Trek Character Gallery: Deep Space Nine
http://members.easyspace.com/stcg/ds9.html

Star Trek Continuum: Deep Space Nine - Images & Videos
www.startrekcontinuum.com/ds9/listarchives.html

Star Trek Continuum: Deep Space Nine Episode Guide
www.startrekcontinuum.com/ds9/quadrant.asp?ssector=log.asp

Star Trek Continuum: Deep Space Nine Media Archives
www.startrekcontinuum.com/ds9/quadrant.asp?ssector=archives.asp

Star Trek Deep Space Nine Books
www.geocities.com/Area51/Nebula/6309/QRY-
STARTREK_DeepSpaceNine_1.html

Star Trek Frontier: Deep Space Nine
www.geocities.com/Area51/Dimension/7551/main_ds9.html

Star Trek Millenium: Deep Space Nine (Station) Pictures
http://home.bip.net/s_t_m/ds9pics.htm

Star Trek Millenium: Deep Space Nine Crew Pictures
http://home.bip.net/s_t_m/ds9cpics.htm

Star Trek Millenium: Defiant Pictures
http://home.bip.net/s_t_m/defpics.htm

Star Trek News (II): Deep Space Nine
www.geocities.com/Area51/Dimension/9268/deepspacenine.html

Star Trek Relationshippers: Deep Space Nine Profiles
www.geocities.com/~teepee47/relprof-ds9.html

Starbase 6503: Deep Space Nine Database Page
www.geocities.com/Area51/Corridor/6503/STDS9.html

The Dysonsphere: Deep Space Nine: Picture Gallery
http://home1.swipnet.se/~w-10546/ds9/DS9gallery.htm

Ultimate Star Trek Collection: Deep Space Nine
http://startrek.fns.net.fsn.net/ds9/ds9.html

United Federation of Planets . . . Deep Space Nine
www.gh.cs.su.oz.au/~matty/Trek/ds9.html

USS Concordant . . . Deep Space Nine
http://goliat.eik.bme.hu/~wraith/ds9/ds9tsr.html

USS Quetzalcoatl: Deep Space Nine
http://members.xoom.com/_XOOM/Tona_Q/NCC-20942/ds9-e.htm

Star Trek: Voyager

The fourth Trek series, focusing on the adventures of a lone Federation ship in the vastly unexplored Delta Quadrant has grown increasingly popular. The sites listed here with introduce you to the USS Voyager and her crew.

"Realization" (An Unused Voyager Script)
www.stikfigure.com/willmartin/realization.htm

AAA Star Trek: Voyager Gallery
http://eonmagazine.com/startrek/voyager%20gallery%20page%202.html

Alexander Enberg (Ensign Vorik) Fan Page
http://members.aol.com/BrentFemme/enberg.html

AllExperts.Com: Ask a question about Voyager
www.allexperts.com/tv/voyager.shtml

Anti-Voyager Newsgroup
alt.flame.star-trek.voyager

August's Fanfic Collection (Voyager Fan Fiction)
http://members.tripod.com/~Appelsini/fanfic.html

Captain Kathryn Janeway's Web Site: Voyager Greeting Cards
http://www4.bravenet.com/postcard/post.asp?userid=ys71524

Crew's Reviews - DS9 & Voyager Episode Reviews
www.geocities.com/Hollywood/Academy/6325/reviews.html

Delta Blues
www.treknews.com/deltablues

Delta Quadrant Alien Database
www.geocities.com/Area51/Rampart/3448/aliens.html

Delta Quadrant, The
www.netcom.ca/~seska

FanFiction.Net: Voyager
www.fanfiction.net/text/browse-
listfiles.cfm?category=StarTrek%3A+Voyager

Fashion Voyager
http://home.att.net/~fashion.voyager

Federation of Obssessed Voyager Fans: Sites List
www.webring.org/cgi-bin/webring?ring=voyfan;list

FedNet: Fanfic by Jeffrey Harlan
www.geocities.com/Area51/Rampart/3219/FedNet/fanfic/index.html

FedNet: Pictures: Voyager
www.geocities.com/Area51/Rampart/3219/FedNet/pics/4.html

Garak's Star Trek Tailor Shop: Voyager Quotes
www.geocities.com/Hollywood/Academy/6325/voyquote.html

Great Seven/Kes Debate, The
www.geocities.com/Area51/Rampart/3448/poll.html

Holodeck 1 (Voyager Photos)
www.geocities.com/Area51/Nebula/1876/Crew.htm

Inside Voyager
www.geocities.com/Area51/Stargate/7559/index.html

JetC14 Fan Fiction Archive
http://web.ukonline.co.uk/sammi.w2/jetc/jetc14fanfic.htm

JuPiter Station (II)
www.geocities.com/~jupiterstation

JuPiter Station (II): J/P Sounds
www.geocities.com/~jupiterstation/JuPSounds.htm

Katie's Star Trek Site
www.geocities.com/Hollywood/8007

KoaliTion Headquaters
http://user.aol.com/jyorraku/ktmain.html

Kret Rats P/T Home Page
http://members.tripod.com/~Maihe

Kret Rats: Voyager Promo Pics
http://members.tripod.com/~Maihe/promopics.html

KTH Media Archive (Kim/Torres)
www.fortunecity.com/tattooine/russ/259/media.html

Lanna's P/T Picks
www.geocities.com/TelevisionCity/Set/6627

Leila's Voyager Page
www.geocities.com/Area51/Cavern/9441

Leila's Voyager Page: Backgrounds
www.geocities.com/Area51/Cavern/9441/epback.html

Main Engineering: Pictures: Voyager
http://mainengineering.simplenet.com/pictures_voy.html

My Star Trek Voyager Page
http://members.aol.com/mergez/scifi/voyager/voyager.html

Official Archive of the Paris/Torres Collective
www.geocities.com/~ptcarchive

Outpost 21: Voyager
www.steve.simplenet.com/voy

Outpost 21: Voyager Episode Guide
www.steve.simplenet.com/episode_guides/voy

Psi Phi's Star Trek: Voyager Archive
www.psiphi.org/voy

Quantum Slipstream
www.geocities.com/Area51/Dunes/8431

Red Dwarf & Star Trek Gallery: Voyager
www.geocities.com/Hollywood/4196/vpg.htm

Sabarwolf's Star Trek Picture Archive: Voyager
http://members.tripod.com/~sabarwolf/stvoy.html

Sector 0-0-1: Episode Guides: Voyager
http://members.aol.com/NCC2364/guide/voy.html

Security/Tactical Station: Voyager News
www.excelsior.free-online.co.uk/sttc

So why finally a woman captain?
www.trekplanet.com/janeway.html

Star Trek - The Collective: Voyager
www.sttc.co.uk/news-voy.html

Star Trek Character Gallery: Voyager
http://members.easyspace.com/stcg/voyager.html

Star Trek Continuum: Voyager Episode Guide
www.startrekcontinuum.com/voy/quadrant.asp?ssector=log.asp

Star Trek Continuum: Voyager Media Archives
www.startrekcontinuum.com/voy/quadrant.asp?ssector=archives.asp

Star Trek Frontier . . . Voyager
www.geocities.com/Area51/Dimension/7551/main_voyager.html

Star Trek Millenium: USS Voyager Pictures
http://home.bip.net/s_t_m/vpics.htm

Star Trek Millenium: Voyager Crew Pictures
http://home.bip.net/s_t_m/voycpics.htm

Star Trek News (II): Voyager
www.geocities.com/Area51/Dimension/9268/voyager.html

Star Trek Relationshippers: Voyager Profiles
www.geocities.com/~teepee47/relprof-voy.html

Star Trek Voyager - Lower Decks
http://ljc.simplenet.com/lowerdecks

Star Trek Voyager Books
www.geocities.com/Area51/Nebula/6309/QRY-
STARTREK_Voyager_1.html

Star Trek Voyager Women
www.sherylfranklin.com/trekwomen_voyager.html

The Dysonsphere: Voyager: Picture Gallery
http://home1.swipnet.se/~w-10546/voy/VOYgallery.htm

VOYAGER - MICROSOFT INTERNET EXPLORER   _ □ ×

File Edit View Go Favorites Help

⇦ Back   ⇨ Forward   ⊗ Stop   ↻ Refresh   ⌂ Home   ◉ Search   ⋇ Favorites   ◷ History   ◷ Channels   ⊡ Fullscreen   ✉ Mail   🖶 Print   ✎ Edit

ADDRESS http://startrek.fns.net.fsn.net/voy/voy.html

TOS
TAS
TNG
DS9
INDEX

The voyages of the Starship U.S.S. Voyager.
(setting -- the 24th century)

The fourth and newest STAR TREK series, which hit U.S. airwaves in January 1995, is the first to feature a female Captain -- Kathryn Janeway. Set aboard the starship U.S.S. Voyager NCC-74656, the ship and crew are marooned over 70,000 light years from Federation space and struggling to find a way home. The U.S.S. Voyager was carried beyond the explored limits of space while in pursuit of a rebel Maquis vessel, and out of necessity, the two marooned ships combined into a mismatched crew of Starfleet officers and Maquis rebels.

U.S.S. VOYAGER

The main crew members of the U.S.S. Voyager are: Captain Kathryn Janeway (Kate Mulgrew), Vulcan Starfleet Tactical/Security Officer Tuvok (Tim Russ), a Holographic Doctor (Robert Picardo) and the former rebel leader as Janeway's First Officer Chakotay (Robert Beltran). A native of this region of space takes on the roles of Guide/Cook/Handyman, Neelix (Ethan Philips), with his Ocampa companion Kes (Jennifer Lien) alongside. A half Klingon ex-rebel serves as Chief Engineer B'Elanna Torres (Roxann Biggs-Dawson), and a recent Academy graduate is Ops/Communications Officer Harry Kim (Garrett Wang). The ship's pilot is field-commissioned Lieutenant Tom Paris (Robert Duncan McNeill). A borg drone separated from the collective has also joined the crew and has been named Seven of Nine (Jeri Ryan).

Ultimate Star Trek Collection: Voyager
http://startrek.fns.net.fsn.net/voy/voy.html

Ultimate TV Show List: Voyager
www.ultimatetv.com/UTVL/show.html?1086

United Federation of Planets . . . Voyager
www.gh.cs.su.oz.au/~matty/Trek/voyager.html

USS Concordant . . . Voyager
http://goliat.eik.bme.hu/~wraith/voy/voytsr.html

USS Prometheus: Voyager News & Upcoming Episodes
www.geocities.com/Area51/Rampart/3448/news.html

USS Prometheus: Voyager Photo Gallery
www.geocities.com/Area51/Rampart/3448/download.html

USS Quetzalcoatl: Voyager
http://members.xoom.com/_XOOM/Tona_Q/NCC-20942/voy-e.htm

USS Voyager
www.aplus.com/seth/trek

USS Voyager Crew Log
www.geocities.com/Area51/Dimension/9644/voycrew.html

Voyager Director Credits
www.psiphi.org/voy/ep/directors.html

Voyager Extreme
www.geocities.com/TimesSquare/Hangar/2213

Voyager Fanatics Webring
www.geocities.com/Area51/Chamber/2434/ring.html

Voyager Fanatics Webring: Sites List
www.webring.org/cgi-bin/webring?ring=stv&list

Voyager Image Archive
www.aplus.com/seth/trek/voyimage.html

Voyager Jeffries' Tubes: Episode Guide
www.geocities.com/Area51/Dimension/9644/voy_eps.html

Voyager Journey Guide
www.geocities.com/Area51/Dimension/9644/voyjourney.html

Voyager Mail (@voyager.zzn.com)
http://voyager.zzn.com

Voyager Musician Credits
www.psiphi.org/voy/ep/music.html

Voyager Newsgroup
alt.tv.star-trek.voyager

Voyager Novels
www.aplus.com/seth/trek/novels.html

Voyager Online Cast/Crew Transcripts
www.psiphi.org/voy/transcripts.html

Voyager Pictures
www.geocities.com/Area51/Corridor/1364/voyager.html

Voyager Producer Credits
www.psiphi.org/voy/ep/producers.html

Voyager Shrine Webring: Sites List
www.webring.org/cgi-bin/webring?ring=voyagershrine;list

Voyager Tour, The
www.geocities.com/Area51/Shadowlands/7129/voygreeting.html

Voyager Writer Credits
www.psiphi.org/voy/ep/writers.html

Voyager's Delights
www.capecod.net/~druddy

Voyager's Delights: Photo Gallery
www.capecod.net/~druddy/photo.htm

Star Trek: New Frontier

New Frontier is the name used to describe a "new Trek series" that exists only in book form. New Frontier has an entirely new ship, captain and crew. Written by Peter David, the New Frontier series from Pocket Books is incredibly popular.

Amazon.Com: Star Trek - New Frontier - Books 1-4
www.amazon.com/exec/obidos/ASIN/0671019783/remixparadisesho

Guide to Star Trek: New Frontier
http://www1.ridgecrest.ca.us/~curtdan/NewFrontier/Excalibur.cgi?FILE=Enter

Guide to Star Trek: New Frontier: Hyperpedia
http://www1.ridgecrest.ca.us/~curtdan/NewFrontier/Excalibur.cgi?FILE=Hypedia_GN

New Frontier Crew Pictures
www.geocities.com/Area51/Corridor/5363/excalibur.html

Discussing
STAR TREK

Whether you want to discuss warp theory or the latest *Seven of Nine* costume, this chapter offers you the chance to share your thoughts with fellow fans. You can join a chat room, post messages in a forum, get your own Trek-oriented e-mail address, and even share your own crossover ideas. Fire up your computer, access a "cyberspace channel," and open your "hailing frequencies"!

Anti-Star Trek Sites

For every fan there's an "anti-fan," someone who despises the object of the fan's obsession. Star Trek is no exception. Although, Star Trek has millions of fans worldwide, there are also a lot of people who don't like it, and even enjoy making fun of it. Here are some sites devoted to the "bashing" of Star Trek as whole or an aspect of it. These sites are presented in this chapter, because perhaps more than any other Trek-related sites, these are bound to spark discussion.

Anti-Voyager Newsgroup
alt.flame.star-trek.voyager

Anti-Wesley Crusher Newsgroup
alt.wesley.crusher.die.die.die

I Hate Star Trek Page
http://members.tripod.com/~Desslok/dietrek/trkstink.htm

MAAT - The March Against Anti-Trekism
www.geocities.com/~deadlockdomain/maat.html

NDS - Neelix Death Squad
www.geocities.com/Area51/Rampart/1470

Punch Captain Kirk
www.well.com/user/vanya/kirk.html

Star Trek vs. Babylon 5 Newsgroup
alt.startrek.vs.babylon5

Star Trek vs. Battlestar Gallactica Newsgroup
 alt.startrek.vs.battlestar-gallactica

Star Trek vs. Lost In Space Newsgroup
 alt.startrek.vs.lost-in-space

Star Trek vs. Star Wars
 www.startrekvsstarwars.8m.com

Star Trek vs. Star Wars Newsgroup
 alt.startrek.vs.starwars

Why Star Trek Sucks
 www.flash.net/~twinkle/psycho/DARK/scholarly/trek.htm

Chat Rooms

Online "chat" is a live, typewritten conversation with one or more persons in cyberspace. The sites below offer chat rooms or links to them. Whether you speak Klingon or English in your ready room, these chat rooms will give you the chance to communicate with other Trekkers.

B'Elanna Torres Chat
 www.angelfire.com/az/chadtrek/chat2.html

Bad Guys of Star Trek, The
 http://members.tripod.com/~Tvamp

Borg Collective, The
 www.theborgcollective.com

Dancing Doctor's Domain, The
 www.lustchip.com/dancingdoctor

Incredible Internet Guide Series
 www.brbpub.com/iig

JuPiter Station (II)
 www.geocities.com/~jupiterstation

KirkChat Live Chat
 www.geocities.com/Area51/Rampart/4537/live.htm

Kommunity ChaTter (Kim/Torres)
 http://user.aol.com/jyorraku/chat.html

Main Engineering
 http://mainengineering.simplenet.com

Odo-Chat
 www.renefiles.com/comlink7.html

Official Jeri Lynn Ryan Homepage, The
 www.jerilynn.com

Q Continuum (I)
 www.geocities.com/Area51/Zone/4431/frames1.htm

Q Continuum (I): Q's Live Chat
 www.geocities.com/Area51/Zone/4431/chat.html

Shuttle Bay 5
 www.geocities.com/Area51/Corridor/8109/sb5.htm

Spiner's Domain
www.spiner.org

Star Trek - Dark Fire: SubSpace
www.datania.com/star-trek/subspace.html

Star Trek - Main Engineering: Chat Room
http://mainengineering.simplenet.com/chat.html

Star Trek - The Collective
www.geocities.com/Area51/Dimension/9644

Star Trek Admiral's Universe
www.startrekker.net/index.shtml

Star Trek Continuum
www.startrek.com

Star Trek Continuum: Chat Rooms
www.startrekcontinuum.com/schq/quadrant.asp?ssector=loungeintro
.asp

Star Trek Continuum: Klingon Great Hall Chat
www.startrekcontinuum.com/kli/Quadrant.asp?ssector=greathall.asp

Star Trek Empire, The
http://home.earthlink.net/~dstubbs

Star Trek Portal
www.strek.com

Star Trek Stuff @ Trekplanet.Com
www.trekplanet.com/startrek.html

Star Trek: The Animated Series
http://mainengineering.simplenet.com/tas_main.html

Star Trek: The Sci-Fi Channel Special Edition
www.scifi.com/startrek

Starfleet Chat
http://earth.beseen.com/chat/rooms/d/510666

Starfleet Database
http://www2.prestel.co.uk/majeed

Subspace Array: WarpChat
http://subspace.virtualave.net/array/chat/index.html

Subspace Communications
http://subspace.virtualave.net

TrekExpress.Com
www.trekexpress.com

TrekExpress.Com: Chat
www.trekexpress.com/chat.htm

Trekker One
www.angelfire.com/nc/TrekkerOne/index.html

TrekWeb.com
www.trekweb.com

UCESS - United Coalition of Earthwide Starfleet Simulations
www.geocities.com/Area51/Rampart/4776/ucess.html

United Interstellar Planets
www.uip.org

Vash's Q Chat Page
www.tedric.demon.co.uk/qchat.html

Vortaphiles
http://www0.delphi.com/Vortaphiles

Webtrekker
www.geocities.com/Area51/Rampart/8138/webtreker.html

Conventions

Find out about past and upcoming Star Trek and science fiction conventions by visiting these web sites.

AAA Star Trek: Conventions
http://eonmagazine.com/startrek/conventions%20page%201.html

About.Com: Star Trek Conventions Listings
http://startrek.about.com/blcon.htm?pid=2833&cob=home

ConNotation - The UK, European & World Science Fiction Convention Listing
www.smof.com/conlist.htm

Creation Convention Central
www.creationent.com/calendar.html

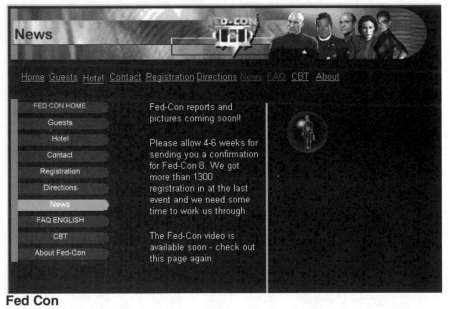

Fed Con
www.fedcon.de

Kristin's Space Central - Convention Reports & More
www.geocities.com/Hollywood/5347/index.html

Lisa's
Sci-Fi
Conventions
HOME PAGE

This site best viewed with Netscape / IE 4.0 or higher
(a computer and modem also help)

Hi! My name is Lisa and I've been a sci-fi fan for almost
seven years. One of the best parts of being a sci-fi fan is
attending conventions! If you still think conventions (or
"cons") are like William Shatner's "Get a Life" sketch,
think again!

If you've never been to a Star Trek or sci-fi convention,
this page is the next best thing. I've included lots of
convention information, pictures from cons I've attended
and tips on attending a convention (if you decide to take
the plunge!)

Lisa's Sci-Fi Conventions Home Page
www.homestead.com/NYTrekker/main.html

My Star Trek Voyager Page
http://members.aol.com/mergez/scifi/voyager/voyager.html

Sci Fi TV/Star Trek/Babylon 5 Conventions Webring
http://pw2.netcom.com/~brucas/sftvcons/index.html

Science Fiction Conventions Webring
www.io.com/~lsc2/sfcons.html

Star Trek - The Collection
www.geocities.com/Hollywood/Set/6458

Star Trek Nexus: Convention Info
http://members.aol.com/treknexus/trektime.htm

Trekker One
www.angelfire.com/nc/TrekkerOne/index.html

TrekNEWS Fandom: Conventions
www.treknews.com/fandom/conventions/index.html

TrekTape.Com (Convention Footage)
www.trektape.com

World-Wide Collectors Digest: Star Trek Conventions
www.wwcd.com/shows/trek-home.html

Crossovers

One of the most popular sources of discussion for any subject that has a fan following is crossovers. What if Captain Picard fought Darth Vader? What if a Borg Cube encountered the Death Star? Etc. The following sites give you the opportunity to read about and discuss crossovers.

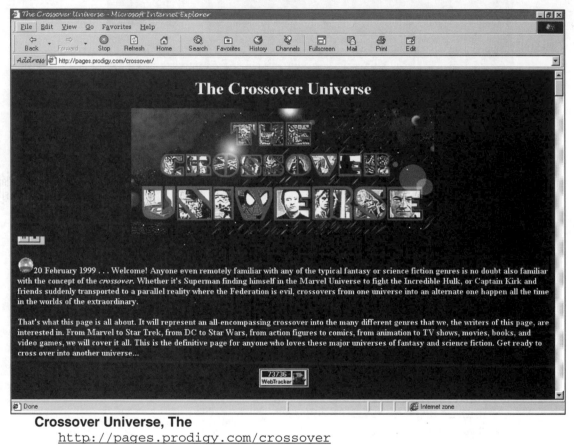

Crossover Universe, The
http://pages.prodigy.com/crossover

Jesse's Star Trek Crossover Page
http://members.easyspace.com/trekxover

Optical Data Network: Babylon 5/Star Trek Crossover
www.alphalink.com.au/~til/B5-ST.htm

USS Athena
www.weddingdaybridals.com/USS_Athena/index.htm

X-Files/Star Trek X-Overs
www.busprod.com/aclaybor/xover/categ/startrek.htm

E-Mail Services

Do you have a boring e-mail address? Would you prefer one that shows your love for Star Trek? You can "Make it so" by checking out these sites.

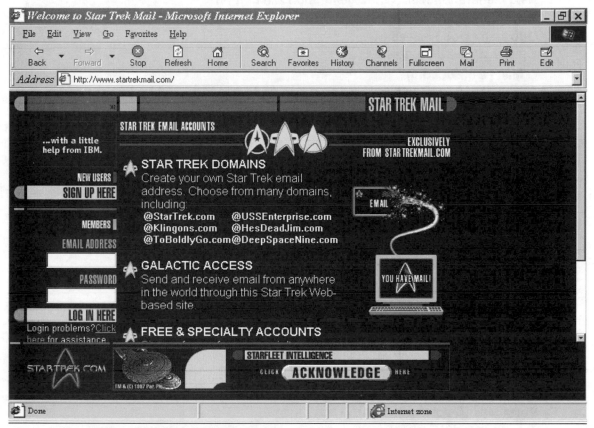

Bajor Mail (@bajor.zzn.com)
http://bajor.zzn.com

Beam Me Up Mail (@beammeup.zzn.com)
http://beammeup.zzn.com

Cardassia Mail (@cardassia.zzn.com)
http://cardassia.zzn.com

Deep Space Nine Mail (@deepspacenine.zzn.com)
http://deepspacenine.zzn.com

Defiant Mail (@defiant.zzn.com)
http://defiant.zzn.com

Dominion Mail (@dominion.zzn.com)
http://dominion.zzn.com

Enterprise Mail (@enterprise.zzn.com)
http://enterprise.zzn.com

Federation Mail (@federation.zzn.com)
http://federation.zzn.com

Janeway Mail (@janeway.zzn.com)
http://janeway.zzn.com

Kirk Mail (@kirk.zzn.com)
http://kirk.zzn.com

Klingons Mail (@klingons.zzn.com)
http://klingons.zzn.com

Next Generation Mail (@nextgeneration.zzn.com)
http://nextgeneration.zzn.com

Odo Mail (@odo.zzn.com)
http://odo.zzn.com

Q Mail (@q.zzn.com)
http://q.zzn.com

Spock Mail (@spock.zzn.com)
http://spock.zzn.com

Star Trek Mail (multiple @ domains)
www.startrekmail.com

Starfleet Mail (@starfleetmail.zzn.com)
http://starfleetmail.zzn.com

SubSpaceMail.Com
www.subspacemail.com

TNG Mail (@tng.zzn.com)
http://tng.zzn.com

Trek Epals - Get a Star Trek E-mail Pal
http://startrek.about.com/blpals.htm?pid=2833&cob=home

Trekkers Mail (@trekkers.zzn.com)
http://trekkers.zzn.com

Trekkies Mail (@trekkies.zzn.com)
http://trekkies.zzn.com

Vorta Mail (@vorta.zzn.com)
http://vorta.zzn.com

Voyager Mail (@voyager.zzn.com)
http://voyager.zzn.com

WarpMail
http://warpmail.enterwarp.com

Warpspeed Mail (@warpspeed.zzn.com)
http://warpspeed.zzn.com

Worf Mail (@worf.zzn.com)
http://worf.zzn.com

Electronic Greeting & Post Cards

Send a greeting through subspace . . . er, cyberspace using electronic "post cards." These sites offer you the chance to brighten someone's day with an e-mail greeting featuring Star Trek characters.

Borg Collective, The: Postcards from the Collective
www.theborgcollective.com/frames/postcards.htm

Captain Kathryn Janeway's Web Site: Voyager Greeting Cards
http://www4.bravenet.com/postcard/post.asp?userid=ys71524

Captain's Holocards
www.geocities.com/Area51/Nebula/1876/Holocards.htm

Infinitely Imzadi: Electronic Postcards
www.fortunecity.com/tattooine/pratchett/66/imzadicards.htm

Main Engineering: Postcard Center
http://mainengineering.simplenet.com/postcards.html

Seska & Martha Hackett Post Cards
www.marthahackett.com/postcards/card.html

Seven of Nine E-Mail Postcards
www.fine-art-gallery.com/postcard.html

Shuttle Bay 5: Postcard System
www.geocities.com/Area51/Corridor/8109/postcard_center.html

Spiner's Domain: Virtual Post Office
http://www3.all-yours.net/program/start20?write17400607

Star Trek: The Animated Series: Greeting Cards
http://mainengineering.simplenet.com/tas_greetingcards.html

Starbase 28: Communications
www.geocities.com/~jacobjou/postcard.html

Trekplanet Postcards
www.trekplanet.com/postcards.html

Fan Clubs

The membership of fan clubs has increased tremendously with the advent of the Internet. Use these sites to join fan clubs and find Trek pals who share your interests.

5th House, The - The Official Majel Barrett Roddenberry Fan Club
http://home.sprynet.com/~joining/joining.html

Aron Eisenberg Fan Club
http://hometown.aol.com/SoupTime/Aron_Eisenberg-Nog_FanClub.htm

Federation CyberSpace - The Official Web Site fo the IFT
www.iftcommand.com

Federation Intelligence - International Star Trek Fan Organization
http://fedintel.net

Gamma Knights - A Star Trek/Maquis Fan Club
www.maquis.com/cells/gammaknights

House of Martok - The Official JG Hertzler Fan Club
www.martok.org

Leonard Nimoy Club Online
www.nimoy.com

NANITES: The Official Nana Visitor Fan Club
www.nanites.com

Official John Colicos Fan Club (Kor)
www.klingon.org/Colicos/pages

Romulan Star Empire International Inc
www.rsempire.org

Seska & Martha Hackett Fan Club
www.marthahackett.com

Shakaar Society
www.shakaar.demon.co.uk/index.html

Shatner.Com: The Official Worldwide Fan Club
www.shatner.com

Spock's Pages
http://ourworld.compuserve.com/homepages/SpocksPages

Star Trek - The Official Fan Club of Australia
www.startrek.com.au/startrek_club.html

Star Trek Fan Club Organia (Portuguese)
http://organia.skynet.com.br

STARFLEET - The International Star Trek Fan Association
www.sfi.org

United Federation of Kids
www.ufk.org

United Federation of Phoenix
www.U-F-P.org

USS Nighthawk
http://hometown.aol.com/ussnghthwk/index.html

William Shatner Fan Club
http://users.aol.com/maxnova/shatner.htm

Mailing Lists

The purpose of mailing lists is to stay abreast of a topic and/or discuss it. When you subscribe to a mailing list, you automatically receive all messages sent to the subscribers of that list. Some lists are open, meaning that you can send a message to the list and all of ts subscribers receive a copy of your message. Others are moderated closely, meaning that you only receive messages from the list, but cannot post any to it. Typically, the title of the list is indicative of the list's subject. Here are some mailing list URLs as well as some sites that offer them from their main page.

AAA Star Trek
www.eonmagazine.com/startrek

August's Fanfic Collection (Voyager Fan Fiction)
http://members.tripod.com/~Appelsini/fanfic.html

Captain Janeway Mailing List
www.onelist.com/subscribe.cgi/CaptainJaneway

Captain on the Bridge
http://warp9.to/captainonthebridge

Dancing Doctor's Domain, The
www.lustchip.com/dancingdoctor

Dancing Doctors List (Devoted to Gates McFadden)
www.lustchip.com/dancingdoctor/join.htm

Database PADD
http://lcars.simplenet.com/padd

DeForest Kelley Mailing List
www.kilroywashere.com/sarah/list.htm

Desktop Starships
www.desktopstarships.com

Dukat's Romantic Fan Fiction
www.kardasi.com/qd/contents.htm

Friends of Brent Spiner (FOBS) Mailing List
www.spiner.org/community/maillist.htm

George Takei Mailing List
www.onelist.com/subscribe/Takei

Hielko's Star Trek Download Site
http://come.to/hielko

Incredible Internet Guides Mailing List
www.incredibleguides.com/mailing_list.htm

JuPiter Station (II)
www.geocities.com/~jupiterstation

Klingon Language Institute
www.kli.org

LCARS - Federation Databank
http://LCARSCom.Net

Main Engineering
http://mainengineering.simplenet.com

Playtrek
www.playtrek.cjb.net

Seska & Martha Hackett Fan Club
www.marthahackett.com

Shuttle Bay 5
www.geocities.com/Area51/Corridor/8109/sb5.htm

Sound Sector, The
www.geocities.com//Hollywood/6275/index.html

Species 8472 Archive
http://come.to/8472real

Spiner's Domain
www.spiner.org

Star Trek Admiral's Universe
www.startrekker.net/index.shtml

Star Trek Empire, The
http://home.earthlink.net/~dstubbs

Star Trek Empire: 3D Chess
http://www2.cybercities.com/s/startreke/games/index.htm

Star Trek Page
www.geocities.com/Hollywood/4401

Star Trek Singularity
http://sts.alphalink.com.au

Star Trek: The Experience
www.startrekexp.com

Starfleet Collective Database
http://lcars.simplenet.com

Starfleet Database
http://www2.prestel.co.uk/majeed

Subspace Array: CommList
http://subspace.virtualave.net/array/email/index.html

Subspace Communications
http://subspace.virtualave.net

Message Boards

Message boards are forums where people can post and read notes about a particular subject. Message boards are only accessible from the site on which they are maintained, meaning that the amount of participants is less than that of newsgroups. The following sites offer Trek-related message boards:

AAA Star Trek
www.eonmagazine.com/startrek

Assimilation Forum
http://disc.server.com/Indices/5634.html

Borg Collective, The
www.theborgcollective.com

Borg Collective, The: Collective Consciousness
http://theborgcollective.com/cgi-bin/miva?frames/com_area.mv

Core, The: Forum (for Trek Webmasters)
http://www3.bravenet.com/forum/show.asp?userid=bs111061

Ezri Dax/Nicole deBouer Message Board
www.insidetheweb.com/mbs.cgi/mb146847

Incredible Internet Guide for Trekkers Message Board
www.insidetheweb.com/mbs.cgi/mb481433

JuPiter Station (II)
www.geocities.com/~jupiterstation

Klingon Costuming Message Board
www.egroups.com/group/klingon_costuming

KoaliTion Message Board (Kim/Torres)
www.netbabbler.com/goto/?forumid=6337

Kret Rats P/T Home Page
http://members.tripod.com/~Maihe

Kronos One
www.kronos.u-net.com/index.htm

Main Engineering
http://mainengineering.simplenet.com

Main Engineering: Com Area
http://mainengineering.simplenet.com/bboard.hts

Playmates Discussion & Classifieds Message Boards
www.liii.com/~joisite/figure/boards.htm

Psi Phi's Star Trek: Voyager Archive
www.psiphi.org/voy

Psi Phi's Voyager Discussion Area
www.psiphi.org/BBS/get/VOY.html

Sector001.Com - United Space Federation
www.sector001.com

Sector001.Com: Message Boards
www.sector001.com/boards

Sid City - The Official Web Site of Alexander Siddig/Siddig El Fadil
www.sidcity.com

Species 8472 Archive
http://come.to/8472real

Spiner's Domain
www.spiner.org

Spiner's Domain: Brent Spiner Forum
http://apps.vantagenet.com/aforums/thread.asp?id=19971211163257

Star Trek - The Collective
www.geocities.com/Area51/Dimension/9644

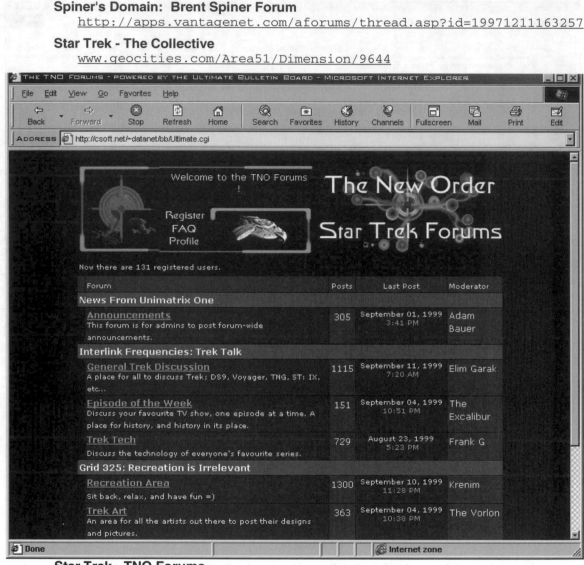

Star Trek - TNO Forums
http://csoft.net/~datanet/bb/Ultimate.cgi

Star Trek Admiral's Universe
www.startrekker.net/index.shtml

Star Trek Forum Darkfire
www.datania.com/cgi-bin/miva?star-trek/forum.mv

Star Trek Portal
www.strek.com

Star Trek: The Sci-Fi Channel Special Edition
www.scifi.com/startrek

Starfleet Collective Database
http://lcars.simplenet.com

Starfleet Collective Database: Comm Panel
http://lcars.simplenet.com/bbs

Starfleet Database
http://www2.prestel.co.uk/majeed

Starship Creator Message Board
www.simonsays.com/startrek/library/creator/bbs.cfm

Subspace Array: CommForum
http://subspace.virtualave.net/array/wwwboard/index.html

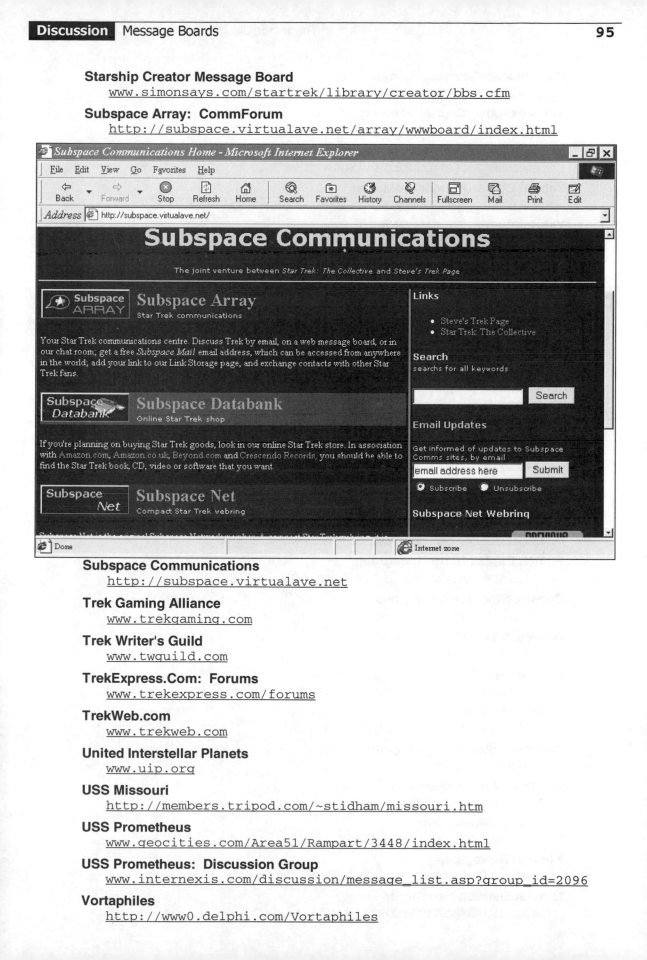

Subspace Communications
http://subspace.virtualave.net

Trek Gaming Alliance
www.trekgaming.com

Trek Writer's Guild
www.twguild.com

TrekExpress.Com: Forums
www.trekexpress.com/forums

TrekWeb.com
www.trekweb.com

United Interstellar Planets
www.uip.org

USS Missouri
http://members.tripod.com/~stidham/missouri.htm

USS Prometheus
www.geocities.com/Area51/Rampart/3448/index.html

USS Prometheus: Discussion Group
www.internexis.com/discussion/message_list.asp?group_id=2096

Vortaphiles
http://www0.delphi.com/Vortaphiles

Wil Wheaton Discussion Board, The
   www.insidetheweb.com/mbs.cgi/mb129977

Yahoo! Clubs: Captain Janeway's Crew
   http://clubs.yahoo.com/clubs/captainjanewayscrew

Yahoo! Clubs: Jeri Ryan's Net
   http://welcome.to/jerilynn

Yahoo! Clubs: Klingon Costumes
   http://clubs.yahoo.com/clubs/klingoncostumes

Yahoo! Clubs: Starfleet's Net
   http://welcome.to/starfleetsnet

Newsgroups

Newsgroups are like mailing lists, only the messages do not end up in your e-mailbox. Rather, you must "log on" to the newsgroup or access it through a site like DejaNews (www.deja.com). If you type "news:" in front of a newsgroup URL and type it in your browser's address bar, you may be able to set up a newsgroup for viewing.

Bajoran Newsgroup
   alt.startrek.bajoran

Borg Newsgroup
   alt.startrek.borg

Brent Spiner Newsgroup
   alt.fan.brent-spiner

Doctor Bashir Newsgroup
   alt.fan.doctor.bashir.grind.thrust.drool

French Captain/Borg Newsgroup
   alt.french.captain.borg.borg.borg

General Star Trek Newsgroup
   alt.binaries.startrek

General Star Trek Newsgroup II
   alt.startrek

German Star Trek Technology Newsgroup
   de.rec.sf.startrek.technologie

Jadzia Dax Newsgroup
   alt.fan.jadzia.dax.slug.slug.slug

Japanese Star Trek Newsgroup
   japan.startrek

Jeri Ryan Newsgroup
   alt.fan.jeri-ryan

Kira Nerys Newsgroup
   alt.fan.major.kira.pant.pant.pant

Klingon Newsgroup
   alt.shared-reality.startrek.klingon

Next Generation Newsgroup I
   alt.tv.star-trek.tng

Next Generation Newsgroup II
alt.tv.star-trek.next-gen

Original Series Newsgroup
alt.tv.star-trek.tos

Q Newsgroup
alt.fan.q

Romulan Newsgroup
alt.startrek.romulan

Star Trek Fandom Newsgroup
rec.arts.startrek.fandom

Star Trek Information Newsgroup
rec.arts.startrek.info

Star Trek Miscellaneous Newsgroup
rec.arts.startrek.misc

Star Trek Reviews Newsgroup
rec.arts.startrek.reviews

Star Trek vs. Babylon 5 Newsgroup
alt.startrek.vs.babylon5

Star Trek vs. Star Wars Newsgroup
alt.startrek.vs.starwars

Starfleet Newsgroup
alt.org.starfleet

Trill Newsgroup
alt.startrek.trill

UK Star Trek Newsgroup
uk.media.tv.sf.startrek

Unknown (I)
aus.sf.star-trek

Unknown (II)
uiuc.misc.trek

Unknown (III)
alt.startrek.uss-amagosa

Unknown (IV)
alt.startrek.writing-staff

Vulcan Newsgroup
alt.startrek.vulcan

Surveys

Which Trek film is the best? Who's the best captain? These and more questions are yours to answer in the Trek-oriented polls, quizzlets, and surveys that dot the 'net. Usually, you can view up to the minute results with the click of a button.

Absolut Star Trek: Polls
www.solace.mh.se/~el302/startrek/polls.html

Bad Guys of Star Trek, The
   http://members.tripod.com/~Tvamp

Dukat Polls
   www.kardasi.com/gd/dukat_polls.htm

Fashion Voyager: Survey Says
   www.geocities.com/Area51/Dimension/5966/survey/index.html

Great Seven/Kes Debate, The
   www.geocities.com/Area51/Rampart/3448/poll.html

Posid's Starbase 616
   www.geocities.com/Area51/Vault/5657

Q Continuum (I)
   www.geocities.com/Area51/Zone/4431/frames1.htm

Star Trek - The Collective
   www.geocities.com/Area51/Dimension/9644

Star Trek Empire, The
   http://home.earthlink.net/~dstubbs

Star Trek News
   www.geocities.com/Hollywood/6952

Star Trek Portal
   www.strek.com

TrekExpress.Com: Voting Center
   www.trekexpress.com/trekexpresscgi/vcenter.cgi

TrekWeb.com
   www.trekweb.com

Ultimate Star Trek Graphic Gallery, The
   www.geocities.com/Area51/Corridor/4914/index1.html

USS Prometheus: Survey
   www.geocities.com/Area51/Shadowlands/7129/polltests.html

STAR TREK
Multimedia
Sites

Using various record devices, Trekkers throughout the cyberuniverse have recorded and uploaded sights and sounds from the various Trek productions. Hear soundbytes from just about every character, watch RealVideo clips, and more using the multimedia sites listed in this chapter.

Audio

MIDIs

MIDI files are music files. Oftentimes, these files are used to interact with an instrument, such as keyboard. Web sites often collect their MIDIs together, placing them on one page, then arranging them by category on that page. Other sites may list MIDIs with other sound formats, usually WAVs.

Borg Collective, The: MIDI Music Archive
www.theborgcollective.com/frames/midi.htm

Desktop Starships: Sound Files
www.desktopstarships.com/sounds.html

Farpoint Station
www.farpointstation.org

Hielko's Star Trek Download Site: MIDIs
http://members.tripod.lycos.nl/hielko/midi.htm

Kronos One
www.kronos.u-net.com/index.htm

Main Engineering: Sounds
http://mainengineering.simplenet.com/sounds.html

Ressikan Flute, The: MIDI Files
www.geocities.com/Area51/9140/midi.html

Rura's Star Trek Gallery: MIDIs
http://vision.simplenet.com/tomparis/mid.html

Spocks' Pages: MIDI Files
http://ourworld.compuserve.com/homepages/SpocksPages/stmidi.htm

Star Trek Stuff: Music
http://members.xoom.com/Neelix/music.html

STARBASE 721
http://Travel.To/Starbase721

Starbase DS7: Star Trek Files
www.sbds7.com/files/files.html

Starfleet Headquarters: The Turbo Lift
http://home.earthlink.net/~cobarry/download.html

Trek Files: MIDI
http://trekfiles.strek.com/Sounds/Midi

Trekker One: Trekker Three: Star Trek Sounds
www.angelfire.com/nc/TrekkerThree/index.html

USS Roo Holodeck 1
www.geocities.com/Area51/4948/holodeck.html

Yes, Yet Another Star Trek Page
www.geocities.com/Area51/Vault/6442

MP3s

MP3s are the latest technology in quality sound reproduction, and are suitable for exacting sound duplication. Due to their size, most MP3 files are only accessible using an FTP utility. If you are having trouble downloading an MP3 file, try right-clicking and choosing "Save target as."

Farpoint Station
www.farpointstation.org

Hielko's Star Trek Download Site: MP3s
http://members.tripod.lycos.nl/hielko/mp3.htm

Spiners' Domain: Brent Spiner Techno Mixes
www.spiner.org/funstuff/techno.htm

Star Trek MP3 Player, The
www.mdigital.bizland.com/trekplay.html

Music

From the majestic sounds of Jerry Goldsmith to the audio efforts of such Trek stars as Leonard Nimoy and Brent Spiner, the Star Trek Universe has produced its share of music. To explore this side of the Star Trek galaxy, set your coordinates based on the sites below.

All-Movie Guide: Jerry Goldsmith
http://allmovie.com/cg/x.dll?UID=10:51:20|PM&p=avg&sql=B91941

All-Music Guide: Brent Spiner
http://allmusic.com/cg/x.dll?UID=10:51:20|PM&p=amg&sql=BP||||14885

All-Music Guide: Jerry Goldsmith
http://allmusic.com/cg/x.dll?UID=10:51:20|PM&p=amg&sql=BP|||||3075

All-Music Guide: Leonard Nimoy
http://allmusic.com/cg/x.dll?UID=10:49:42|PM&p=amg&sql=BP||||24674

Borg Collective, The: MIDI Music Archive
www.theborgcollective.com/frames/midi.htm

Filk Tunes & Parodies
www.physik.uni-regensburg.de/~krt04517/Forbes/rofilk.html

GNP/Crescendo Record Co Inc
www.gnpcrescendo.com

In Search of Middle C: The Music of Leonard Nimoy
www.calweb.com/~ejr/spock_sings.html

Leonard Nimoy Albums Page
www.geocities.com/Hollywood/Set/1931/records.html

Ressikan Flute, The - The Music of Star Trek
www.geocities.com/Area51/9140

Spiners' Domain: Brent Spiner Techno Mixes
www.spiner.org/funstuff/techno.htm

Star Trek Soundtracks
www.geocities.com/Area51/Cavern/6053/sts

Tim Russ Sings the Voyager Love Boat Theme
www.geocities.com/~teepee47/tim_russ/multimedia.html

Voyager Musician Credits
www.psiphi.org/voy/ep/music.html

RealAudio

RealAudio (.ra or .au) format sound files are a suitable format for interviews or longer audio episodes. A Real Player is available at www.realplayer.com.

Ferengi Commerce Commission: Sound Page
http://belegost.mit.edu/steve/treksou.html

Main Engineering: Sounds
http://mainengineering.simplenet.com/sounds.html

Official DeForest Kelley Web Site, The: Sounds
>   www.kilroywashere.com/sarah/sounds.htm

Q Continuum (I): Sound Clips
>   www.geocities.com/Area51/Zone/4431/frames2.htm

Star Trek in Real Audio
>   www.cybercomm.nl/~sytze/startrek.htm

Star Trek Universe: Star Trek in Real Audio
>   www.kroesen.demon.nl/startrek/rkstaudio.html

WAVs

WAVs are the most common sound format for the computer. Usually, WAV format is used for quotes downloaded from other media such as videos. WAV format is also a good medium for delivering sounds on web sites.

Beverly Crusher WAV Files
>   www.geocities.com/Area51/Zone/7932

| ADDRESS | http://www.staga.force9.co.uk/sound/sound.htm |

SOUND FILES

★The Star Trek Animated GIF Archive

★Top 50 Trek Sites
★The Core Awards
★Tutorials and Tips

★FREE E-MAIL
★FREE Software
★More FREE Stuff
★Make Money

★Sound Files
★Background Images
★Fonts

★Add Your Link
★The Elite Trek Sites
★Link To The Core

★The Core Forum
★Feedback
★E-Mail

One good way to make your site better is to add some sound effects when the page loads or when a link is clicked. Below are some sounds that you can use to do just that.

Most of the sound files below are used with permission from Star Trek In Sound and Vision. You should be able to find something there if you can't find it below.

Computer Sound Effects

File Name	Size	Description
computer1.wav	4kb	A single computer beep
computer2.wav	9kb	A longer computer beep
computer3.wav	19kb	Another long computer beep
computer4.wav	11kb	Yet another computer beep
computer5.wav	56kb	A really long computer beep
computer6.wav	14kb	Another Enterprise beep
computer7.wav	12kb	A well known computer beep
computer8.wav	6kb	A short beep

Core, The: Sound Files
>   www.staga.force9.co.uk/sound/sound.htm

Desktop Starships: Sound Files
>   www.desktopstarships.com/sounds.html

Federation Sound Archive: Crusher
>   www.domaindlx.com/timbo/crusher.html

Federation Sound Archive: Data
>   www.domaindlx.com/timbo/data.html

Federation Sound Archive: Guinan
>   www.domaindlx.com/timbo/guinan.html

Federation Sound Archive: LaForge
>   www.domaindlx.com/timbo/laforge.html

Federation Sound Archive: O'Brien
www.domaindlx.com/timbo/obrien.html

Federation Sound Archive: Q Continuum
www.domaindlx.com/timbo/q.html

Federation Sound Archive: Riker
www.domaindlx.com/timbo/riker.html

Federation Sound Archive: Tasha
www.domaindlx.com/timbo/tasha.html

Federation Sound Archive: Troi
www.domaindlx.com/timbo/troi.html

Federation Sound Archive: WAVs
www.domaindlx.com/timbo/thewavs.html

Federation Sound Archive: Wesley
www.domaindlx.com/timbo/wesley.html

Federation Sound Archive: Worf
www.domaindlx.com/timbo/worf.html

Ferengi Commerce Commission: Sound Page
http://belegost.mit.edu/steve/treksou.html

Ismaela's Unauthorized Brent Spiner Fan Page: Brent's Voice Files
www.geocities.co.jp/Broadway/1776/vozcarpe.html

Kronos One
www.kronos.u-net.com/index.htm

KTH Media Archive (Kim/Torres)
www.fortunecity.com/tattooine/russ/259/media.html

LCARS - Federation Databank
http://LCARSCom.Net

Main Engineering: Sounds
http://mainengineering.simplenet.com/sounds.html

Maximum Defiant: Multimedia: Sounds
www.maximumdefiant.com/multi/sounds/index.html

Official DeForest Kelley Web Site, The: Sounds
www.kilroywashere.com/sarah/sounds.htm

Outpost 21: Audio
www.steve.simplenet.com/audio/index_nf.html

Q Continuum (I): Sound Clips
www.geocities.com/Area51/Zone/4431/frames2.htm

Sector 0-0-1: Sounds
http://members.aol.com/NCC2364/wav

Sector001.Com: Sounds
www.sector001.com/filelib_sounds.htm

Star Trek & Beyond: Starfleet Seconday IMG Array
www.geocities.com/Tokyo/Bay/8946/trek.htm

Star Trek: The Next Generation - Federation Sound Archive
www.deathray.net/soundarchive

Starbase 6503: Next Generation Database
www.geocities.com/Area51/Corridor/6503/STTNG.html

Starbase 6503: The Original Series Database
www.geocities.com/Area51/Corridor/6503/STTOS.html

STARBASE 721
http://Travel.To/Starbase721

Starbase DS7: Star Trek Files
www.sbds7.com/files/files.html

Trek Worlds: Trek Sounds
www.geocities.com/Area51/Zone/3000/index_wav.htm

Trekker One: Trekker Three: Star Trek Sounds
www.angelfire.com/nc/TrekkerThree/index.html

Tuvok Appreciation: WAVs
www.geocities.com/Hollywood/Studio/4436/tuvokwav.html

Ultimate Star Trek Graphic Gallery, The
www.geocities.com/Area51/Corridor/4914/index1.html

Wally's Weird Star Trek Tribute
www.wallys.com/startrek/startrek.htm

Yes, Yet Another Star Trek Page
www.geocities.com/Area51/Vault/6442

Video

AVIs

*AVI is a PC-based video format. Most Windows systems include the software to view these files. If you are a Windows user, try double-clicking on AVI files to view them. If that doesn't work, visit Shareware.Com (*www.shareware.com*) or Filez (*www.filez.com*) and search for "AVI Player" to find a program that will work for you.*

Main Engineering: Video
http://mainengineering.simplenet.com/video.html

Q Continuum (I): Q Movies
www.geocities.com/Area51/Zone/4431/q-movies.htm

Shuttlebay 5: Video
www.geocities.com/Area51/Corridor/8109/video.htm

Star Trek Continuum: Deep Space Nine - Images & Videos
www.startrekcontinuum.com/ds9/listarchives.html

Star Trek Continuum: Deep Space Nine Media Archives
www.startrekcontinuum.com/ds9/quadrant.asp?ssector=archives.asp

Star Trek Continuum: Next Generation - Images & Videos
www.startrekcontinuum.com/tng/listarchives.html

Star Trek Continuum: Next Generation Media Archives
www.startrekcontinuum.com/tng/quadrant.asp?ssector=archives.asp

Star Trek Continuum: Original Series - Images & Videos
www.startrekcontinuum.com/tos/listarchives.html

Star Trek Continuum: Original Series Media Archives
www.startrekcontinuum.com/tos/quadrant.asp?ssector=archives.asp

Starfleet Headquarters: The Holodeck
http://home.earthlink.net/~cobarry/movies.html

Tim Russ Sings the Voyager Loveboat Theme
www.geocities.com/~teepee47/tim_russ/multimedia.html

MPEGs

MPEG is a less common video format. Nonetheless, there are some Trek files available in MPEG format.

Maximum Defiant: Multimedia: Movies
www.maximumdefiant.com/multi/movies/index.html

Space Battles & Other FX
http://fly.to/spacebattles

QuickTime (MOV Files)

QuickTime video format was originally created for the Macintosh. The software to view QuickTime files is standard on most Macintoshes as well as some PC systems. If you are a PC user and you have trouble opening a QuickTime file, visit Shareware.Com (www.shareware.com) or Filez (www.filez.com), and search for "QuickTime Player" to locate a program that you may download to view your QuickTime files.

Computer Core Dump: Star Trek Movies
www.ccdump.org/STMovies.html

Kronos One
www.kronos.u-net.com/index.htm

Maximum Defiant: Multimedia: Movies
www.maximumdefiant.com/multi/movies/index.html

Outpost 21: Video
www.steve.simplenet.com/video/index_nf.html

Q Continuum (I): Q Movies
www.geocities.com/Area51/Zone/4431/q-movies.htm

Shuttlebay 5: Video
www.geocities.com/Area51/Corridor/8109/video.htm

Starfleet Headquarters: The Holodeck
http://home.earthlink.net/~cobarry/movies.html

United Federation of Planets . . . Deep Space Nine
www.gh.cs.su.oz.au/~matty/Trek/ds9.html

United Federation of Planets . . . First Contact
www.gh.cs.su.oz.au/~matty/Trek/firstcontact.html

United Federation of Planets . . . Generations
www.gh.cs.su.oz.au/~matty/Trek/generations.html

United Federation of Planets . . . Voyager
www.gh.cs.su.oz.au/~matty/Trek/voyager.html

RealVideo

The Real Video format is a good computer medium for somewhat longer files, interviews for example. A Real Player is available at www.realplayer.com.

Hielko's Star Trek Download Site: Real Media
http://members.tripod.lycos.nl/hielko/rm.htm

Main Engineering: Video
http://mainengineering.simplenet.com/video.html

Official Jeri Lynn Ryan Homepage, The: FAQ
www.jerilynn.com/faq.htm

Space Battles & Other FX
http://fly.to/spacebattles

Star Trek: The Next Generation - Trailers
http://members.xoom.com/the8472s/tng/tng.html

Star Trek: The Original Series - Trailers
http://members.xoom.com/the8472s/tos/tos.html

Tim Russ Sings the Voyager Love Boat Theme
www.geocities.com/~teepee47/tim_russ/multimedia.html

ONLINE STAR TREK
Galleries

One of the most common features found on Star Trek-related web sites, galleries are places where you can view, print and download images. The sites included in this chapter contain images at the URLs listed here or through links on the main page. Look for buttons or text links labeled "Pictures," "Gallery," or "Images."

Almost all images found online are "downloadable" -- that is, you can save the image on your computer for viewing later. However, not all web site owners want you to download the "pix" they offer. Usually, in these cases, the webmaster will say "nay" somewhere on the site.

Images from the Star Trek films and series are owned by Paramount Pictures (www.paramount.com), which is the studio that produces both. It is not a good idea to download "their" stuff and use it in a distasteful or commercial manner -- or any manner that would not be approved of in this galaxy or the next.

This chapter contains links to sites that offer animations, original artwork and subject-specific galleries. For galleries of images from a particular Trek series, see the Best Star Trek Series Sites chapter.

Animated GIFs

Animated GIFs are essentially a series of GIF or image files that have been combined to create a short animation. Animated GIFs are commonly used in banner advertisements on the Web. Trekkers have created a wide variety of Trek-oriented animated GIFs, everything from computer displays to starship fly-bys have been animated in GIF format. Visit these sites to see what all this animation is about.

Ern Yoka's Animated GIFs
www.geocities.com/Area51/Nebula/8818/animated.html

Federation Place: Software
www.fedplace.de/startrke.htm

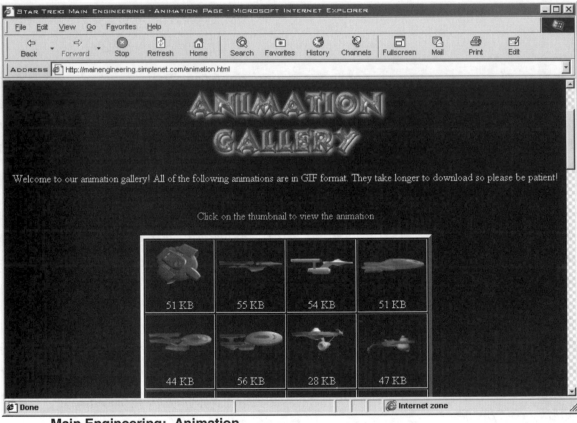

Main Engineering: Animation
http://mainengineering.simplenet.com/animation.html

Star Trek Utopia: Defiant Animation Page
http://members.aol.com/defiant41/gif/gif.html

Star Trek: The Animated Series: Animations
http://mainengineering.simplenet.com/tas_animations.html

STID - Star Trek Information Depository
www.tntie.com/trek_id

The Protonic Pages - The Further Adventures of Captain Proton
www.geocities.com/Area51/Rampart/1812/ProtonAnimations.html

Trek Worlds: Animated GIFs
www.geocities.com/Area51/Zone/3000/index_gifs.htm

Trek Worlds: Trek GIFs Collection
www.geocities.com/Area51/Zone/2200/trekgifsmenu.htm

USS Hornet NCC-1714: Cargobay 3
www.geocities.com/SiliconValley/Way/3761/cargobay.html

Original Artwork

View beautiful, artistic renditions of Star Trek characters, locations, and concepts by visiting these sites.

Blair Art Studios: Art of Technology
www.drublair.com

Borg Collective, The: Star Trek Fan Art
www.theborgcollective.com/frames/fan_art.htm

Gallery of Klingon Warriors
www.hotink.com/warriors

Ismaela's Unauthorized Brent Spiner Fan Page: Fan Art
www.geocities.co.jp/Broadway/1776/cumple.html

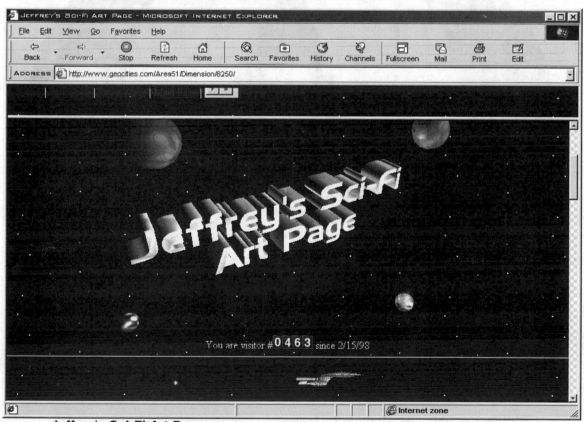

Jeffrey's Sci-Fi Art Page
www.geocities.com/Area51/Dimension/8250

Kelpie's Star Trek Fan Art Gallery
www.geocities.com/Area51/Labyrinth/8873/fanart.htm

Lake Ogopogo
www.geocities.com/Tokyo/Temple/3535

Lightspeed Fine Arts Inc
www.lightspeedfineart.com

Main Engineering: Art Gallery
http://mainengineering.simplenet.com/art_gallery.html

Official Jeri Lynn Ryan Homepage, The: Fan Art
www.jerilynn.com/fanart.htm

Radioactive
www.tu-chemnitz.de/~jger/joerg.html

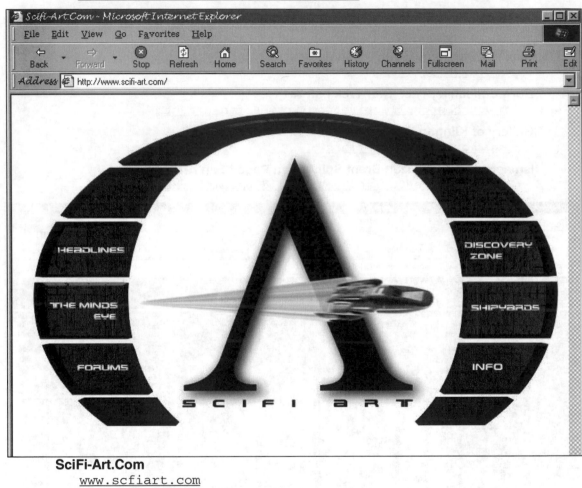

SciFi-Art.Com
www.scfiart.com

Scott Benson's Badge & Uniform Art
www.cjnetworks.com/~tfrazier/stbenson.html

Seventh Order, The: Art Gallery
www.7thorder.org/7art.htm

Star Trek Art Gallery
www.cjnetworks.com/~tfrazier/stgalery.html

Star Trek Artists' Webring: Sites List
www.webring.org/cgi-bin/webring?ring=start;list

Star Trek Utopia: Original Artwork
www.geocities.com/Area51/Dimension/8041/art2.html

Star Trek Utopia: Star Trek vs. Star Wars Images
http://hometown.aol.com/defiant41/trekwar/index.html

Star Trek: The Original Art Site
www.geocities.com/Area51/Vault/7414/viewer.html

Star Trek: Voyager (Still 3D Images)
www.geocities.com/SoHo/Lofts/6676/voyager.htm

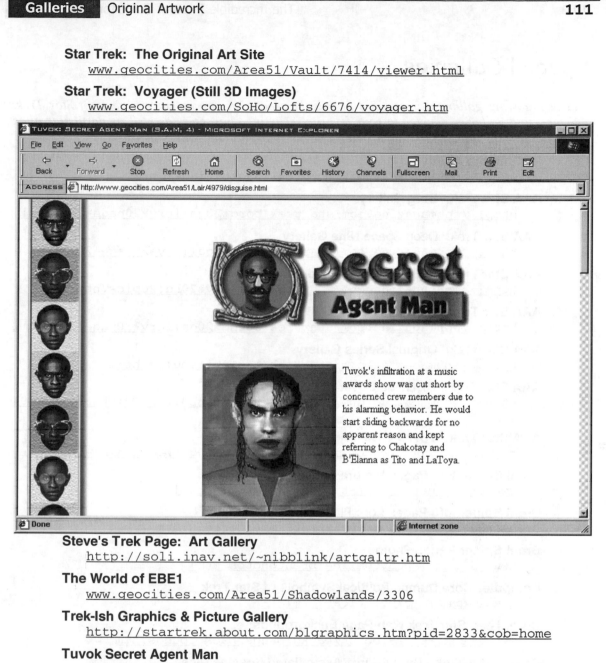

Steve's Trek Page: Art Gallery
http://soli.inav.net/~nibblink/artgaltr.htm

The World of EBE1
www.geocities.com/Area51/Shadowlands/3306

Trek-Ish Graphics & Picture Gallery
http://startrek.about.com/blgraphics.htm?pid=2833&cob=home

Tuvok Secret Agent Man
www.geocities.com/Area51/Lair/4979/disguise.html

Ultimate Star Trek Graphic Gallery, The
www.geocities.com/Area51/Corridor/4914/index1.html

Wolf359
http://members.aol.com/wolfpak359

You Can't Do That on Star Trek!
http://washington.xtn.net/~philipb/youcant.htm

Special Galleries

The following galleries are special in that they focus on one or more aspects of Star Trek. You'll find galleries devoted to your favorite recurring characters as well as particular alien races. Use the name of the site to determine the subject of the gallery listed.

3D Starship Archive
www.amtc.net/users/~ziroc/trek/3dships/index.htm

AAA Star Trek: Borg Gallery
http://eonmagazine.com/startrek/borg%20gallery%20page%201.html

AAA Star Trek: Deep Space Nine Gallery
http://eonmagazine.com/startrek/ds9%20gallery%20page%201.html

AAA Star Trek: High Definition Gallery
http://eonmagazine.com/startrek/gallery%20hd%20pics.html

AAA Star Trek: Next Generation Gallery
http://eonmagazine.com/startrek/sttng%20gallery%20page%201.html

AAA Star Trek: Original Series Gallery
http://eonmagazine.com/startrek/1701shipthumbs.html

AAA Star Trek: TV Guide Cover Gallery
http://eonmagazine.com/startrek/GALLERY%20TV%20GUIDE%20PAGE%201.html

AAA Star Trek: Voyager Gallery
http://eonmagazine.com/startrek/voyager%20gallery%20page%202.html

Brent Spiner Fan Page: Picture Collections
www.asahi-net.or.jp/~ti3y-itu/pictures.html

Brent Spiner Info Page: Lore Pics
http://members.aol.com/BrentFemme/lorepix.htm

Brent Spiner Page: Photos
www.millennianet.com/lee/brentphotos.html

Computer Core Dump: Political Symbols of Star Trek
www.ccdump.org/political.html

Core, The: Star Trek Web Page Backgrounds
www.staga.force9.co.uk/backgrounds/backgrounds.htm

Dave's Star Trek - Borg Page: Assimilated Species Pics
www.geocities.com/Area51/Nebula/6309/asspics.htm

Dominion Gallery
www.geocities.com/Area51/Nebula/4349/g_dominion.html

DS9 Personnel Gallery
www.geocities.com/Area51/Nebula/4349/g_ds9.html

Federation Ship Images Gallery
http://vision.simplenet.com/tomparis/shipimage.html

Garek Gallery
www.geocities.com/Area51/Nebula/4349/g_garak.html

Gul Dukat Gallery
www.geocities.com/Area51/Nebula/4349/g_dukat.html

Imzadi Pictures
www.freespeech.org/feydreams/galle1.html

Infinitely Imzadi: Images of Imzadi
www.fortunecity.com/tattooine/pratchett/66/imzadicards.htm

Joan's Secret Little Star Trek: Insurrection Scrapbook
www.geocities.com/Area51/Crater/9082

Kamar Sutra: Elim Garak Gallery
http://elimgarak.com/art/garakart.html

Locotus' Hang: NCC-1701 Pictures
www.geocities.com/Area51/Labyrinth/8852/pic1.htm

Locutus' Hang: Borg Pictures
www.geocities.com/Area51/Labyrinth/8852/pic6.htm

Locutus' Hang: NCC-1701-A Pictures
www.geocities.com/Area51/Labyrinth/8852/pic2.htm

Locutus' Hang: NCC-1701-D Pictures
www.geocities.com/Area51/Labyrinth/8852/pic3.htm

Locutus' Hang: NCC-1701-E Pictures
www.geocities.com/Area51/Labyrinth/8852/pic4.htm

Mego Star Trek Gallery
www.toymania.com/megomuseum/trek

Milky Way Galaxy Map, The
http://members.aol.com/grewsomeco/map.htm

Nicole deBoer - Spellbound: Gallery
www.nikkideboer.com/photos.htm

Official Jeri Lynn Ryan Homepage, The: Pictures
www.jerilynn.com/pics.htm

Optical Data Network: Autographed Photos
www.alphalink.com.au/~til/Autograph.htm

Optical Data Network: Babylon 5/Star Trek Crossover
www.alphalink.com.au/~til/B5-ST.htm

Patrick & His Women!
http://members.easyspace.com/mejensen/patrick/patwomen.html

Rogues' Gallery of Andorians
www.magna.com.au/~lindsay/trek/Rogues.html

Rogues' Gallery of Bolians
www.geocities.com/Area51/Station/1558/Bolians.html

Sector 0-0-1: Dedication Plaques Gallery
http://members.aol.com/NCC2364/plaques

Sector 0-0-1: Insignia Gallery
http://members.aol.com/NCC2364/sign

Sector 0-0-1: Posters & CD-Covers
http://members.aol.com/NCC2364/posters

Star Trek - The Collection
www.geocities.com/Hollywood/Set/6458

Star Trek Catwalk: A Gallery of Star Trek Uniforms
http://members.aol.com/NCC2364/catwalk

Star Trek Millenium: Actors & Aliens Pictures
http://home.bip.net/s_t_m/aaapics.htm

Star Trek Millenium: Deep Space Nine (Station) Pictures
http://home.bip.net/s_t_m/ds9pics.htm

Star Trek Millenium: Pictures of Ships & Bases
http://home.bip.net/s_t_m/osabpics.htm

Star Trek Plates (Gallery & Information)
www.spacenine.demon.co.uk/index.html

Star Trek: The Caption Generation
www.twguild.com/captions

The Gallery (of Gates McFadden & Patrick Stewart)
www.geocities.com/Broadway/Wing/1796/index.html

Totally Kate!: Mulgrew Photos
http://members.tripod.com/~marcia_2/photos.htm

Toymania's Mego Star Trek Gallery
www.toymania.com/megomuseum/trek

Trek Art - The Best Starship Schematics on the Web
www.netcomuk.co.uk/~trekart/index.html

Trek TV Guide Covers
www.geocities.com/Area51/Corridor/5363/trektvguide.html

Ultimate Star Trek Collection: TV Guide Covers
http://startrek.fns.net.fsn.net/download/tvguide.html

USS Hornet NCC-1714: Stellar Cartography
www.geocities.com/SiliconValley/Way/3761/stellarcartography.html

USS Prometheus Images
www.geocities.com/Area51/Shadowlands/7129/pimages.html

USS Prometheus: Voyager Photo Gallery
www.geocities.com/Area51/Rampart/3448/download.html

Vorta Gallery
www.geocities.com/Area51/Nebula/4349/g_vorta.html

Wayoun Gallery
www.geocities.com/Area51/Nebula/4349/g_weyoun.html

Web Backgrounds by Locutus
www.geocities.com/Area51/Labyrinth/8852/graf.htm

Wil Wheaton Picture Gallery
http://pics.teencelebsplus.com/wheaton/wheaton.html

Wolf359: Klingon 3D Stills
http://wolf359a.anet-stl.com/klingon.html

Wolf359: Klingon Ship Portraits
http://wolf359a.anet-stl.com/kport.html

STAR TREK
Software

The Web is full of fun "unofficial" Star Trek stuff to download. Many enterprising fans have created their own Trek wallpaper, themes and more. If your taste for acquisition is even close to that of a Ferengi, this chapter should satisfy your need to acquire.

Cursors

Sick of that boring arrow? Visit these sites to get Trek-oriented cursors.

Hielko's Star Trek Download Site: Cursors
http://members.tripod.lycos.nl/hielko/cursors.htm

Shuttlebay 5: Animated Cursors
www.geocities.com/Area51/Corridor/8109/desktop_ac.htm

Spock's Pages: Star Trek Cursors
http://ourworld.compuserve.com/homepages/SpocksPages/stcursor.htm

Star Trek Stuff: Multimedia
http://members.xoom.com/Neelix/multi.html

Trek Files: Cursors
http://trekfiles.strek.com/Other/Cursors

Fonts

Whether you are creating Trek-looking graphics or simply want to spice up a letter, these sites offer Star Trek typefaces that will make your word processing intergalactic!

Borg Collective, The: Star Trek Fonts
www.theborgcollective.com/frames/fonts.htm

Desktop Starships: Sci-Fi Fonts
www.desktopstarships.com/font.html

Federation Sound Archive: Fonts
www.domaindlx.com/timbo/font.html

Giuseppe Tisotto's Home Page
http://members.xoom.it/totthebest

Hielko's Star Trek Download Site: Fonts
http://members.tripod.lycos.nl/hielko/fonts.htm

Quark's Place: Downloads
www.orlinter.com/users/grandnag/downloads.htm

Spock's Pages: Star Trek Fonts
http://ourworld.compuserve.com/homepages/SpocksPages/stfonts.htm

Star Trek Stuff: Fonts
http://members.xoom.com/Neelix/fonts.html

Star Trek: The Next Generation - Federation Sound Archive
www.deathray.net/soundarchive

Starfleet Headquarters: The Turbo Lift
http://home.earthlink.net/~cobarry/download.html

Tommy of Escondido's Alien Fonts Page
www.geocities.com/TimesSquare/4965

Trek Files: Fonts
http://trekfiles.strek.com/Other/Fonts

Trek Worlds: Odo's Security Font Files
www.geocities.com/Area51/Zone/3000/index_fonts.htm

USS Roo
www.geocities.com/Area51/4948

Icons

Sick of looking at the same recycle bin on your PC desktop? "Trekify" your desktop with the icons you can download from these sites.

Borg Collective, The: Icons & Screensavers
www.theborgcollective.com/frames/icons_etc.htm

Dar's Star Trek Icon Collection
www.geocities.com/~darsplace/star_trek_vault/icons.html

Hielko's Star Trek Download Site: Icons
http://members.tripod.lycos.nl/hielko/icons.htm

Optical Data Network
http://start.at/ODN

Quark's Place: Downloads
www.orlinter.com/users/grandnag/downloads.htm

Sector 0-0-1: Icons
http://members.aol.com/NCC2364/icons

Star Trek Downloads: Icons
http://clgray.simplenet.com/strtrk/download/icons.html

Star Trek Stuff: Multimedia
http://members.xoom.com/Neelix/multi.html

Trek Files: Icons
http://trekfiles.strek.com/Icons

Trek Worlds: Button & Icon Files
www.geocities.com/Area51/Zone/3000/index_icons.htm

Trek Worlds: Quark's Swap Shop
www.geocities.com/Area51/Zone/3000/index_swap.htm

Miscellaneous Software

Whether you're in the mood for games, computer clocks or program add-ons, these sites will help you find them.

Federation Place: Software
www.fedplace.de/startrke.htm

Hielko's Star Trek Download Site: Programs
http://members.tripod.lycos.nl/hielko/progs.htm

Hielko's Star Trek Download Site: WinAmp Skins
http://members.tripod.lycos.nl/hielko/skins.htm

Main Engineering: Fun Stuff
http://mainengineering.simplenet.com/funstuff.html

Star Trek Downloads: Games/Programs
http://clgray.simplenet.com/strtrk/download/games.html

Star Trek Internet Interactive - Macintosh Multimedia
www.pol.com/people/interact

Star Trek MP3 Player, The
www.mdigital.bizland.com/trekplay.html

STID - Star Trek Information Depository
www.tntie.com/trek_id

Trek Family: Games & Miscellaneous
www.geocities.com/Area51/8466/Games_and_Misc.html

Trek Files
http://trekfiles.strek.com

Trek Worlds: Quark's Swap Shop
www.geocities.com/Area51/Zone/3000/index_swap.htm

Ultimate Star Trek Collection: Star Trek WinAmp Skins
http://startrek.fns.net.fsn.net/download/skins.html

YSK's Star Trek Page
www.geocities.com/Area51/Corridor/3546

Screensavers

Instead of flying toasters or colored squiggles, you can have a Trek-oriented screensaver to boldly go across your monitor.

Borg Collective, The: Icons & Screensavers
www.theborgcollective.com/frames/icons_etc.htm

Farpoint Station
www.farpointstation.org

Hielko's Star Trek Download Site: Screensavers
http://members.tripod.lycos.nl/hielko/scr.htm

Spock's Pages: Star Trek Screensavers
http://ourworld.compuserve.com/homepages/SpocksPages/stss.htm

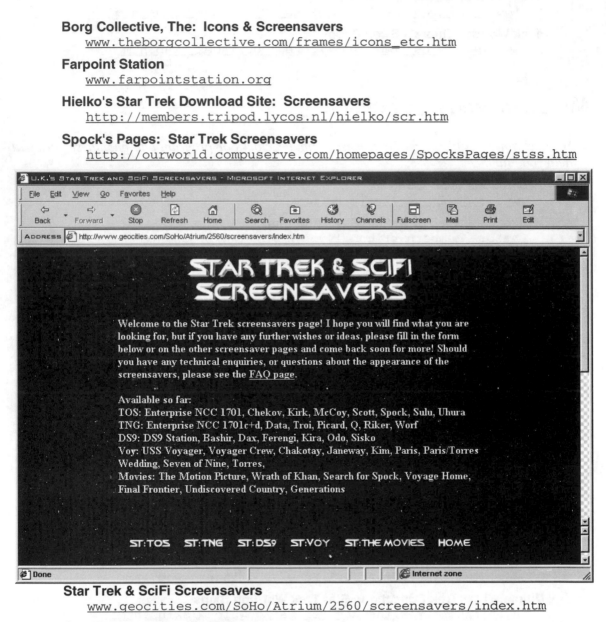

Star Trek & SciFi Screensavers
www.geocities.com/SoHo/Atrium/2560/screensavers/index.htm

Star Trek Downloads: Themes
http://clgray.simplenet.com/strtrk/download/themes.html

Trek Files: Screensavers
http://trekfiles.strek.com/Screen_Savers

UK's Star Trek & Sci-Fi Screensavers
www.geocities.com/SoHo/Atrium/2560/screensavers/index.htm

Themes

Themes are files that are designed to transform the visual appearance of your Windows desktop environment. Countless themes have been created, including at least one for just about every television program. These sites offer Trek-related themes that will make your desktop look stellar.

Beverly Crusher WAV Files
www.geocities.com/Area51/Zone/7932

BHBplus's Original Star Trek Desktop Themes & Links
http://members.aol.com/BHBplus/index17.html

Borg Collective, The: Themes & Wallpaper
www.theborgcollective.com/frames/windows_wallpaper.htm

Desktop Starships: Sci-Fi Themes
www.desktopstarships.com/themes.html

DS9 Windows Desktop Theme
http://users.dx.com.au/wormhole/themes.html

Farpoint Station
www.farpointstation.org

Federation Place: Software
www.fedplace.de/startrke.htm

Ferengi Commerce Commission: Themes
http://belegost.mit.edu/steve/trekthe.html

Giuseppe Tisotto's Home Page
http://members.xoom.it/totthebest

Hielko's Star Trek Download Site: Themes
http://members.tripod.lycos.nl/hielko/themes.htm

Kronos One
www.kronos.u-net.com/index.htm

Quark's Place: Downloads
www.orlinter.com/users/grandnag/downloads.htm

Star Trek Downloads: Themes
http://clgray.simplenet.com/strtrk/download/themes.html

Star Trek: The Next Generation - Federation Sound Archive
www.deathray.net/soundarchive

Starfleet Headquarters: The Turbo Lift
http://home.earthlink.net/~cobarry/download.html

Trek Files: Desktop Themes
http://trekfiles.strek.com/Desktop_Themes

Ute & Joan's Star Trek Desktop Themes
http://tatooine.fortunecity.com/ellison/236/index.html

VLAD - Voyager LCARS Active Desktop
www.startrekvlad.tsx.org

Wallpaper

In computing terms, "wallpaper" refers to images used to decorate the desktop of your computer. Whether you want to see a Borg cube beneath your icons or the Enterprise travelling at high warp, these sites have got all the Trek-oriented wallpaper you need.

Borg Collective, The: Themes & Wallpaper
www.theborgcollective.com/frames/windows_wallpaper.htm

Desktop Starships
www.desktopstarships.com

Leila's Voyager Page: Backgrounds
www.geocities.com/Area51/Cavern/9441/epback.html

Mark's Star Trek Desktop Calendars
www.geocities.com/Area51/Zone/3318

Maximum Defiant: Backgrounds
www.maximumdefiant.com/bgrounds/index.html

Optical Data Network: First Contact Mosaic
www.alphalink.com.au/~til/Mosaics/FirstContactMosaic.jpg

Optical Data Network: Generations Mosaic
www.alphalink.com.au/~til/Mosaics/GenerationsMosaic.jpg

Quality Star Wars & Star Trek Desktop Pictures
www.spacestar.net/users/gandalf

SciFiArt.Com: Mind's Eye
www.scifi-art.com/mindseye

Shuttlebay 5: Wallpaper
www.geocities.com/Area51/Corridor/8109/desktop_wp.htm

Star Trek & Beyond: Starfleet Imaging Array
www.geocities.com/Area51/Chamber/2468/stng1.htm

Star Trek in Sound & Vision
www.stinsv.com

Trek Files: Wallpaper
http://trekfiles.strek.com/Wallpaper

Trek Worlds: Trek Backgrounds
www.geocities.com/Area51/Zone/3000/index_bgs.htm

Foreign Sites
DEVOTED TO STAR TREK

Although Star Trek is now a part of American popular culture, it has become successful across the planet as well. Whether you're a foreign language student wanting to write a paper about your favorite television show or simply someone who's curious about Star Trek abroad, this chapter is your passport to foreign fun.

Some foreign sites do not have English versions readily available. These are marked with a star (✪) so that you are aware of this factor before accessing the page listed. AltaVista (www.altavista.com) has an excellent translation figure that you can use as well. In lieu of a universal translator, we've compiled some Internet-related foreign terms to assist in your navigation of these pages. If you have any additions or corrections to our foreign terms, please send them to Trek_Changes@klingons.zzn.com so that we may include them in the next edition. Sites from countries where English is the primary language are not listed here. Rather they are mixed in within appropriate categories throughout the book.

Use your find command (usually Ctrl+F) to search for the terms if you are looking for something specific. For example, if you are searching for links on a French site, you might use the find command to search for "liens."

French Sites

French	English
acceuil	previous
aide	help
courrier électronique	e-mail
faites-en votre page d'accueil	make this site your home page
gallerie	gallery
gallerie photo	photo gallery
liens	links
livre d'invites	guestbook
mot de passe	password
nom d'utilisateur	user name
selectionnez une image pour la voir en plein	click on a thumbnail to get a full screen view.
suivante	next
support technique	technical support
systeme	system
usager	user

Michelle Forbes Central
www.jsp.umontreal.ca/~chabotma/Michelle.html

✪ **Star Trek - TSF: Departement Navigation**
http://skyvador.citeweb.net/tsf/frame.htm

✪ **Star Trek - TSF: USS Concordia**
www.startrek-tsf.org/uss/concordia

✪ **Star Trek sur Dav's Clone**
www.multimania.com/davclone/star.html

German Sites

German	English
anmelden	login
benutzername	user name
biographie	biography
Bitte, markieren Sie diese Seite	please bookmark this page
bucher	books
charaktere	character
E-mail-Adresse	e-mail address
episoden	episode
filmographie	filmography
gaestebuch	guestbook
hilfe	help
kontakt	contact
letzes update	last update
mache Sie das zu Ihrer Home Page	make this site your home page
mit frames	with frames

ohne frames	without frames
passwort	password
passwort vergessen	password reminder
plakat	Poster
seite	site
seiten	sites
sternenflotte	Starfleet
technische hilfe	technical support

CJ Tassilo Michelle Forbes Home Page
www.physik.uni-regensburg.de/~krt04517/Forbes

✪ **Crosis (German)**
www.crosis.de

✪ **Das Star Trek Universum**
http://aia.wu-wien.ac.at/Startrek/titelseite.html

✪ **Deutscher StarTrek-Index**
http://startrek.www.de

Fed Con
www.fedcon.de

✪ **Ferengi Rules of Acquisition**
http://aia.wu-wien.ac.at/Startrek/ferengi-regeln.html

German Star Trek Culture Newsgroup
de.rec.sf.startrek.kulturen

German Star Trek Technology Newsgroup
de.rec.sf.startrek.technologie

✪ **Gul Dukat's Homepage**
http://members.aol.com/malaimo/index.htm

✪ **Klingon Embassy**
www.klingon-embassy.de

✪ **Miles O'Brien's Homepage**
http://home.t-online.de/home/MilesOBrien/space.htm

✪ **Moquebarek Online**
http://members.xoom.com/Moquebarek

Patrick Stewart Online: Biography
www.tu-berlin.de/~stewart-page/ps-bio-deutsch.html

✪ **Saar Trek**
www.saarnet.de/startrek

✪ **Star Trek (German)**
www.geocities.com/TimesSquare/Dungeon/2251/trekkie.htm

✪ **Star Trek Chronology**
http://aia.wu-wien.ac.at/Startrek/chronologie.html

✪ **Star Trek Film Information**
http://aia.wu-wien.ac.at/Startrek/Filme/filme.html

✪ **Star Trek German Web Sites Link List**
http://wirtschaft.aon.at/cashtips/3_c_81-1.html

○ **Star Trek Meeting Point**
http://members.tripod.de/prom

○ **Star Trek Pages - M' My Torres**
www.homestead.com/MaTorres/index.html

Star Trek: The Lost Mission
www.geocities.com/Athens/Acropolis/8246

Starfleet Roleplaying in German Newsgroup
alt.starfleet.rpg.german

○ **StarTrek.At**
www.startrek.at/index1.htm

Sternenbasis 11
www.geocities.com/Hollywood/6370/index.html

○ **Terminal IV**
http://tv.freepage.de/terminal4

○ **www.STARTREK.de.cx**
www.startrek.de.cx

Italian Sites

Italian	English
assitenza tecnica	technical support
galleria	gallery
guida	help
nome dell'Utente	user name
pagina	page
parola d'Ordine	password
prossimi 5	next 5
rendi questa pagina la tua pagina iniziale	make this site your home page
siti	sites
sito	site
supporto tecnico	technical support

○ **Comando Centrale Cardassiano**
http://senatodellerazze.org/cardassia

○ **Comitato d'azion Klingon**
www.geocities.com/Hollywood/5844

○ **Dabok Emporium**
http://come.to/dabok

○ **Fondiazone Vulcaniana**
www.geocities.com/Area51/4033/fondazione.html

○ **Organizzazione Libera Bajor (Italian)**
http://members.xoom.it/Bajor_it

Patrick Stewart Online: Biography
www.tu-berlin.de/~stewart-page/ps-bio-italy.html

⊙ **Webtrek Italia**
www.webtrekitalia.com

Klingon (Translated) Sites

Klingon Assault Group (KAG) of Australia
www.ozemail.com.au/~kagaus

Polish Sites

⊙ **Serwis Star Trek**
www.startrek.cavern.com.pl/index2.html

⊙ **USS Shadow**
http://surf.to/ussshadow

Portuguese Sites

Portuguese	English
ajuda	help
cadastre esta pagina	bookmark this page
clique	click
clique aqui	click here
imagens	images
nome do usuario	user name
senha	password
sons	sounds

suporte tecnico	technical support
textos	text

✪ KG Home Page
http://members.tripod.com/kgcorp/st.html

Star Trek Fan Club Organia (Portuguese)
http://organia.skynet.com.br

✪ Star Trek Page
www.geocities.com/Hollywood/4401

Russian Sites

✪ Russian Star Trek
http://user.cityline.ru/~rex

Spanish Sites

Spanish	English
asistencia tecnica	technical support
avuda	help
conexion	login
contrasena	password
figuras de acción	action figures
firmar el libro de visitas	sign the guestbook
galeria photographia	photo gallery
leer el libro de visitas	read the guestbook
mecanismos de búsqueda	search engines
nombre del usuario	user name
puntua este site	rate this site
recordatorio de contrasena	password reminder
recursos	resources
Si encontraste un link que no funciona por	if you found a non working link, please click
sirvase marcar esta pagina	please bookmark this page

Denise Crosby: Spanish Tribute
http://moviepeople.hollywood.com/people.asp?p_id=P|17807

✪ MiniFAQ - Star Trek en Espana
http://bbs.seker.es/~alvy/MiniFAQ_Star_Trek_ES.html

✪ Nemesis
www.gruponemesis.com

✪ Pagina Principal - Star Trek
www.clx.cl/startrek

Patrick Stewart Online: Biography (Spanish)
www.tu-berlin.de/~stewart-page/ps-bio-spain.html

USS Quetzalcoatl
http://members.xoom.com/Tona_Q/NCC-20942

STAR TREK
Merchandise
Online

If you want your Star Trek collection to grow, the Web can certainly help you accomplish it. With e-commerce becoming more and more common, your options for making purchases are increasing exponetially. It doesn't take a positronic brain to figure out that some of the best deals are available online. Whether you're obsessed with Trek action figures or you want to dress like a Klingon, the sites in this chapter will help you make it so.

Action Figures

Whether you're looking for information on 6", 12" or Mego Trek action figures, you can find it on the Internet. Use your kung fu grip on the mouse to click your way to these sites.

ActionAce.Com: Star Trek Merchandise
http://shop.actionace.com/cgi-bin/ActionAce.storefront/900267755/Catalog/1108

Cougar Enterprise's Action Figure Store - Star Trek
http://members.aol.com/efc999/startrek.htm

Greg's Star Trek Playmates Toys Page
http://home.rmi.net/~lustig/toys.html

Ian's Star Trek Memories
www.magna.com.au/~lindsay/trek/Trek.html

Justin's Star Trek Action Figure Page
www.liii.com/~joisite/figure

Mego Star Trek Gallery
www.toymania.com/megomuseum/trek

Mikey's Star Trek Action Figure Page
www.geocities.com/Area51/Vault/6934

Mikey's Star Trek Action Figure Trade Page
www.geocities.com/Area51/Vault/6934/trade.html

Mikey's Star Trek Action Figures for Sale Page
www.geocities.com/Area51/Vault/6934/sale.html

New Eye Studio: Playmates Items
www.neweyestudio.com/stnrfig1.htm

Playmates Toys Home Page
www.playmatestoys.com

Playtrek
www.playtrek.cjb.net

Recipes for Customizing Playmates Star Trek Action Figures
www.magna.com.au/~lindsay/trek/Recipes.html

Rene Boruguet's Action Figure Page
http://members.aol.com/RDBousquet/StarTrk.html

Star Trek Action Figure List (Variations, Oddities & Rarities)
http://hometown.aol.com/strtrkker/INDEXe.HTM

Star Trek Figures for Sale
http://hometown.aol.com/lazeebums/index.html

StarTrekToys.Com
www.startrektoys.com

TJ's Cards & Comics: Star Trek Collectibles
http://tjccc.com/strekpg.htm

Toymania's 3/4 Inch Star Trek Action Figure Archive
www.toymania.com/334archives/trek/index.shtml

Toymania's Mego Star Trek Gallery
www.toymania.com/megomuseum/trek

Autographed Items

These sites offer items autographed by the stars of Star Trek. If you want a picture of Picard and Patrick's signature on your wall or one from anyone else from the Trek universe, these are the sites for you.

Grace Lee Whitney Official Autograph Site
www.graceleewhitney.tf

Official John Colicos Fan Club (Kor)
www.klingon.org/Colicos/pages

Science Fiction Autographs & More
http://autograph.gamescrash.com/index.shtml

Uhura.Com
www.uhura.com

Buy

Whether you want to spend your microcosmic allowance on Trek merchandise or buy a gift for your favorite Trekaholic, the Web has been assimilated by online stores ready to charge your phasers and your credit cards.

800-Trekker
www.800-trekker.com/trek.htm

A Wrinkle In Time: Star Trek Photos
www.awit.com

AAA Star Trek Novels Store
www.geocities.com/TimesSquare/Chasm/7857/Startrek/trekstore.htm

AAA Star Trek: Trek Shop
http://affiliate.iee.net/aaastartrek

Alien Battle Swords
www.deathstar.org/~sword/aliensword.html

American Covers Inc - Star Trek Lenticular Motion Mouse Mats
www.softsolutions.com/promo/aci/startrek.htm

BigStar.Com - Buy Star Trek Movies
www.bigstar.com/misc/startrek.ff?aff=9531&banid=20531

Clicket.Com: Star Trek
www.clicket.com/stgallery/stgal.asp?ain=999999

Clicket.Com: Star Trek Costumes & Accessories
www.clicket.com/stgallery/stgal.asp?ain=368956

Cougar Enterprise's Action Figure Store - Star Trek
http://members.aol.com/efc999/startrek.htm

eBay Listings: Star Trek
http://listings.ebay.com/aw/listings/list/category155/index.html

Flying Pirate Collectibles: Star Trek Bounty
www.galactictradingpost.com/trek2~1.htm

GiftTrek.Com
www.gifttrek.com

GNP/Crescendo Record Co Inc
www.gnpcrescendo.com

Kinder's Comics (Sells Comics, Action Figures, CCGs, etc.)
http://megabits.net/~kinder

Klingon Language Institute
www.kli.org

Lightspeed Fine Arts Inc
www.lightspeedfineart.com

Lincoln Enterprises Star Trek Catalog
www.roddenberry.com/1tc1_01.htm

Mikey's Star Trek Action Figures for Sale Page
www.geocities.com/Area51/Vault/6934/sale.html

New Eye Studio: Playmates Items
www.neweyestudio.com/stnrfig1.htm

New Eye Studio: Star Trek Catalog
www.neweyestudio.com/stsub.htm

New Eye Studio: Star Trek Model Kits
www.neweyestudio.com/stc1m.htm

New Eye Studio: Star Trek Uniforms
www.neweyestudio.com/stc2u.htm

Nightmare Factory: Star Trek Department
www.nightmarefactory.com/startrek.html

Reel.Com: Star Trek II
www.reel.com/content/moviepage.asp?MMID=1701

Reel.Com: Star Trek III
www.reel.com/content/moviepage.asp?MMID=1702

Reel.Com: Star Trek IV
www.reel.com/Content/moviepage.asp?mmid=1411

Reel.Com: Star Trek V
www.reel.com/Content/moviepage.asp?mmid=1733

Reel.Com: Star Trek VI
www.reel.com/Content/moviepage.asp?mmid=3040

Reel.Com: Star Trek: First Contact
www.reel.com/content/moviepage.asp?MMID=12493

Reel.Com: Star Trek: Generations
www.reel.com/Content/moviepage.asp?mmid=7697

Reel.Com: Star Trek: The Motion Picture
www.reel.com/Content/moviepage.asp?mmid=1696

Star Trek at Another Universe.Com
www.anotheruniverse.com/store/categories/StarTrek.asp

Star Trek at the Sci-Fi Channel Store
http://store.scifi.com/categories/StarTrek.asp

Star Trek Figures for Sale
http://hometown.aol.com/lazeebums/index.html

Star Trek Memorabilia Catalog
http://arizona.speedchoice.com/~sraney

Star Trek Online from Home Entertainment
www.startrek.co.uk/main-frameset.html

Star Trek Pins
www.startrekpins.com

Star Trek Store
www.startrekstore.com

Star Trek Virtual Bookstore
www.trekbooks.com

Starbase-1
www.starbase-1.com

Starland
www.starland.com

StarTrekToys.Com
www.startrektoys.com

Subspace Databank
http://subspace.virtualave.net/databank/index.html

Thomas Models
www.thomasmodels.com

TJ's Cards & Comics: Star Trek Collectibles
http://tjccc.com/strekpg.htm

TrekCollect.Com: Star Trek Collectibles
www.trekcollect.com/startrek.htm

TrekTape.Com (Convention Footage)
www.trektape.com

TrekWeb.com
www.trekweb.com

Tribbles & Beyond
www.tribbles.com

Uhura.Com
www.uhura.com

Unified Terran Empire
www.nemonet.com/users/rclow/html/home.htm

WilliamShatner.Com
www.williamshatner.com

Cards

With or without bubblegum trading cards are still a popular pasttime. Star Trek has had more than one series of cards. These sites are dedicated to the various trading card series for Trek and the collecting of them.

Cosmic Dave's "The Star Trader"
http://homes.acmecity.com/tv/thursday/324/stcards

Star Trek Trading Cards Newsgroup
rec.games.trading-cards.startrek

Star Trek Universe Cards
www.atlaseditions.com/trekuniverse1/index.html

Costumes & Apparrel

Want to dress like a Klingon or get into a Starfleet uniform? These sites will help you do just that! Everything from costuming tips to vendors that offer ready-made outfits await you on the World Wide Web.

Clicket.Com: Star Trek
www.clicket.com/stgallery/stgal.asp?ain=999999

Clicket.Com: Star Trek Costumes & Accessories
www.clicket.com/stgallery/stgal.asp?ain=368956

GiftTrek.Com
www.gifttrek.com

JK2 Costumers
http://home.earthlink.net/~jk2costumers

Kang's Page: Costume Design
www.islandnet.com/~timespac/klingon/kampbell.html

Klingon Costuming Message Board
www.egroups.com/group/klingon_costuming

Lincoln Enterprises Star Trek Catalog
www.roddenberry.com/1tc1_01.htm

New Eye Studio: Star Trek Uniforms
www.neweyestudio.com/stc2u.htm

Nightmare Factory: Star Trek Department
www.nightmarefactory.com/startrek.html

Phaser-1's Star Trek Uniforms
www.geocities.com/Area51/Keep/7522

So, you want to be a Cardassian or just look like one?
http://members.aol.com/primeview/makeup.html

Star Trek Uniforms
www.geocities.com/Area51/Keep/7522

Uhura.Com
www.uhura.com

Yahoo! Clubs: Klingon Costumes
http://clubs.yahoo.com/clubs/klingoncostumes

Models & Modeling

Modeling has gone from simply planes, trains and automobiles to starships and alien craft. Webbuilders are building sites to showcase their models and sell them. Satisfy your modeling fix with these sites.

Abe's Star Trek Model Page
www.abeduran.com

Beyond Antares - Modelling Star Trek
www.betechdata.no/Antares/index.htm

CultTVman's Science Fiction Modelling Page
www.culttvman.com

Griffworks' Shipyards
http://hometown.aol.com/griffworks/shipyards.html

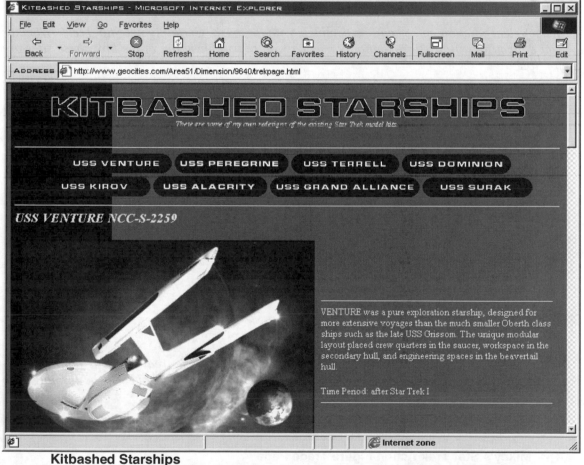

Kitbashed Starships
www.geocities.com/Area51/Dimension/9640/trekpage.html

Markus Nee's Starship Model Page
http://www-personal.umich.edu/~markusn/art/starships.html

New Eye Studio: Star Trek Model Kits
www.neweyestudio.com/stc1m.htm

Pedro's Shiporama
www.shiporama.org

Star Cast - Science Fiction Model Kits
http://members.aol.com/StarCastSF/starships.htm

Starship Builder's Guide
www.ao.net/~chas_art/sbg

Starship Modeler: Ships of the Federation
www.starshipmodeler.com/trek/trekfeds.htm

Starships Only
www.nymac.com/starships

Thomas Models
www.thomasmodels.com

Toys

What science fiction epic would be complete without toys? Certainly not Star Trek! Whether you collect toys in pristine condition or can't wait to tear them out of the box, these sites are for you

ActionAce.Com: Star Trek Merchandise
http://shop.actionace.com/cgi-bin/ActionAce.storefront/900267755/Catalog/1108

Borg Action Figures & Toys
www.geocities.com/Area51/Nebula/6309/plates/staftoys.html

Klingon Teddy Bears
http://members.tripod.com/~klingonbear/index.html

StarTrekToys.Com
www.startrektoys.com

The Star Trek Toy Reference Area
www.newforcecomics.com/trekref

Trade

Conduct trade negotiations through cyberspace! Establish a treaty with a fellow cyber-traveller and trade your goods. With this list of sites, your cargo hold will be teeming with activity.

Cosmic Dave's "The Star Trader"
http://homes.acmecity.com/tv/thursday/324/stcards

Mikey's Star Trek Action Figure Trade Page
www.geocities.com/Area51/Vault/6934/trade.html

Star Trek Trading Center Webring
www.geocities.com/Area51/Station/7010/startrek/tradering.html

STAR TREK
Fun, Games &
Roleplaying

The Star Trek franchise has been applied to many different games. Everything from arcade to computer to online games has been designed using the Star Trek universe. If you're a gamer or want to be, you'll find all the resources in this chapter you need to get involved in a game and improve your playing performance.

Cheat Codes

Don't throw your joystick into your monitor. Check out these "cheat code" sites to help you solve those difficult spots in your Star Trek games.

AAA Star Trek: Cheat Codes for Games
http://eonmagazine.com/startrek/CHEATERS%20PAGE%201.html

Game Nexus: Star Trek - Borg Walk Through
www.gamenexus.com/hints/borg.htm

Game Nexus: Star Trek - Judgement Rites Walkthrough
www.gamenexus.com/hints/startrekjr.htm

Game Nexus: Star Trek - The Next Generation Walk Through
www.gamenexus.com/hints/startrekng.htm

Game Nexus: Star Trek 25th Anniversary Walk Through
www.gamenexus.com/hints/startrek.htm

Game Nexus: Starfleet Academy Cheats
www.gamenexus.com/hints/sfacheat.htm

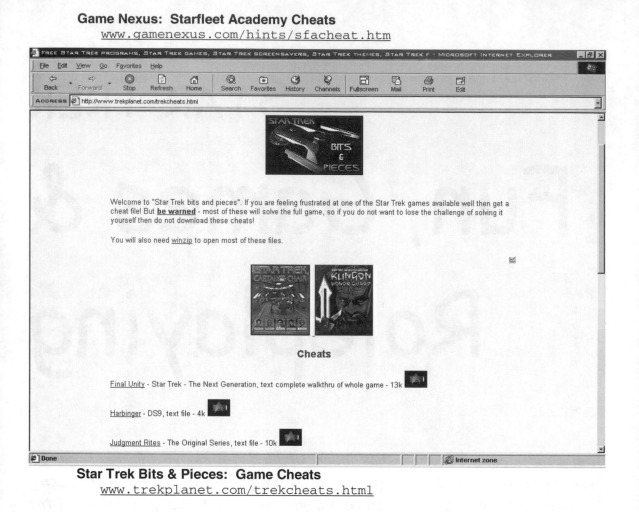

Star Trek Bits & Pieces: Game Cheats
www.trekplanet.com/trekcheats.html

Collectible Card Games (CCGs)

Collectible Card Games (also known as Customizable Card Games and CCGs) are trading cards that can be used to play a game. With the popularity of Magic: The Gathering, it was only a matter of time before CCGs developed for popular franchises, such as Star Trek. Two different companies have released official Star Trek CCGs. These web sites will introduce you to the world of Trek CCGs and enhance your game.

Bot's Unofficial ST:CCG Spot
www.geocities.com/Area51/Corridor/8024

Decipher.Com: Q Continuum Expansion Set: Card List
www.decipher.com/startrek/cardlists/qcontinuum/index.html

Dream Center (Information about CCG Dream Cards)
www.wcs-net.com/~winters/dcframeset.html

Jesse's ST:CCG Site
www.geocities.com/TimesSquare/Arena/3530/noframes/index.html

Computer Games

Star Trek has ventured into about every medium possible, and computer games is no exception. In fact, some of the Star Trek computer games have gone so far as to include new footage with popular actors, adding bits and pieces to the Star Trek universe.

BlazingKnight's ShipYards (Starship Creator)
www.geocities.com/starbase721

Game Nexus: Star Trek - Borg Walk Through
www.gamenexus.com/hints/borg.htm

Game Nexus: Star Trek - Judgement Rites Walkthrough
www.gamenexus.com/hints/startrekjr.htm

Game Nexus: Star Trek - The Next Generation Walk Through
www.gamenexus.com/hints/startrekng.htm

Game Nexus: Star Trek 25th Anniversary Walk Through
www.gamenexus.com/hints/startrek.htm

Game Nexus: Starfleet Academy Cheats
www.gamenexus.com/hints/sfacheat.htm

Interplay: Star Trek
www.interplay.com/startrek/index.html

Klingon Academy Webring
www.geocities.com/Area51/Rampart/7191/sfaka/index.html

KlingonAcademy.Com
www.klingonacademy.com

Star Trek Bits & Pieces: Game Cheats
www.trekplanet.com/trekcheats.html

Star Trek: Starfleet Starship Creator
www.simonsays.com/startrek/library/creator

Starship Creator Message Board
www.simonsays.com/startrek/library/creator/bbs.cfm

Trek Files: Games (Reviews)
http://trekfiles.strek.com/Games

Humor

Everything from top ten lists to one-liners to scripted parodies of Star Trek can be found online. So whether you want to tickle your funny bone or your borg implant, visit these sites.

Borg Tag Lines
http://www2.prestel.co.uk/majeed/sfdbase/databank/borgmtag.htm

Borgisms
http://www2.prestel.co.uk/majeed/sfdbase/databank/borgisms.htm

Dar's Star Trek Humor Vault
www.geocities.com/~darsplace/star_trek_vault/humor.html

Delta Quadrant Resort, The
www.geocities.com/Area51/Station/5192/index.html

Fashion Voyager
http://home.att.net/~fashion.voyager

Federation Foil, The
www.geocities.com/Hollywood/1271

Filk Tunes & Parodies
www.physik.uni-regensburg.de/~krt04517/Forbes/rofilk.html

Garak's Star Trek Tailor Shop: Goofs & Jokes
www.geocities.com/Hollywood/Academy/6325/funnies.html

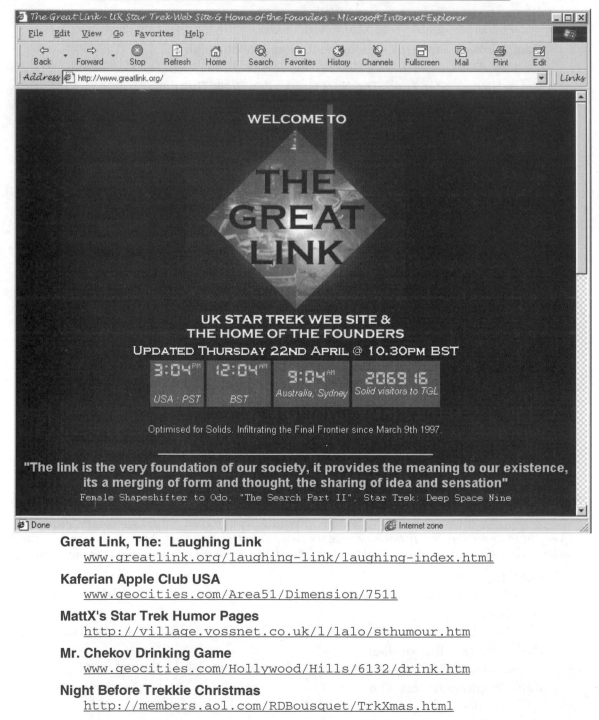

Great Link, The: Laughing Link
www.greatlink.org/laughing-link/laughing-index.html

Kaferian Apple Club USA
www.geocities.com/Area51/Dimension/7511

MattX's Star Trek Humor Pages
http://village.vossnet.co.uk/l/lalo/sthumour.htm

Mr. Chekov Drinking Game
www.geocities.com/Hollywood/Hills/6132/drink.htm

Night Before Trekkie Christmas
http://members.aol.com/RDBousquet/TrkXmas.html

Odo's Bucket Page
www.mindspring.com/~blittle/odosbucket/trek.html

Odo's Top Ten Pet Peeves About Being Solid
http://www2.uic.edu/~rcasti1/odo_t10.html

Operation SNAFU (Blooper & Gaff Information for TNG)
www.ugcs.caltech.edu/st-tng/trivia/snafu.html

Q Continuum (II): Q Humor
www.worc.u-net.com/alt.fan.q/humor.html

Sev Trek - A Cartoon Satire
www.sev.com.au/toonzone/sevtrek.htm

Star Park: A Trek in the Park (South Park meets Star Trek!)
www.jedinet.com/starpark/parkers

Star Trash
http://members.xoom.com/startrash

Star Trek & The Road Runner
http://tempura.cs.uq.edu.au/personal/bof/Television/trekrunner.
html

Star Trek Drinking Game
gopher://wiretap.spies.com/00/Library/Media/Trek/stdrink%09%09%
2B

Star Trek Frontier . . . Humor
www.geocities.com/Area51/Dimension/7551/humor.html

Star Trek Jokes: Borg
http://www2.prestel.co.uk/majeed/sfdbase/databank/Jokesbor.htm

Star Trek Jokes: Klingon
http://www2.prestel.co.uk/majeed/sfdbase/databank/Jokeskli.htm

Star Trek Stuff: Humor
http://members.xoom.com/Neelix/humor.html

Star Trek Top Ten Lists part 1
gopher://wiretap.spies.com/00/Library/Media/Trek/top10.st1%09%0
9%2B

Star Trek Top Ten Lists part 2
gopher://wiretap.spies.com/00/Library/Media/Trek/top10.st2%09%0
9%2B

Star Trek with Dilbert Management
http://members.aol.com/RDBousquet/TrkDilbert.html

Star Trek: The Night Before Christmas
www.dmrtc.net/~thompsde/xmas.html

Steve's Trek Page: Adopt a Trek Pet
http://soli.inav.net/~nibblink/adptmain.htm

Targ TV
http://members.aol.com/LaurThur/TARGTV.html

The Borg vs. Microsoft Windows
http://www2.prestel.co.uk/majeed/sfdbase/databank/borgwin.htm

The Page that Turns You Into a Tribble
www.geocities.com/SoHo/6012/tribble.html

Top Infinite Reasons Kirk is Better Than Picard, The
www.geocities.com/Area51/Rampart/4537/krkbest.html

Trek Love
www.lunaticlounge.com/treklove

Trekker One: Trekker Five: Star Trek Humor
www.angelfire.com/nc/TrekkerFive/index.html

Tuvok Secret Agent Man
www.geocities.com/Area51/Lair/4979/disguise.html

Ultimate Star Trek Collection: Star Trek Humor
http://startrek.fns.net.fsn.net/humor/sthumor.html

Voyager Jokes
www.aplus.com/seth/trek/jokes.html

Wally's Weird Star Trek Tribute
www.wallys.com/startrek/startrek.htm

Worf's Star Trek Site: Humor
www.bazza.com/sj/trek/humour

Online & Java-Based Games

Web browsing has become so advanced that we can even play games within a web page itself. Althought we've still got a ways to go before we can step into our own holodecks, the Web can certainly keep us occupied. Check out these online and Java-based games.

Create Your Own Star Trek Plot (Java Game)
www.geocities.com/Area51/Cavern/3227/trek.html

Garak's Star Trek Tailor Shop: Dominion Checkers
www.geocities.com/Hollywood/Academy/6325/checkers.html

Garak's Star Trek Tailor Shop: Quiz
www.geocities.com/Hollywood/Academy/6325/quiz.html

Main Engineering: Game Room
http://mainengineering.simplenet.com/games.html

Pinch Captain Picard
www.geocities.com/Area51/Rampart/4537/pinch.html

Six Degrees of William Shatner!
www.geocities.com/Area51/Rampart/4537/6degree.html

Star Trek Continuum: Recreation Room
www.startrekcontinuum.com/RecRoom/quadrant.asp?ssector=recroom.asp

Star Trek Puzzle
www.trekplanet.com/puzzletrek.html

Star Trek: The Animated Series: Mah Jong
http://mainengineering.simplenet.com/tas_minipai/tas_minipai.html

Play-by-E-Mail Games (PBEMs)

In the past, people played roleplaying games through snail mail, using postage to send game directions and moves to one another. Now, with the advent of e-mail, players can communicate almost instantaneously. To join a play-by-e-mail Trek game, log on to the sites listed here.

Allied Electronic Simulations (AES)
www.aesim.com

Federation Realms
www.federationrealms.com

Seventh Order, The
www.geocities.com/~ardeth

Star Trek - Godspeed
www.geocities.com/TelevisionCity/Station/5420/Godspeed2.html

Star Trek: Shadow Operations
http://home.talkcity.com/InfiniteLoop/bskyrilvree

USS Athena
www.weddingdaybridals.com/USS_Athena/index.htm

USS Hope
www.uss-hope.freeserve.co.uk/index.html

Roleplaying Groups

Roleplaying groups are exactly that -- groups that roleplay. The following sites belong to such groups for Star Trek.

Klingon Assault Group (KAG) Domain, The
www.kag.org

Klingon Assault Group (KAG) of Australia
www.ozemail.com.au/~kagaus

Live Action Roleplaying in the Star Trek Universe
www.geocities.com/Area51/Nebula/6613

Roleplaying With Star Trek
http://members.xoom.com/rwst

Romulan Invasions Squadron
http://cflmain.com/romulans

Star Trek: Genesis Sim Group
http://members.aol.com/stgenesis/index.htm

Roleplaying Resources

For good roleplaying, the participant should know what they're doing, and what they are talking about. These sites are excellent for administering a game or for embellishing a character with authentic detail and knowledge.

Allied Electronic Simulations (AES)
www.aesim.com

Bravo Fleet RPG
www.bravofleet.com

Federation Sim Group
www.fsg-sims.com

Interstellar Simming Organization
www.simming.org

Siencia Colony SIM
www.geocities.com/Area51/4900/index.html

Star Trek Roleplaying
www.ufed.org

Star Trek: Genesis Sim Group
http://members.aol.com/stgenesis/index.htm

UCESS - United Coalition of Earthwide Starfleet Simulations
www.geocities.com/Area51/Rampart/4776/ucess.html

United Federation of Kids
www.ufk.org

United Interstellar Planets
www.uip.org

United Space Federation Internet Simulations
www.sector001.com/inter.htm

USS Amazon
www.ussamazon.cjb.net

USS Saturn
www.angelfire.com/ca2/lexacus/index.html

Sim Groups (SIMs)

Sim Groups meet in chat rooms at certain times and roleplay live.

30 Years of Star Trek Trivia Cards
www.geocities.com/Area51/Vault/4060/engstga.html

Bob's LCARS Database
www.geocities.com/bobstrek

Star Trek TOS Trivia
www.geocities.com/TelevisionCity/3555/startrivia.html

TriviaTrek.Com
www.triviatrek.com

Star Trek: The Experience

Las Vegas has everything -- including Star Trek! Thanks to the Hilton's Star Trek: The Experience you can meet Klingons without going to a Trek convention.

A Funny Thing Happened on the Way to the Simulator
http://members.aol.com/treborp2/home/Story.HTML

A Review of Star Trek: The Experience at the Las Vegas Hilton
http://pages.prodigy.com/crossover/trekhilt.htm

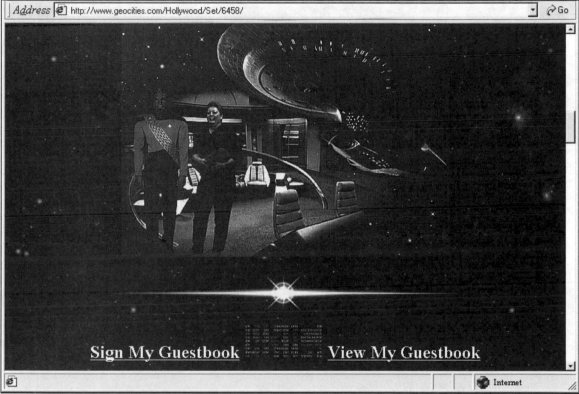

Star Trek - The Collection
www.geocities.com/Hollywood/Set/6458

Star Trek: The Experience
www.startrekexp.com

Star Trek: The Experience - at the Las Vegas Hilton
www.pcap.com/startrek.htm

Starbase Vegas
www.vegaslounge.com/startrek

Starbase Vegas: FAQ
www.vegaslounge.com/startrek/questions.html

Trivia

Test your Trek knowledge and challenge your friends using the trivia found at the sites below.

30 Years of Star Trek Trivia Cards
www.geocities.com/Area51/Vault/4060/engstga.html

AAA Star Trek: Trivia Contest
http://eonmagazine.com/startrek/iqindex.html

Bob's LCARS Database
www.geocities.com/bobstrek

Star Trek TOS Trivia
www.geocities.com/TelevisionCity/3555/startrivia.html

TriviaTrek.Com
www.triviatrek.com

Reading

ABOUT STAR TREK

Can't get enough Star Trek? Well, put on your reading glasses (or VISOR as the case may be) and log on to the sites in this chapter. Whether you want articles, e-zines, episode guides, or fan fiction, it's online and it's listed here.

Articles

It's no surprise that Star Trek is written about. It's popularity demands it. As such, there are numerous places on the Web where you can read articles that have been published regarding Star Trek. Use the titles in this list like a table of contents to clue you in as to the subject of the article listed.

Armin Shimmerman Articles
www.walrus.com/~quark/armin/articles.html

CNN Showbiz: Let Picard be your guide to the universe
www.cnn.com/SHOWBIZ/9606/20/tech.guide/index.html

CNN Showbiz: New Star Trek film aims for the gut, not just the head
www.cnn.com/SHOWBIZ/9611/22/star.trek/index.html

CNN Showbiz: Patrick Stewart Celebrates His First Decade With First Contact
www.cnn.com/SHOWBIZ/9611/28/patrick.stewart

E! Online: Q&A with Patrick Stewart
www.eonline.com/Hot/Qa/Stewart

Nicole deBoer - Spellbound: Articles & Interviews
www.nikkideboer.com/interviews.htm

Totally Kate!: Mulgrew Articles
http://members.tripod.com/~marcia_2/articles.htm

Yahoo! Internet Life - Star Trek Special: The Dope on Data
www.zdnet.com/yil/content/mag/startrek/datanew.html

Yahoo! Internet Life: The Star Trek Universe Online
www.zdnet.com/yil/content/mag/9812/trek.html

Comics

The history of Star Trek comics is a rather complicated one. The license to produce official Star Trek comics has changed hands many times. DC has had the license twice, Marvel twice as well, and Malibu had the license to produce a Deep Space Nine comic for a short period. Now Wildstorm, an imprint of DC Comics, has the license. Find out more about the Trek comics and their history by visiting these sites.

AAA Star Trek: Star Trek Comics
http://eonmagazine.com/startrek/comics%20page%201.html

Mania Magazine: Review of Star Trek/X-Men Comic
www.anotheruniverse.com/comics/features/trekxmen.html

Review: Star Trek/X-Men - Second Contact 1
www.enteract.com/~katew/reviews/xmensttng1.htm

Star Trek Comics Checklist
www.landfield.com/faqs/star-trek/comics-checklist/part1

E-Zines

E-Zines are essentially homegrown magazines that are published electronically. Just about every popular topic has a "zine" devoted to it, and Star Trek is no exception. Check out these Star Trek e-zines!

Database PADD
http://lcars.simplenet.com/padd

Dateline: Starfleet
www.data1701d.com

Federation Foil, The
www.geocities.com/Hollywood/1271

Sector001.Com: Publications
www.sector001.com/filelib_pubs.htm

thIngn jev, the (Klingon Newsletter)
www.cyberramp.net/~klingon/jev/jev.htm

Episode Guides

Episode guides are extremely useful to anyone trying to watch every episode or find out what he or she missed. Episode guides range from bare bones descriptions to full blown synopsis. With this list of sites, you won't need to purchase any commercial episode guides -- you'll only need to log onto the Web.

Andrew Tong's Next Generation Episode Guide
www.ugcs.caltech.edu/st-tng/episodes.html

Concise Star Trek Episode Guide, The
www.geocities.com/Area51/1125

Delta Blues
www.treknews.com/deltablues

DS9 Episode Guide 98
www.geocities.com/TimesSquare/4818/ds92.htm

Eric's Excruciatingly Detailed Star Trek (TOS) Plot Summaries
www.treasure-troves.com/startrek

Galactic Handbook for All Starfleet Cadets
http://welcome.to/galactic_handbook

MJ's Star Trek Web Site
www.surfshop.net/~majtown/NoFrames1.html

Outpost 21: Deep Space Nine Episode Guide
www.steve.simplenet.com/episode_guides/ds9

Outpost 21: Next Generation Episode Guide
www.steve.simplenet.com/episode_guides/tng

Outpost 21: Voyager Episode Guide
www.steve.simplenet.com/episode_guides/voy

Sci-Fi Channel Star Trek Episode Search
www.scifi.com/startrek/episodes

Sector 0-0-1: Episode Guides: Deep Space Nine
http://members.aol.com/NCC2364/guide/ds9.html

Sector 0-0-1: Episode Guides: Next Generation
http://members.aol.com/NCC2364/guide/tng.html

Sector 0-0-1: Episode Guides: The Original Series
http://members.aol.com/NCC2364/guide/tos.html

Sector 0-0-1: Episode Guides: Voyager
http://members.aol.com/NCC2364/guide/voy.html

Star Trek Continuum: Deep Space Nine Episode Guide
www.startrekcontinuum.com/ds9/quadrant.asp?ssector=log.asp

Star Trek Continuum: Next Generation Episode Guide
www.startrekcontinuum.com/tng/quadrant.asp?ssector=log.asp

Star Trek Continuum: Original Series Episode Guide
www.startrekcontinuum.com/tos/quadrant.asp?ssector=log.asp

Star Trek Continuum: Voyager Episode Guide
www.startrekcontinuum.com/voy/quadrant.asp?ssector=log.asp

Star Trek Episode Guide
http://members.tripod.com/~Xronos/trek.htm

Starfleet Supply: Next Generation Episode Guide
www.geocities.com/Area51/Stargate/7952/sttnge.html

Voyager Jeffries' Tubes: Episode Guide
www.geocities.com/Area51/Dimension/9644/voy_eps.html

Essays

The following sites offer essays, some factual, some opinionated, on various aspects of the Star Trek mythos. Use the titles of the sites to determine the content of the essays.

A Funny Thing Happened on the Way to the Simulator
http://members.aol.com/treborp2/home/Story.HTML

A Grammatical Sketch & Dictionary of the Andorian Language
http://randyb.byu.edu/alioth/sketch.html

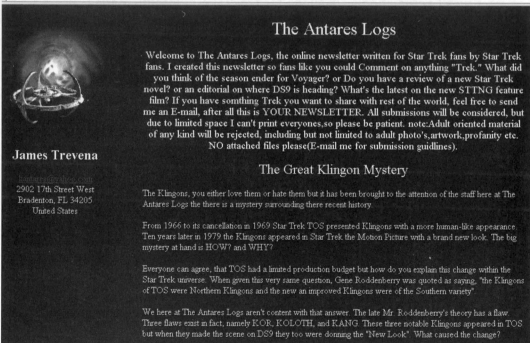

Antares Logs, The
http://members.tripod.com/~LtAntares/TheAntaresLogs.html

Cardassians - Now We Like Them, Now We Don't
http://startrek.about.com/library/weekly/aa031799.htm?pid=2833&
cob=home

Garak's Star Trek Tailor Shop: Fan-Written Articles
www.geocities.com/Hollywood/Academy/6325/weyoun.html

Gay Trek
www.the-spa.com/cj/gay.htm

Identity, Paranoia & Technology on the Next Generation
http://eng.hss.cmu.edu/cyber/startrek.html

Improvement of Human Technology by Borgification, The
www.geocities.com/Area51/Chamber/8121

KIDC: Intergalactic Delicacies
www.klingon.org/KIDC/pages/intergalactic_cuisine.html

Multilingual Star Trek
gopher://wiretap.spies.com/00/Library/Media/Trek/language.st%09%09%2B

Physics of Star Trek, The: Could Warp Drive Work?
www.newscientist.com/nsplus/insight/startrek/warp.html

Sector 001: Alternate Timelines
www.powernet.net/~jcrafton/timealt.html

So why finally a woman captain?
www.trekplanet.com/janeway.html

Star Trek for Dummies
http://members.tripod.com/~pete1701

Star Trek Papers
www.stwww.com/papers/index.html

Summary of the Physiological Roots of Andorian Culture
www.geocities.com/Area51/Station/1558/Fish.html

The Number 47 - The Saga of One Special Number in One Big Television Legend
www.stanford.edu/~schlock/the47s.html

Trek is Everywhere - References to Trek in Other Media
www.voicenet.com/~vmaiocco/Trek%20is%20Everywhere.html

Treknology.Com
www.treknology.8m.com

USS Quetzalcoatl: Essays & Articles
http://members.xoom.com/_XOOM/Tona_Q/NCC-20942/trek-ne.htm

What if the Star Trek Universe Had Its Own Superhero Team?
http://pages.prodigy.com/crossover/jlads92.htm

Why Star Trek Sucks
www.flash.net/~twinkle/psycho/DARK/scholarly/trek.htm

Fan Fiction

Fan Fiction is fiction written by fans about the subject of which they are a fan. In this case, many Trekkers have put their creative impulses to good use in creating some excellent "unofficial" stories of just about every Trek character. To read these "new" adventures, you need only visit the pages listed here.

Adventures of the USS Phantom
http://ussphantom.8m.com

August's Fanfic Collection (Voyager Fan Fiction)
http://members.tripod.com/~Appelsini/fanfic.html

Bay's Picard/Crusher Stories
www.geocities.com/TelevisionCity/Stage/8486/Stories.html

Borg Collective, The: Fan Fiction
www.theborgcollective.com/frames/fan_fiction.htm

Chakotay/Paris Slash Ring: Sites List
www.webring.org/cgi-bin/webring?ring=cpslash;list

Data & Tasha Fanfic Page, The
www.geocities.com/Area51/Stargate/1206

DolittleMD's Page of Procrastination
http://members.xoom.com/DolittleMD/main.htm

Dukat's Romantic Fan Fiction
www.kardasi.com/qd/contents.htm

FanFiction.Net: Deep Space Nine
www.fanfiction.net/text/browse-
listfiles.cfm?category=StarTrek%3A+Deep+Space+Nine

FanFiction.Net: Next Generation
www.fanfiction.net/text/browse-
listfiles.cfm?category=StarTrek%3A+The+Next+Generation

FanFiction.Net: Other Star Trek Fiction
www.fanfiction.net/text/browse-
listfiles.cfm?category=StarTrek%3A+Other

FanFiction.Net: The Original Series
www.fanfiction.net/text/browse-
listfiles.cfm?category=StarTrek%3A+The+Original+Series

FanFiction.Net: Voyager
www.fanfiction.net/text/browse-
listfiles.cfm?category=StarTrek%3A+Voyager

FedNet: Fanfic by Jeffrey Harlan
www.geocities.com/Area51/Rampart/3219/FedNet/fanfic/index.html

Forever Imzadi
www.geocities.com/Paris/Metro/4010

Garak's Star Trek Tailor Shop: Fan Fiction
www.geocities.com/Hollywood/Academy/6325/stories.html

Gul Traglor's Cardassian Fan Fiction
http://homestead.com/Cardassian/Cardie0.html

Imzadi - Their Hearts Beat As One
http://members.xoom.com/invilil

Infinitely Imzadi
www.geocities.com/Area51/Hollow/2955

Infinitely Imzadi: Fan Fiction
www.geocities.com/Area51/Hollow/2955/fanfic.htm

Interactive Kirk Novels, The
http://books.dreambook.com/phineasbog/kirkbook.html

Jesse's Star Trek Crossover Page
http://members.easyspace.com/trekxover

JetC14 Fan Fiction Archive
http://web.ukonline.co.uk/sammi.w2/jetc/jetc14fanfic.htm

Judy Gale's Fan Fiction Archive
www.geocities.com/Area51/Corridor/4957/index.html

JuPiter Station (II)
www.geocities.com/~jupiterstation

Kret Rats: P/T Fan Fiction
http://members.tripod.com/~Maihe/stories.html

Kret Rats: P/T Fan Poetry
http://members.tripod.com/~Maihe/poems.html

Lady K'Lyssia's Realms of Imagination
www.geocities.com/klyssia

Lady Kardasi's Domain
www.kardasi.com

Lanna's P/T Picks
www.geocities.com/TelevisionCity/Set/6627

Millenium Pictures
http://members.tripod.co.uk/m_p

My Caitian World
www.concentric.net/~Psgibbs/index_.htm

New Worlds Ring
www.geocities.com/Area51/2403/nwr.htm

Official Archive of the Paris/Torres Collective
www.geocities.com/~ptcarchive

Paradox761's Star Trek FanFic Page
http://members.tripod.com/~Paradox761/index.html

Past Futures: Chronicles of the Nebular Alliance
http://members.home.net/transwarp

PJ in NH's Fan Fiction
http://unix.worldpath.net/~kelhapam

Q Fan Fiction Library
www.knownspace.demon.co.uk/qindex.htm

Quantum Slipstream
www.geocities.com/Area51/Dunes/8431

Running Horse's Voyager Page
http://members.tripod.com/~dianerhsmith/index.html

Sam's Voyage Into the Unknown: Fan Fiction Page
www.geocities.com/Area51/Shire/7170/samfanfic.html

Star Trek - The Adventures of Argus
Www.USSArgus.com

Star Trek Fan Fiction Romance Ring: Sites List
www.webring.org/cgi-bin/webring?ring=ginomo&list

Star Trek Institute for Romantics
www.angelfire.com/in/telania/index.html

Star Trek News (II): Fan Fiction
www.geocities.com/Area51/Dimension/9268/storypage.html

Star Trek Slash Ring: Sites List
www.webring.org/cgi-bin/webring?ring=stslash;list

Star Trek Voyager - Lower Decks
http://ljc.simplenet.com/lowerdecks

Star Trek: Defender
www.startrekdefender.cwc.net

Star Trek: The Lost Mission
www.geocities.com/Athens/Acropolis/8246

Starbase 28: The Holonovel
www.geocities.com/~jacobjou/holonove.html

Starfleet Missions II
www.amtc.net/users/~ziroc/sfm2p/index.htm

Tales by Wolfen (Fan Fiction)
http://members.tripod.com/~wolf_fen/wolftales.htm

The Nexus: Star Trek Fiction
www.mcm.edu/~tardiffj/fiction/story1.htm

The Site for TOS Stories
www.ludwig.ucl.ac.uk/st/StarTrek/Stories/stories.html

The Tom Paris Fanfic Archive - Paris Nights
www.ParisNights.de

Trek Writer's Guild
www.twguild.com

TrekExpress.Com: Fan Fiction
www.trekexpress.com/fanfic/fanfic.htm

Tricorder Readings
www.geocities.com/Area51/Corridor/9352

UK's Star Trek Stories, Artwork, Links & More!
www.geocities.com/SoHo/Atrium/2560

USS Missouri
http://members.tripod.com/~stidham/missouri.htm

Vorta Vortex
http://members.tripod.com/~vortavixen/vortex.htm

Voyager's Delights
www.capecod.net/~druddy

Voyager's Delights: Fan Fiction
www.capecod.net/~druddy/fan%20fiction.htm

Worf/Troi Domain, The
http://members.aol.com/reid756/wtdomain.html

X-Files/Star Trek X-Overs
www.busprod.com/aclaybor/xover/categ/startrek.htm

FAQs

FAQ stands for Frequently Asked Questions. FAQ files are collections of these questions and their answers. The following are FAQs for Star Trek. Use the title to determine the subject.

Alien Voices (Audiobooks) FAQ
www.knownspace.demon.co.uk/alienvfaq.txt

AllExperts.Com: Ask a Question about Deep Space Nine
www.allexperts.com/tv/ds9.shtml

AllExperts.Com: Ask a question about Voyager
www.allexperts.com/tv/voyager.shtml

Big Bill's Star Trek Stuff
www.kruse.demon.co.uk/index.htm

FAQ: DeForest Kelley
www.kilroywashere.com/sarah/faq.htm

Frequently Asked Questions about Jeri Ryan
www.jerilynn.com/faq.htm

Holodeck & Computers FAQ
http://members.aa.net/~skeksis/Star_Trek/FAQs/holodeck-faq.html

Kes FAQ
www.vliet.org/jl/kesfaq.html

Klingon Fan Clubs & Groups FAQ
www.khemorex-klinzhai.de/faqs/kli-faq.html

Klingon Language Institute
www.kli.org

Odo/Kira FAQ
http://members.tripod.com/~OdoGoddess/OdoGoddess/okfaq.txt

Spiners' Doman: Brent Spiner FAQ
www.spiner.org/facts/stats.htm

Star Trek Actors' Other Roles FAQ
www.cris.com/~Carman

Starbase Vegas: FAQ
www.vegaslounge.com/startrek/questions.html

Stardates in Star Trek FAQ
www.cs.umanitoba.ca/~djc/startrek/stardates

Ten Forward Lounge: Stardate Mini-FAQ
www.interlog.com/~pcarr/star_trek/stardate.html

The Flagship: Star Trek X: FAQ
http://bsd.interstat.net/~tomveil/stx/faq.html

Transporters, Replicators & Phasing FAQ
http://members.aa.net/~skeksis/Star_Trek/FAQs/transport-faq.html

Utopia Planitia Starship Database
http://utopia.solareclipse.net

Warp & Subspace FAQ
http://members.aa.net/~skeksis/Star_Trek/FAQs/warp-faq.html

Warp Velocities FAQ
http://members.aa.net/~skeksis/Star_Trek/FAQs/warp_velocities-faq.html

Historical Information

The sites below offer background material on the fictitious Star Trek universe as well as information about the creation of the show and its various incarnations.

Borg Collective, The: What is Star Trek?
www.theborgcollective.com/frames/trek_main.htm

Deep Space Nine Bible
gopher://wiretap.spies.com/00/Library/Media/Trek/deep9.bib%09%09%2B

Our Star Trek Universe Timeline - How We Remember It
www.geocities.com/Area51/Corridor/5363/sttimeline.html

Star Trek History
www.clark.net/pub/aheisey/startrek/history/home.html

Star Trek Timeline
gopher://wiretap.spies.com/00/Library/Media/Trek/startrek.tl%09%09%2B

USS Quetzacoatl: Star Trek Universe
http://members.xoom.com/_XOOM/Tona_Q/NCC-20942/trek-e.htm

Interviews

Visit the sites below to read interviews with the cast and crew of the various Star Trek series. Use the title to determine the subject of the interview.

AAA Star Trek: Interviews
http://eonmagazine.com/startrek/INTERVIEWS%20PAGE%201.html

Great Link, The: Interviews
www.greatlink.org/convention-reps/con-index.html

Infinitely Imzadi: Interviews
www.geocities.com/Area51/Hollow/2955/interviews.htm

Inside Voyager:
Interview with Jimmy Flowers, Author of The Incredible Internet Guide for Trekkers
http://www.geocities.com/Area51/Stargate/7559/holodeck.htm

Kate Speaks Out - Interviews with Kate Mulgrew
www.geocities.com/Area51/Nebula/1876/Kate2.htm

Maximum Defiant: Ronald Moore Speaks!
www.maximumdefiant.com/misc/moore.html

Nicole deBoer - Spellbound: Articles & Interviews
www.nikkideboer.com/interviews.htm

Official Jeri Lynn Ryan Homepage, The: Interviews
www.jerilynn.com/interv.htm

Official Robert Picardo Homepage, The: Interviews
http://members.aol.com/rpicardo/intervie.html

Patrick Stewart Online: Interviews
www.tu-berlin.de/~stewart-page/interviews.html

Physics of Star Trek, The: Interview with the Author (Lawrence Krauss)
www.newscientist.com/nsplus/insight/startrek/krauss.html

Totally Kate!: Mulgrew Television, Radio & Online Interviews
http://members.tripod.com/~marcia_2/intervew.htm

TrekToday's Interview with Insurrection Game Designers
www.trektoday.com/e3/insurrection.shtml

Whisper of Alien Voices (Interview with John de Lancie)
www.knownspace.demon.co.uk/alienv.htm

Yahoo! Internet Life: The Star Trek Universe Online
www.zdnet.com/yil/content/mag/9812/trek.html

Yahoo! Internet Life: Star Trek Special: Spiner Speaks
www.zdnet.com/yil/content/mag/startrek/spiner9612a.html

News

Stay on top of priority transmissions and monitor subspace channels with these sites. Use these pages to find out the latest goings-on in the world of Star Trek -- onscreen and off.

AnotherUniverse.Com: Mania Magazine
www.anotheruniverse.com/mania

Dark Horizons
www.darkhorizons.com

Database PADD
http://lcars.simplenet.com/padd

Dateline: Starfleet
www.data1701d.com

DEN, The - Daily Entertainment Network
www.theden.com

Hollywood Online
www.hollywood.com

Inside Voyager
www.geocities.com/Area51/Stargate/7559/index.html

Maximum Warp
http://homepages.enterprise.net/davies/trek

Psi Phi's Star Trek: Voyager Archive
www.psiphi.org/voy

Quinn's News Stand (from Garak's Star Trek Tailor Shop)
www.geocities.com/Hollywood/Academy/6325/news.html

Security/Tactical Station: Voyager News
www.excelsior.free-online.co.uk/sttc

Series 5 News from The Universe
http://startrek-universe.simplenet.com/vseries.html

Star Trek - The Collective: Ready Room
www.excelsior.free-online.co.uk/sttc

Star Trek News
www.geocities.com/Hollywood/6952

Star Trek News (II)
www.geocities.com/Area51/Dimension/9268/index.html

Star Trek News Newsgroup
rec.arts.startrek.current

Star Trek Newsletter
www.geocities.com/Area51/Dimension/7551/news.html

Star Trek Nexus: News Network
http://members.aol.com/trekannex/treknews.htm

Star Trek Portal
www.strek.com

Star Trek Singularity
http://sts.alphalink.com.au

Starfleet Database
http://www2.prestel.co.uk/majeed

Starfleet Intelligence
www.angelfire.com/mt/sfintelligence/index.html

The Universe
http://startrek-universe.simplenet.com

Trek Scoop
www.tgeweb.com/trek/scoop.htm

TrekExpress.Com: Gossip
www.trekexpress.com/gossip.htm

TREKNEWSnetwork

TrekNews.Com
www.treknews.com

"The first and only daily updated guide to all things Trek"

TrekToday.Com
www.trektoday.com

TrekWeb.com
www.trekweb.com

YSK's Star Trek Page
www.geocities.com/Area51/Corridor/3546

Novels & Non-Fiction

Star Trek has appeared in just about every form of media, and print is no exception. Here are some sites that focus on the novels and non-fiction books of Star Trek.

AAA Star Trek Novels Store
www.geocities.com/TimesSquare/Chasm/7857/Startrek/trekstore.htm

Brad & Kathi Ferguson's Home Away from Home Page (Author Site)
www.fred.net/thirteen

Christie Golden's Home Page (Author Site)
www.sff.net/people/christie.golden

Classic Trek on the 'Net: Novel Reviews by Trekkie Guy
www.geocities.com/Area51/Rampart/9065/review.htm

David & Leonore Dvorkin's Introductory Pages (Author Site)
www.dvorkin.com

Esther Friesner's Web Site (Author Site)
www.sff.net/people/e.friesner

Guide to Star Trek: New Frontier
http://www1.ridgecrest.ca.us/~curtdan/NewFrontier/Excalibur.cgi
?FILE=Enter

Incredible Internet Guide Series
www.incredibleguides.com

Jean Lorrah's Home Page
(Author - "Metamorphosis" & "The Vulcan Academy Murders"
www.simegen.com/Jean

Jerry Oltion (Author Site)
www.sff.net/people/J.Oltion

Jimmy Flowers Online (Author Site)
http://go.to/jimmyflowers

ADDRESS http://www.wildsidepress.com/johnbib1.htm

Wildside Press
Online Catalog
Bibliography
For Booksellers
CD-ROMS
Message Board
Mailing List

Corporate
Investor Relations

Publishing Services
Publishing Solutions
Guidelines

Science Fiction
John Betancourt Page
Science Fiction Links
The Writers' Page
Author's Own Bookstore

JOHN GREGORY BETANCOURT:
A SELECTED BIBLIOGRAPHY

Novels

- Star Trek The Next Generation: Double Helix, Book I: Infection (Pocket Books) *Forthcoming.*

- Hercules: The Wrath of Poseidon (Tor Books)
  First published June, 1997. $4.99 (U.S.).

- Hercules: The Vengeance of Hera (Tor Books)
  First published September, 1997. $4.99 (U.S.).

- Star Trek Deep Space 9: Heart of the Warrior (Pocket Books)
  First published October, 1996. $5.99 (U.S.).
- The Hag's Contract (TSR, Inc.)
  First published June, 1996. $5.99 (U.S.). Set in TSR's "Birthright" universe, it's an old-fashioned sword & sorcery adventure, complete with giant snakes, epic battles, intrigue, ghosts, and of course wizards, assassins, kings, and warriors.
- Lois & Clark: Exile, by "M.J. Friedman" (TSR, Inc.)
  First published May, 1996. $5.99 (U.S.). A Superman novel, written with Michael Jan Friedman (I did the first draft, he did the final). For kids.

John Gregory Betancourt (Author Site)
www.wildsidepress.com/jgb.htm

John Vornholt (Author Site)
www.sff.net/people/vornholt

Josepha Sherman (Author - "Vulcan's Forge")
www.sff.net/people/Josepha.Sherman

Mark Okrand Forum (Author - "Klingon Dictionary")
www.startrekcontinuum.com/earth/quadrant.asp?ssector=exokr.asp

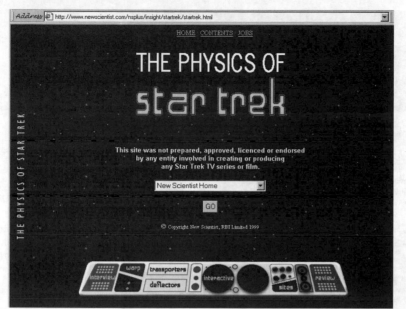

Physics of Star Trek, The
www.newscientist.com/nsplus/insight/startrek/startrek.html

Physics of Star Trek, The: Interview with the Author (Lawrence Krauss)
www.newscientist.com/nsplus/insight/startrek/krauss.html

Psi Phi's Deep Space Nine Novels
www.psiphi.org/DS9/books.html?ix

Star Trek - The Books
www.simonsays.com/startrek

Star Trek Bantam Books
www.geocities.com/Area51/Nebula/6309/QRY-BANTAMBooks_1.html

Star Trek Book List
www.geocities.com/Hollywood/Boulevard/6608

Star Trek Deep Space Nine Books
www.geocities.com/Area51/Nebula/6309/QRY-
STARTREK_DeepSpaceNine_1.html

Star Trek Next Generation Books
www.geocities.com/Area51/Nebula/6309/QRY-
STARTREK_NextGeneration_The_1.html

Star Trek Original Series Books
www.geocities.com/Area51/Nebula/6309/QRY-
STARTREK_OriginalSeries_The_1.html

Star Trek Virtual Bookstore
www.trekbooks.com

Star Trek Voyager Books
www.geocities.com/Area51/Nebula/6309/QRY-
STARTREK_Voyager_1.html

The Hub - The Unauthorized Star Trek Novel Pages
www.suneater.org

To Seek Out New Life (Home Page for The Biology of Star Trek)
www.thebiologyofstartrek.com

Vulcan Phil's Review of Star Trek Novels
http://hometown.aol.com/vulcanphil/TrekNovels.html

Warped Factors: A Neurotic's Guide to the Universe
http://hometown.aol.com/Assimiltr/warped.html

Poetry

Star Trek has had a tremendous impact on people. One example of this impact is that it has inspired 'Net denizens to write poetry. Visit these sites to read Trek-oriented poetry.

Garak's Star Trek Tailor Shop: Fan Fiction
www.geocities.com/Hollywood/Academy/6325/stories.html

Leila's Voyager Page: Poetry
www.geocities.com/Area51/Cavern/9441/poetry.html

Quotes

Most Star Trek fans can readily quote their favorite characters and episodes. Thus, it's no surprise that there are pages devoted to quotes from Star Trek.

Garak's Star Trek Tailor Shop: Deep Space Nine Quotes
www.geocities.com/Hollywood/Academy/6325/ds9quote.html

Garak's Star Trek Tailor Shop: Miscellaneous Quotes
www.geocities.com/Hollywood/Academy/6325/tngquote.html

Garak's Star Trek Tailor Shop: Voyager Quotes
www.geocities.com/Hollywood/Academy/6325/voyquote.html

Worf's Star Trek Site
www.bazza.com/sj/trek

Reference

Details of the various Klingon family lines, the flags used in the Trek universe, and more await you in these online, reference-oriented Trek texts.

Cardassian Intelligence: Dominion War Summary
www.geocities.com/Hollywood/Academy/6325/dominion.html

Cardassians - The Unofficial Encyclopedia
http://members.aol.com/primeview/enctable.html

Flags in Star Trek
www.dallas.net/~cpinette/startrek/trekflags.html

Galactic Handbook for All Starfleet Cadets
http://welcome.to/galactic_handbook

Independent Klingon Line Registry, The
www.netvista.net/~mmaksel/iklr

Location of Vulcan: The Final Word
gopher://wiretap.spies.com/00/Library/Media/Trek/vulcan.loc%09%09%2B

Maximum Warp
http://homepages.enterprise.net/davies/trek

NCC 1701D Database
www.lwix.demon.co.uk

Richter Scale of Cultural Development, The
http://members.aol.com/grewsomeco/richter.htm

http://www.geocities.com/Area51/Chamber/2541/TrekDrinks.html

The Picard Cocktail
8 oz. of Earl Grey Tea hot
1 oz. of Grand Marnier liqueur

Vulcan Mind Meld Probe

1 part ouzo
1 part rum (151 proof)

serve in a shot glass

Star Trek Beverages
www.geocities.com/Area51/Chamber/2541/TrekDrinks.html

Star Trek Frontier: Starfleet's General Orders
www.geocities.com/Area51/Dimension/7551/generalorders.html

Star Trek Geography
www.geocities.com/Area51/Labyrinth/8332/Galaxy

Star Trek Locations
gopher://wiretap.spies.com/00/Library/Media/Trek/location.st%09%09%2B

Starbase 16
http://starbase16.virtualave.net

Starfleet Command: Articles of the Federation
www.clearlight.com/~sfc/documents/aof.html

Reviews

Whether you're writing a critical paper on Star Trek or simply want to get a second opinion, these sites offer reviews of various Star Trek productions.

AAA Star Trek: Reviews
http://eonmagazine.com/startrek/REVIEWS%20PAGE%201.html

A Review of Star Trek: The Experience at the Las Vegas Hilton
http://pages.prodigy.com/crossover/trekhilt.htm

Being Mark Farinas
www.1pc.net/trotsky

Classic Trek on the 'Net: Novel Reviews by Trekkie Guy
www.geocities.com/Area51/Rampart/9065/review.htm

Crew's Reviews - DS9 & Voyager Episode Reviews
www.geocities.com/Hollywood/Academy/6325/reviews.html

Film.Com: Star Trek Film Reviews
www.film.com/search/index.jhtml?query=Star+Trek&src=film

Hollywood.Com: First Contact
www.hollywood.com/videoguide/movies/startrek

Mania Magazine: Review of Star Trek/X-Men Comic
www.anotheruniverse.com/comics/features/trekxmen.html

Movie Review Query Engine: First Contact - Reviews
www.mrqe.com/lookup?^Star+Trek%3a+First+Contact+(1996)

Movie Review Query Engine: Generations - Reviews
www.mrqe.com/lookup?^Star+Trek%3a+Generations+(1994)

Movie Review Query Engine: Insurrection - Reviews
www.mrqe.com/lookup?^Star+Trek%3a+Insurrection+(1998)

Movie Review Query Engine: Star Trek II - Reviews
www.mrqe.com/lookup?^Star+Trek%3a+The+Wrath+of+Khan+(1982)

Movie Review Query Engine: Star Trek III - Reviews
www.mrqe.com/lookup?^Star+Trek+III%3a+The+Search+for+Spock+(1984)

Movie Review Query Engine: Star Trek IV - Reviews
www.mrqe.com/lookup?^Star+Trek+IV%3a+The+Voyage+Home+(1986)

Movie Review Query Engine: Star Trek Motion Picture - Reviews
www.mrqe.com/lookup?^Star+Trek%3a+The+Motion+Picture+(1979)

Movie Review Query Engine: Star Trek V - Reviews
www.mrqe.com/lookup?^Star+Trek+V%3a+The+Final+Frontier+(1989)

Movie Review Query Engine: Star Trek VI - Reviews
www.mrqe.com/lookup?^Star+Trek+VI%3a+The+Undiscovered+Country+(1991)

Review: Star Trek/X-Men Second Contact 1
www.enteract.com/~katew/reviews/xmensttng1.htm

Roddenberry's Masterpiece: Game Reviews
www.geocities.com/Area51/4396/reviews.html

Star Trek II: The Wrath of Khan Review
http://clgray.simplenet.com/strtrk/stmovie/stii.html

Star Trek III: The Search for Spock Review
http://clgray.simplenet.com/strtrk/stmovie/stiii.html

Star Trek IV: The Voyage Home Review
http://clgray.simplenet.com/strtrk/stmovie/stiv.html

Star Trek Reviews Newsgroup
rec.arts.startrek.reviews

Star Trek V: The Final Frontier Review
http://clgray.simplenet.com/strtrk/stmovie/stv.html

Star Trek VI: The Undiscovered Country Review
http://clgray.simplenet.com/strtrk/stmovie/stvi.html

Star Trek: Generations Review
http://clgray.simplenet.com/strtrk/stmovie/stvii.html

Star Trek: The Motion Picture Review
http://clgray.simplenet.com/strtrk/stmovie/sti.html

STAR TREK: Hypertext
www.st-hypertext.com

Starfleet Intelligence
www.angelfire.com/mt/sfintelligence/index.html

The Hub - The Unauthorized Star Trek Novel Pages
www.suneater.org

Trek Files: Games (Reviews)
   http://trekfiles.strek.com/Games

TrekToday: Review of Free Enterprise
   www.trektoday.com/articles/free_enterprise.shtml

TrekWeb.Com: Reviews
   http://trekweb.com/Reviews

Vulcan Phil's Review of Star Trek Novels
   http://hometown.aol.com/vulcanphil/TrekNovels.html

Schedules & Airdates

Everything from syndication reports to airdates to star-centric television grids are available online. Use these sites to plot your stardates.

Sector001.Com: News
   www.sector001.com/trekframe.htm

Star Trek Portal
   www.strek.com

Star Trek: The Sci-Fi Channel Special Edition
   www.scifi.com/startrek

Syndication Notes (for Next Generation)
   www.ugcs.caltech.edu/st-tng/trivia/syndication.html

TV Now: Avery Brooks TV Schedule
   www.tv-now.com/stars/avbrook.html

TV Now: Brent Spiner TV Schedule
   www.tv-now.com/stars/spiner.html

Address   http://www.tv-now.com/stars/mulgrew.html   ▾   ⟳ Go

TVNow presents

Kate Mulgrew
On TV
Jan. 27 - Feb. 29

[Primetime TV Picks]   Eastern Time Zone Used   [Star's Filmography]

Manions of America, Part 1
95 minutes- Part 1 of 3

A 19th-century Irish rebel, Rory O'Manion (Pierce Brosnan), leaves the Englishwoman (Kate Mulgrew) he loves and his poverty-stricken homeland when he decides to find a better life in the United States.

Sat Feb 5 10:00A RC- Romance Classics

TV Now: Kate Mulgrew TV Schedule
www.tv-now.com/stars/mulgrew.html

TV Now: Leonard Nimoy TV Schedule
www.tv-now.com/stars/nimoy.html

TV Now: Patrick Stewart TV Schedule
www.tv-now.com/stars/pstew.html

TV Now: Robert Beltran TV Schedule
www.tv-now.com/stars/beltran.html

TV Now: Robert Picardo TV Schedule
www.tv-now.com/stars/picardo.html

TV Now: William Shatner TV Schedule
www.tv-now.com/stars/shatner.html

Ultimate TV Show List: Voyager
www.ultimatetv.com/UTVL/show.html?1086

USS Prometheus: Voyager News & Upcoming Episodes
www.geocities.com/Area51/Rampart/3448/news.html

Scripts

These sites contain Star Trek-related scripts.

"Child's Play" (An Unused Next Generation Script)
www.el-dorado.ca.us/~dmnews/script/childs_play.html

"Realization" (An Unused Voyager Script)
www.stikfigure.com/willmartin/realization.htm

Transcripts

The following sites of transcripts of Internet chats and televised interviews with the cast of the various Star Trek series. Use the title of the site to determine the subject of the transcript.

A Touch of Kate: Kate Mulgrew Transcripts
http://members.tripod.com/~sofa_spud/km/kmtrans.html

Armin Shimmerman Chat Transcripts
www.walrus.com/~quark/armin/chats.html

Address 🕮 http://www.geocities.com/Hollywood/6952/   ⌄ ⟳ Go

[Discussion Board]   [Ron Moore Posting Archive]   [Dispatches]

Star Trek News

Deep Space Nine (July 29)   Voyager (February 11)

News Bar   (Sunday, February 13)

Weekly
Features
   Buzz

This Week's
Episode

Voyager
"Collective"

Janeway and
Seven of
Nine are
forced to
bargain with
the surviving

Gates McFadden Guest Stars on "The Practice"
Gates McFadden guest starred as a judge on the February 13th episode of "The Practice" (Armin Shimmerman and Louise Fletcher are other Trek actors who have previously taken on such roles). It would not be completely surprising if this became a recurring role as most judges on both David E. Kelley's "The Practice" and "Ally McBeal" recur on both shows, and the ending of the episode implied a rivalry between McFadden's character and that of Lara Flynn Boyle.

The Rock Brings Up Voyager's Ratings
On UPN, a special appearance by the World Wrestling Federation's ``The Rock'' helped ``Star Trek: Voyager'' (6.6 household rating, 10 share in overnights) to pin down its best numbers since last February.
(Variety)

Ethan Phillips Confirms Kes' Return
Ethan Phillips has confirmed that Jennifer Lien will be returning to Voyager as a guest star in the next episode to be filmed.

Star Trek News
www.geocities.com/Hollywood/6952

Voyager Online Cast/Crew Transcripts
www.psiphi.org/voy/transcripts.html

Finding
More Star Trek Online

Are you on a voyage to seek out new Star Trek information and explore new web sites? Well, it's a neverending journey and a fantastic voyage. This chapter collects sources, such as link lists, directories, webrings, search engines and other tools that will help you discover the "strange new life" that appears on the Web everyday.

Databases

Data isn't just a character on Star Trek. Thankfully, data about Data and other Star Trek entities can be found using these databases.

All-Movie Guide
www.allmovie.com

All-Music Guide
www.allmusic.com

Antares Station: Federation Database
www.antaresstation.freeserve.co.uk/database/ie4/index.htm

Internet Movie Database
www.imdb.com

NCC 1701D Database
www.lwix.demon.co.uk

Utopia Planitia Starship Database
http://utopia.solareclipse.net

Directories

Directories are more extensive link lists, usually complete with categorized links making your browsing much more efficient. Directories can be a great place to discover new sites and surf aimlessly.

HandiLinks to Science Fiction - Star Trek
http://sflare.com/portal.shtml

Science Fiction Resource Guide
http://sflovers.rutgers.edu/Web/SFRG

Space Station: Solar Flare
http://sflare.com/portal.shtml

Trek Express
www.trekexpress.com

TrekExpress.Com: Link Centre
www.trekexpress.com/links

Link Lists

Link lists on a web page are lists of other, separate web sites that deal with the same topic. Typically these lists are not organized in any particular fashion. Usually, the person putting up the link list has approved these "linked sites," and you will automatically open the "linked" site when you click on it. Most Trek sites offer some sort of link list. These are some of the best.

24th Century Webring, The: Sites List
www.webring.org/cgi-bin/webring?ring=jonasa&list

Alpha Quadrant: Sites List
www.webring.org/cgi-bin/webring?ring=star_trek_ring&list

Ambassador Spock's Logical Sci-Fi Picks Ring: Sites List
www.webring.org/cgi-bin/webring?ring=logic;list

Babylon 5, Star Trek, X-Files! Oh My! Webring: Sites List
http://nav.webring.com/cgi-bin/navcgi?ring=b5stxfring;list

Becky's Star Trek Webring: Sites List
www.webring.org/cgi-bin/webring?ring=becktrek;list

Best Star Trek Webring in the Galaxy: Sites List
http://nav.webring.com/cgi-bin/navcgi?ring=startrex;list

Borg Collective, The: Collective Site Links
http://theborgcollective.com/cgi-bin/miva?frames/sitelinks.mv

Captain Janeway's Webring: Sites List
www.webring.org/cgi-bin/webring?ring=kjaneway18;list

Cardassia Forever Webring: Sites List
www.webring.org/cgi-bin/webring?ring=cardassians;list

Chakotay/Paris Slash Ring: Sites List
www.webring.org/cgi-bin/webring?ring=cpslash;list

Designation: Seven of Nine Webring: Sites List
http://nav.webring.com/cgi-bin/navcgi?ring=7of9;list

Dominion War Webring: Sites List
www.webring.org/cgi-bin/webring?ring=dominionwar&list

Enterprise E Webring List
www.webring.org/cgi-bin/webring?ring=enterprise&list

Federation of Obsessed Voyager Fans: Sites List
www.webring.org/cgi-bin/webring?ring=voyfan;list

Federation Task Force Webring: Sites List
www.webring.org/cgi-bin/webring?ring=sttaskforce;list

FhDS9 Ring: Sites List
http://nav.webring.com/cgi-bin/navcgi?ring=fhds9;list

Friends of Brent Spiner Webring: Sites List
www.webring.org/cgi-bin/webring?ring=fobs;list

Gamma Knights' Webring: Sites List
www.webring.org/cgi-bin/webring?ring=gammaknights;list

Gateway to the Wormhole Webring: Sites List
www.webring.org/cgi-bin/webring?ring=gateworm;list

Gorkon's Star Trek Webrings: Sites List
www.webring.org/cgi-bin/webring?ring=gorkon;list

Imperial House of Lords Webring: Sites List
www.webring.org/cgi-bin/webring?ring=imperialhouse;list

Imzadi International Webring: Sites List
www.webring.org/cgi-bin/webring?ring=imzadi;list

Jem' Hadar Webring: Sites List
www.webring.org/cgi-bin/webring?ring=jemhadar&list

Jennifer Lien Webring: Sites List
www.webring.org/cgi-bin/webring?ring=jenlien1&list

K'Mel's Guide to Klingon Cyberspace
www.geocities.com/Area51/1908

Kate Mulgrew Webring: Sites List
www.webring.org/cgi-bin/webring?ring=kmring;list

Katie's Star Trek Webrings: Sites List
www.webring.org/cgi-bin/webring?ring=belanna&list

Klingon Bitch Webrings: Sites List
www.webring.org/cgi-bin/webring?ring=klingonbitch;list

Klingon High Council Webring: Sites List
www.webring.org/cgi-bin/webring?ring=khcw;list

Landing Pad C - Links
www.geocities.com/Hollywood/Academy/6325/padc.htm

LCARS Top Star Trek Sites
http://members.tripod.com/jooky_/ie_index.html

Lieutenant Commander Data Ring: Sites List
www.webring.org/cgi-bin/webring?ring=ltcommdata;list

Locutus' Hang Webring: Sites List
www.webring.org/cgi-bin/webring?ring=joseph&id=45&list

Men of Trek . . . Alliance Webring: Sites List
www.webring.org/cgi-bin/webring?ring=mot;id=8;list

Nicole deBouer Fan Webring: Sites List
www.webring.org/cgi-bin/webring?ring=nicolering;list

Noy Voyager Members Ring: Sites List
www.webring.org/cgi-bin/webring?ring=nowvoy;list

Omnipotent Collective Webring: Sites List
www.webring.org/cgi-bin/webring?ring=qborg&id=87&list

Patrick Stewart Ring, The: Sites List
www.webring.org/cgi-bin/webring?ring=patrick_stewart;list

PJ in NH's Link Page
http://unix.worldpath.net/~kelhapam/links.htm

Q Continuum Webring: Sites List
www.webring.org/cgi-bin/webring?ring=theqcontinuum;list

Quark's Establishment - The Star Trek Universe
www.algonet.se/~quark/st.html

Riker/Troi Webring: Sites List
www.webring.org/cgi-bin/webring?ring=rtring;list

Robert Beltran Webring: Sites List
www.webring.org/cgi-bin/webring?ring=beltran;list

Rude Doggy's Star Trek Ring: Sites List
www.webring.org/cgi-bin/webring?ring=rd1701;list

Save Star Trek Web Community Webring: Sites List
www.webring.org/cgi-bin/webring?ring=savetrek&list

Sci-Fi Gallery Ring, The: Sites List
www.webring.org/cgi-bin/webring?ring=scigalaxy&list

Seven of Nine & Harry Kim Webring: Sites List
www.webring.org/cgi-bin/webring?ring=7kim&list

Spacedock Webring: Sites List
www.webring.org/cgi-bin/webring?ring=ufps;list

Spock Webring: Sites List
www.webring.org/cgi-bin/webring?ring=spock;list

Star Trek Artists' Webring: Sites List
www.webring.org/cgi-bin/webring?ring=start;list

Star Trek Collective Webring: Sites List
www.webring.org/cgi-bin/webring?ring=stc&list

Star Trek Continuum Ring List
www.webring.org/cgi-bin/webring?ring=startrek4&list

Star Trek Fan Fiction Romance Ring: Sites List
www.webring.org/cgi-bin/webring?ring=qinomo&list

Star Trek Nexus
http://members.aol.com/treknexus

Star Trek Photo Gallery Ring: Sites List
www.webring.org/cgi-bin/webring?ring=stpg&list

Star Trek Relationships Ring: Sites List
www.webring.org/cgi-bin/webring?ring=stromance&list

Star Trek Singularity Webring: Sites List
www.webring.org/cgi-bin/webring?ring=STSingularity;list

Star Trek Slash Ring: Sites List
www.webring.org/cgi-bin/webring?ring=stslash;list

Star Trek: WWW
www.stwww.com

Starbase DS9 Webring: Sites List
www.webring.org/cgi-bin/webring?ring=garak&list

STrek's Star Trek Page
http://home.earthlink.net/~strek1/contents.htm

The Tholian Webring: Sites List
http://nav.webring.com/cgi-bin/navcgi?ring=tholianweb;list

Todd's Star Trek Pages
www.cjnetworks.com/~tfrazier/st.html

Tom Paris Ring: Sites List
www.webring.org/cgi-bin/webring?ring=parisring&list

Top 200 Star Trek Sites
www.phantomstar.com/trek.html

Transporter Chief
http://members.xoom.com/Transp_Chief

Transwarp - The Webring: Sites List
www.webring.org/cgi-bin/webring?ring=transwarp;list

Transwarp Travel Agency
www.oneimage.com/~dgustaf/stlinks/stlinks2.htm

Trek Ladies' Webring: Sites List
www.webring.org/cgi-bin/webring?ring=trekladies;list

Ultimate Star Trek Webring, The: Sites List
www.webring.org/cgi-bin/webring?ring=stvoy&list

United Federation of Trek Sites: Sites List
www.webring.org/cgi-bin/webring?ring=federation&list

USS Cochrane Webring: Sites List
www.webring.org/cgi-bin/webring?ring=usscochrane;list

USS Veldran's Sub-Space Links: Sites List
http://nav.webring.com/cgi-bin/navcgi?ring=veldring;list

Voyager Fanatics Webring: Sites List
www.webring.org/cgi-bin/webring?ring=stv&list

Voyager Shrine Webring: Sites List
www.webring.org/cgi-bin/webring?ring=voyagershrine;list

Vulcan Webring: Sites List
www.webring.org/cgi-bin/webring?ring=vulcan;index

WBS Klingon Webring: Sites List
www.webring.org/cgi-bin/webring?ring=wbsklingon&list

Welcome to the 23rd Century & Beyond
www.people.virginia.edu/~cph9c/startrek.html

Worf's Star Trek Ring: Sites List
www.webring.org/cgi-bin/webring?list&ring=worf

Worf's Star Trek Site: Links
www.bazza.com/sj/trek/links.html

Worf/Troi Webring: Sites List
www.webring.org/cgi-bin/webring?ring=worftroi;list

World of Science Fiction Webring, The: Sites List
www.webring.org/cgi-bin/webring?ring=worldscifi&list

Yahoo! . . . Star Trek
http://dir.yahoo.com/News_and_Media/Television/Genres/Science_
Fiction__Fantasy__and_Horror/Star_Trek

Search Engines

There are actually entire search engines devoted to Star Trek. Whether you've created your own Trek site or are looking to find more to add to your bookmarks, use these "engines" to warp your way to more Trek on the 'Net.

Fandom - Star Trek Central
www.fandom.com/star_trek

James Kirk Search Engine
www.webwombat.com.au/trek

Sci-File - The Science Fiction Search Engine
www.sci-file.com/home.shtml

Science Fiction List: Search Engines
www.scifilist.com/websearch.asp

Sector001.Com: Search Engine
www.sector001.com/searchengine

Sha Ka Ree
http://start.at/sha_ka_ree

Trek Portal, The
http://start.at/trekportal

Trek Sites
www.treksites.com

Trekcite!
www.trekcite.co.uk

Trekhoo
www.startrekker.net/trekhoo/index.shtml

Trekseek
www.trekseek.com

Webrings

Webrings are a group of sites organized in a "ring-like" fashion, meaning that by clicking on the "Next" and "Previous" buttons of a webring's logo, you can travel around to the sites that are part of that ring. When you reach the end, the ring automatically takes you back to the first site. Therefore, ring travel forms an endless loop or "ring." Some webring logos also give you the opportunity to view all the sites in the ring by clicking on "List Sites." The link lists for some of the webrings listed here can be accessed using the URLs listed in the Link Lists section earlier in this chapter.

5th Fleet's Webring, The
www.geocities.com/Area51/Shire/7232/ch2.html

Allies In the Alpha Quadrant
http://pages.prodigy.net/stinger77/aitag.html

Alpha Quadrant
www.geocities.com/Area51/Cavern/4451

Ambassador Spock's Logical Sci-Fi Picks Ring: Sites List
www.webring.org/cgi-bin/webring?ring=logic;list

Babylon 5, Star Trek, X-Files! Oh My! Webring
www.geocities.com/Area51/Hollow/9330/webrings.html

Babylon 5, Star Trek, X-Files! Oh My! Webring: Sites List
http://nav.webring.com/cgi-bin/navcgi?ring=b5stxfring;list

Becky's Star Trek Webring
http://members.aol.com/beckyusc/webring

Best Star Trek Webring in the Galaxy: Sites List
http://nav.webring.com/cgi-bin/navcgi?ring=startrex;list

Bomis: Denise Crosby Ring
www.bomis.com/rings/denisecrosby

Captain Janeway's Webring
www.geocities.com/Area51/Stargate/4761/webringjane.htm

Captain Symok's Sci-Fi Ring
http://nav.webring.com/cgi-bin/navcgi?ring=symokring;list

Cardassia Forever Webring
http://edit.webring.com/cgi-bin/membercgi?ring=cardassians&global=1&addform

Cardassia Forever Webring: Sites List
www.webring.org/cgi-bin/webring?ring=cardassians;list

Chakotay/Paris Slash Ring: Sites List
www.webring.org/cgi-bin/webring?ring=cpslash;list

Continuum Webring
www.geocities.com/Area51/Station/7066

Deep Space Nine Ring
www.geocities.com/Area51/Quadrant/9137/ds9ring.html

Delta Alliance Space Ring
www.stvsd.com/lcars_e/delta_alliance_index.html

Designation: Seven of Nine Webring
http://members.tripod.com/~AuraZ/webring/join.html

Dominion War Webring: Sites List
www.webring.org/cgi-bin/webring?ring=dominionwar&list

Draconian's Star Trek Lair Webring
www.angelfire.com/wa/Draconian/Form.html

Enterprise E Webring
www.geocities.com/Area51/Cavern/2135

Expanding Universe Ring, The
www.geocities.com/Area51/Vault/8994/univers.html

Federation Task Force Webring
www.geocities.com/Hollywood/Academy/6325/Federation_Task_Force.html

FhDS9 Ring
http://members.xoom.com/gegen/ring.html

Friends of Brent Spiner (FOBS) Webring
http://members.xoom.com/ozg2/fobs.htm

Galactic Web Connection Ring, The
www.geocities.com/SouthBeach/Surf/2144/galactic.html

Gamma Knights' Webring
http://edit.webring.com/cgi-bin/membercgi?ring=gammaknights&global=1&addform

Gegen's Star Trek Webring
http://members.xoom.com/gegen/ring.html

Gorkon's Star Trek Webrings
http://members.aol.com/g0rk0n/ring.html

Imperial & Federation Database Ring
www.geocities.com/Area51/Nebula/3657

Imzadi International Webring
http://people.delphi.com/dpj/ii_ra.htm

Jadzia Dax Memorial Ring
www.jdmemorial.tsx.org

Jean Luc Picard's Star Trek Ring
www.geocities.com/Area51/Zone/3665

JediLinks - Science Fiction Webring
www.geocities.com/Area51/Zone/4283/jedilink.html

Jem' Hadar Webring: Sites List
www.webring.org/cgi-bin/webring?ring=jemhadar&list

Jennifer Lien Webring
www.geocities.com/Area51/Rampart/4311/voyager.html

Kate Mulgrew Webring
www.geocities.com/Area51/Starship/1131/webrings.html

Katie's Star Trek Webring Home Page
www.geocities.com/Hollywood/8007

Kim/Seven Webring
www.geocities.com/TelevisionCity/Studio/2869/code.html

Kim/Torres Webring
www.webring.org/cgi-bin/webring?ring=ktring;list

Klingon Bitch Webring
www.geocities.com/SouthBeach/Cove/7072/KBwebring.html

Klingon High Council Webring
www.geocities.com/Area51/Labyrinth/2995

Klingon Language Webring
http://php.indiana.edu/~clipscom/

LCARS Central Webring
http://kwg.virtualave.net

LCARS Ring
http://freespace.virgin.net/p.dobson/lcarsring

Locutus' Hang Webring
www.geocities.com/Area51/Labyrinth/8852/webring.htm

Men of Trek . . . Alliance Webring: Sites List
www.webring.org/cgi-bin/webring?ring=mot;id=8;list

Mike's Star Trek Ring
www.geocities.com/Area51/Chamber/3015/frames/webr.htm

Millennial Trek Award Ring
http://lcars.simplenet.com/trek2000/join.htm

Neutral Zone Sector 3.0 Webring
http://home.utah-inter.net/dasaxx/ring.htm

New Worlds Ring
www.geocities.com/Area51/2403/nwr.htm

Nicole deBouer Fan Webring
http://members.xoom.com/scifioz/webring.htm

Noy Voyager Members Ring: Sites List
www.webring.org/cgi-bin/webring?ring=nowvoy;list

Omnipotent Collective Webring: Sites List
www.webring.org/cgi-bin/webring?ring=qborg&id=87&list

Paris/Torres (P/T) Fan Ring
www.geocities.com/EnchantedForest/2931/PTRing.htm

Patrick Stewart Ring, The: Sites List
www.webring.org/cgi-bin/webring?ring=patrick_stewart;list

Promenade Directory Webring
http://members.tripod.com/~fuzzy124/Promenade_Directory_web_rin
g.html

Promenade Directory Webring: Sites List
www.webring.org/cgi-bin/webring?list&ring=promenade

Q Continuum Webring: Sites List
www.webring.org/cgi-bin/webring?ring=theqcontinuum;list

Red Alert Webring
www.geocities.com/Area51/Corridor/2917/alert.html

Rude Doggy's Star Trek Ring
www.geocities.com/Area51/Vault/2664/join.html

Ryan's Star Trek Page Webring
http://www2.mmind.net/ryanj/webring/webring.htm

Save the Star Trek Web Community Webring
www.pilaf.com/savetrek

Sci Fi TV/Star Trek/Babylon 5 Conventions Webring
http://pw2.netcom.com/~brucas/sftvcons/index.html

Sci-Fi Connections Webrings
www.geocities.com/Area51/1499/sciring.html

Sci-Fi Galaxy Ring, The
www.cyberstreet.com/users/petei/ring.htm

Sci-Fi/Fantasy Ring
www.geocities.com/Area51/Vault/4639/scififantasyring.html

Science Fiction Conventions Webring
www.io.com/~lsc2/sfcons.html

Science Fiction Fandom Webring
http://fanac.org/sffandom

Science Fiction TV Series Ring
www.geocities.com/TelevisionCity/Stage/1125/Home.html

Spacedock Webring
http://members.tripod.com/~ussenterprise_a

Spock Webring: Sites List
www.webring.org/cgi-bin/webring?ring=spock;list

Star Trek 10 Webring
http://m3.easyspace.com/globaltrek/webring

Star Trek Collective Webring: Sites List
www.webring.org/cgi-bin/webring?ring=stc&list

Star Trek Fan Fiction Romance Ring: Sites List
www.webring.org/cgi-bin/webring?ring=qinomo&list

Star Trek Officers Webring
www.geocities.com/Area51/Orion/9967

Star Trek Photo Gallery Ring
www.soltec.net/~jw591/stpgr

Star Trek Relationships Ring
http://ncc-1701-d.webjump.com/webrings/
1701dwebrings/webring.html

Star Trek RPG Webring
www.geocities.com/Area51/Dimension/1015

Star Trek Slash Ring: Sites List
www.webring.org/cgi-bin/webring?ring=stslash;list

Star Trek: The Next Generation: The French Alternative Webring
www.allolaterre.com/startrek/webring

Starbase DS9 Webring: Sites List
www.webring.org/cgi-bin/webring?ring=garak&list

Starfleet Database Ring
http://ring.starfleet-db.com/y_ring.htm

Subspace Net
http://subspace.virtualave.net/net/index.html

SyFy World Webring
http://treknation.com/syfyworld/webadmin.shtml

Talshiar Ring
www.geocities.com/Hollywood/4463/talring.htm

Terok Nor Promanade Webring
www.geocities.com/Area51/Nebula/7689/norring

The Occupation Ring
www.concentric.net/~ustrek/occring.htm

The Tholian Webring
www.geocities.com/Area51/Cavern/8846

Tom Paris Ring: Sites List
www.webring.org/cgi-bin/webring?ring=parisring&list

Transwarp - The Webring: Sites List
www.webring.org/cgi-bin/webring?ring=transwarp;list

Trek Ladies' Webring: Sites List
www.webring.org/cgi-bin/webring?ring=trekladies;list

Ultimate J & J (Julian & Jadzia) Webring, The
www.geocities.com/Hollywood/4498

Ultimate Star Trek Webring, The
www.geocities.com/Area51/Cavern/4556/USTW/index.html

USS Defiant Webring
www.boingweb.com/startrek/webring.html

USS Veldran's Sub-Space Links
www.geocities.com/Area51/Chamber/7897

Voyager Fanatics Webring
www.geocities.com/Area51/Chamber/2434/ring.html

Voyager LCARS SF Database Ring
http://lcars-access.simplenet.com

Vulcan Webring: Sites List
www.webring.org/cgi-bin/webring?ring=vulcan;index

Warp Core Containment Ring
http://nav.webring.com/cgi-bin/navcgi?ring=starfleet1;list

WBS Klingon Webring
www.geocities.com/Hollywood/Hills/3786/klinweb.html

Winkle Star Trek Webring, The
www.geocities.com/Hollywood/Hills/7035/webring.html

World of Science Fiction Webring, The
www.geocities.com/TelevisionCity/1701/world.html

Building
YOUR OWN
STAR TREK SITE

*Want to build your own Star Trek station on the Web? Well you've come to the right sector! This chapter has everything you need to create your own web site, including design help and free stuff. Just be sure to visit Paramount's home page (*www.paramount.com*) to make sure that you are adhering to copyright laws. While you're at it, you might as well add a link from your site to Parmount's page.*

Let us know about your new site by writing to us at Trek_Changes@klingons.zzn.com -- *we might include your web site in future editions of this book. Feel free to link to the home page for the Incredible Internet Guide for Trekkers as well by visiting* www.incredibleguides.com/trekkers/link2us.htm.

Chat Rooms

Why not add a chat room to your site? Use the free services listed here to add a chat room to your site. You can use it to discuss a particular character, alien race, or even Star Trek as a whole.

Be Seen
www.beseen.com/chat/topics.html

Talk City
www.talkcity.com/irc/apply.html

Guestbooks

If you're building your own web site, it's great to have a guestbook so that you can get feedback from your visitors. The following sites offer free guestbook services.

Bloke.Com
http://guestbook.bloke.com

Dreambook
www.dreambook.com

Free Services from Escati
www.escati.com/freeservices.htm

Komy.Net - Free Web Site Resources
www.komy.net/guestbook

Planet Guestbook
www.planetguestbook.com

Trek City
http://trekcity2.virtualave.net

Trek City Guestbooks
http://romulan.virtualave.net/services/gb

Message Boards

Enhance your site with a message board. Message boards give visitors the opportunity to discuss topics that you determine. Webmasters, visit the sites listed here to register for your own message board.

Delphi Forums
www.delphi.com/dir-app/cfsetup/
beginsetup.asp?webtag=createaforum

Inside the Web
www.insidetheweb.com/messageboard/create.cgi?board=true

MessageMaster
http://207.49.157.180/discussion/legal.asp

Site Design

Customizing your web site and making it sparkle can be a lot of fun. Use the sites listed here to access design resources and tips to make your site stellar!

Animation Online
www.animationonline.com

Banner Generator
www.coder.com/creations/banner

BeSeen.Com
www.beseen.com

Builder.Com
www.builder.com

CoolHomepages.Com
www.coolhomepages.com

Core, The
www.staga.force9.co.uk

Core, The: Star Trek Web Page Backgrounds
www.staga.force9.co.uk/backgrounds/backgrounds.htm

Damn Coyotes JavaScript
www.albedo.net/~oscar/jscript.htm

Enterwarp.com Network: Web Center
http://webcenter.enterwarp.com

FreeCode.Com
www.freecode.com

Media Builder - Animated Banner Maker
www.mediabuilder.com/abm.html

Web Backgrounds by Locutus
www.geocities.com/Area51/Labyrinth/8852/graf.htm

ZapZone
www.zzn.com

Webrings

One of the fastest and best ways to promote any new site is to join webrings. Since a lot of users simply click "next" when using a webring, webrings bring random visitors to your site. See the Finding More Star Trek Online chapter for a list of webrings, and then visit those sites to sign-up once your site is online.

Webspace & Hosting

Want to put up your own web site? Well, you're going to need a place to put it. Use the services listed here to get your own free web space -- the final frontier.

321 Web Site
www.321website.com

FortuneCity.Com
www.fortunecity.com

Free Sites Network
www.fsn.net

Free Web Pages at FreeTown
www.freetown.com/free/index.html

FreeServers.Com
www.freeservers.com

FreeWebspace.Net
www.freewebspace.net

Go Network: Homepage Center
http://homepages.go.com

Homestead
> www.homestead.com/~site/TermsOfService/TermsOfService_out.ffhtm
> l?B_EXISTING_CUSTOMER=FALSE

Trek City
> http://trekcity2.virtualave.net

TrekHosting.Com
> www.trekhosting.com

Tripod
> www.tripod.com/build

WebJump
> www.webjump.com

Worm-Hole.Net
> www.worm-hole.net

ADDRESS 🖉 http://xoom.com/join/services.xihtml

Join XOOM.com!

Which free service do you want to start with?

Unlimited Web Space
If you came here to build a home page, start here!

XOOMCounter with PowerSTATS
Learn about who is visiting your Web site!

XOOMFax
Receive your faxes by Email! It really works!

Chat Rooms
Regardless of where you are hosted, you can get a chat room!

Downloads
Download shareware and cool tools here!

Email
Sign up Today and get a free XOOMMAIL Email account!

Clip Art
When you sign-up, you'll get access to our huge clipart library online!

Greeting Cards
Send and receive e-cards for the holidays or for any occasion!

Electronic Newsletters
Health Tips, Trivia, History and more. Get a 'Wealth of Information' in your e-mailbox everyday!

Classic Movies
Horror to Comedy, we've got movies that you can view right online!

JOIN FREE!
UNLIMITED
WEB SPACE
EMAIL
E-FAXES
E-CARDS
CLIP ART
COUNTERS
CHATROOMS
E-ZINES
SOFTWARE
MOVIES

FREE

Xoom
> http://xoom.com/join/services.xihtml

STAR TREK
Science &
Technology

Starships, transporters and replicators -- oh, my! Immerse yourself in the richly developed technological landscape of the Trek universe by logging on to the sites in this chapter. You'll learn about the theories behind warp drive, uncover detailed specifications on your favorite starships, and more.

Science & Technology - Miscellaneous

The writers of Star Trek refer to some dialog as "technobabble," meaning that the words are not based on reality, rather on the fictitious technology of the Trek universe. To learn more about "replicators," "phasing," etc. visit these sites.

AAA Star Trek: Equipment & Technology
http://eonmagazine.com/startrek/equipment%20page%201.html

Computer Core Dump: Phaser Cannon
www.ccdump.org/phasercannon.html

Computer Core Dump: Phasers
www.ccdump.org/phasers.html

Computer Core Dump: Photon Torpedoes
www.ccdump.org/photontorps.html

Computer Core Dump: Quantum Torpedoes
www.ccdump.org/quantumtorps.html

German Star Trek Technology Newsgroup
de.rec.sf.startrek.technologie

Holodeck & Computers FAQ
http://members.aa.net/~skeksis/Star_Trek/FAQs/holodeck-faq.html

Navigating in Space
www.surfshop.net/~majtown/Nav.htm

Omega LCARS Database II
http://members.spree.com/sci-fi/omegalcars/default.htm

Particles of Star Trek, The
www.midwinter.com/~koreth/particles

Physics of Star Trek, The: Deflector Fields
www.newscientist.com/nsplus/insight/startrek/deflectors.html

Science of Star Trek, The
http://ssdoo.gsfc.nasa.gov/education/just_for_fun/startrek.html

Star Trek Encyclopedia of Technology & Physics
www.treknology.8m.com/encyc.htm

Star Trek Technology Newsgroup
rec.arts.startrek.tech

The Dysonsphere: What is a Dysonsphere?
http://home1.swipnet.se/~w-10546/dysonspheres/Dysonsphere_Index.htm

Transporters, Replicators & Phasing FAQ
http://members.aa.net/~skeksis/Star_Trek/FAQs/transport-faq.html

Treknology.Com
www.treknology.8m.com

TrekTech
www.geocities.com/Area51/Corridor/5363/trektech.html

Tricorders & Other Devices in Star Trek
www.the-spa.com/cj/tricorder.htm

Ultimate Star Trek Collection: Technology
http://startrek.fns.net.fsn.net/a-z/a-z.html

Stardates

The method of timekeeping used in Star Trek is different than that of our society, and though it is not really a "technology," it does involve calculation. "Stardates" are used, often in "Captain's Logs," to mark the date. The following sites focus on stardates. See also the Stardate Listing in the back of this book.

Star Trek Stardates
gopher://wiretap.spies.com/00/Library/Media/Trek/stardate.st%09%09%2B

Ten Forward Lounge: Stardate Mini-FAQ
www.interlog.com/~pcarr/star_trek/stardate.html

Starships

Whether travelling at warp speed, hiding in a nebula, or answering distress calls, the starships of Star Trek are an integral part of the series. To learn more about these awe-inspiring crafts, board the sites below . . .

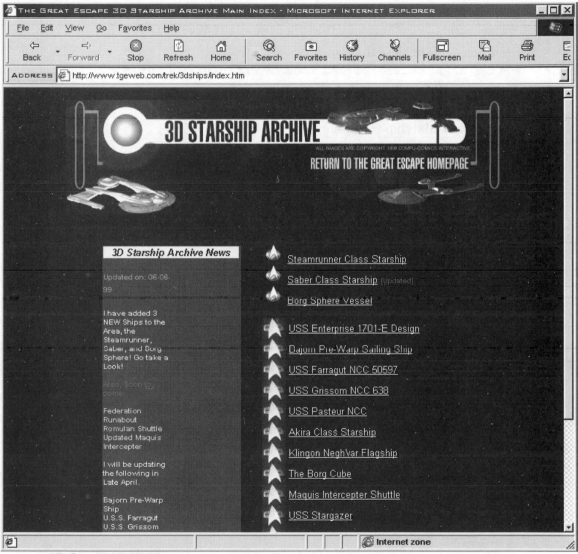

3D Starship Archive
www.amtc.net/users/~ziroc/trek/3dships/index.htm

AAA Star Trek: Ships
http://eonmagazine.com/startrek/ships.html

A History of the Ships Named Enterprise
www.cs.umanitoba.ca/~djc/startrek/SNE.html

Computer Core Dump: Alien Ships
www.ccdump.org/enemyship.html

Computer Core Dump: Starships
www.ccdump.org/ships.html

Defiant Mail (@defiant.zzn.com)
http://defiant.zzn.com

Defiant Pictures
www.geocities.com/Area51/Corridor/1364/defiant.html

Enterprise Mail (@enterprise.zzn.com)
http://enterprise.zzn.com

Excelsior Pictures
www.geocities.com/Area51/Corridor/1364/excelsior.html

Federation Ship Images Gallery
http://vision.simplenet.com/tomparis/shipimage.html

International Federation of Trekkers: Excelsior Campaign
http://excelsior.iftcommand.com

Intrepid Class Starship Development Project
www.maxpowers.com/i

John's Star Trek Universe
www.angelfire.com/nj2/startrek/index.html

Kazon Predator Class Starship
http://startrek.fns.net.fsn.net/ships/predator.html

Locutus' Hang: NCC-1701 Pictures
www.geocities.com/Area51/Labyrinth/8852/pic1.htm

Locutus' Hang: NCC-1701-A Pictures
www.geocities.com/Area51/Labyrinth/8852/pic2.htm

Locutus' Hang: NCC-1701-D Pictrues
www.geocities.com/Area51/Labyrinth/8852/pic3.htm

Locutus' Hang: NCC-1701-E Pictures
www.geocities.com/Area51/Labyrinth/8852/pic4.htm

Main Engineering: Pictures: Starships
http://mainengineering.simplenet.com/pictures_ships.html

Maximum Defiant
www.maximumdefiant.com

NX-6920 Aries
www.geocities.com/TimesSquare/7322/aries.html

Pedro's Shiporama
www.shiporama.org

SciFiArt.Com: Shipyards
http://shipyard.scifi-art.com

Sector 0-0-1: Databank
http://members.aol.com/NCC2364/diagrams

Sector 0-0-1: Dedication Plaques Gallery
http://members.aol.com/NCC2364/plaques

Ship Gallery
http://members.tripod.com/~Silky_Moon/gallery.html

Space Battles & Other FX
http://fly.to/spacebattles

Species 8472 Bioship
http://startrek.fns.net.fsn.net/ships/8472ship.html

Star Trek & Beyond: Starfleet Secondary IMG Array
www.geocities.com/Tokyo/Bay/8946/trek.htm

Star Trek Continuum: Transportation Databanks
www.startrekcontinuum.com/lcars/quadrant.asp?ssector=databanks.
asp&DockingBay=Trans

Star Trek Excelsior
http://www1.ridgecrest.ca.us/~curtdan/Excelsior/SuluPages.cgi?F
ILE=Main

Star Trek Excelsior: Excelsior Bridge
http://www1.ridgecrest.ca.us/~curtdan/Excelsior/SuluPages.cgi?F
ILE=Bridge

Star Trek Excelsior: Timeline
http://www1.ridgecrest.ca.us/~curtdan/Excelsior/SuluPages.cgi?F
ILE=Timeline

Star Trek Frontier: Alien Ships
www.geocities.com/Area51/Dimension/7551/classalien.html

Star Trek Frontier: Federation Starships
www.geocities.com/Area51/Dimension/7551/class.html

Star Trek Millenium: Defiant Pictures
http://home.bip.net/s_t_m/defpics.htm

Star Trek Millenium: Enterprise Pictures
http://home.bip.net/s_t_m/epics.htm

Star Trek Millenium: Pictures of Ships & Bases
http://home.bip.net/s_t_m/osabpics.htm

Star Trek Millenium: USS Voyager Pictures
http://home.bip.net/s_t_m/vpics.htm

Star Trek Ship Names
gopher://wiretap.spies.com/00/Library/Media/Trek/ships.st%09%09
%2B

Star Trek Ship Registry
www.nemonet.com/users/rclow/html/paddship1.htm

Star Trek Ships Expanded
www.cs.umanitoba.ca/~djc/startrek/ships.expanded.html

Star Trek Utopia: Starship Creations
http://members.aol.com/okinawa41/creation/creation.html

Star Trek Utopia: Starships
www.geocities.com/Area51/Dimension/8041/ships.html

Starbase SDL (Starship Design Library)
http://beam.at/StarbaseSDL

Starfleet Headquarters: The View Screen
http://home.earthlink.net/~cobarry/pictures.html

Starship Schematics Database
www.shipschematics.net

Starships Only
www.nymac.com/starships

ADDRESS http://www.netcomuk.co.uk/~trekart/trekart.htm

Trek Art - The Best Starship Schematics on the Web
www.netcomuk.co.uk/~trekart/index.html

Ultimate Star Trek Collection: Starships & Spacecraft
http://startrek.fns.net.fsn.net/ships/ships.html

USS Amazon
www.ussamazon.cjb.net

USS Dreadnought
http://welcome.to/dreadnought

USS Enterprise Memorial
www.geocities.com/Area51/Rampart/4777

USS Hornet NCC-1714
www.geocities.com/Area51/Nebula/1160/HornetframesV2-3.html

USS Jaguar
www.worldkids.net/jaguar

USS Katana
http://members.tripod.com/~USS_Katana/test.htm

USS Missouri
http://members.tripod.com/~stidham/missouri.htm

USS Prometheus Images
www.geocities.com/Area51/Shadowlands/7129/pimages.html

http://www.geocities.com/Area51/4948/

Welcome aboard!

You are visitor number 3 9 4 5 9 7 6

This is the bridge of the USS Roo, Starfleet's newest starship.

USS Roo
www.geocities.com/Area51/4948

USS Stargazer II
www.stargazertwo.com

USS Victory NCC-67019
www.angelfire.com/al/alphafleet

Utopia Planitia Starship Database
http://utopia.solareclipse.net

Voyager Mail (@voyager.zzn.com)
http://voyager.zzn.com

Voyager Pictures
www.geocities.com/Area51/Corridor/1364/voyager.html

Voyager Tour, The
www.geocities.com/Area51/Shadowlands/7129/voygreeting.html

Wolf359: Klingon Ship Portraits
http://wolf359a.anet-stl.com/kport.html

www.STARTREK.de.cx (German)
www.startrek.de.cx

Transporters

Virtually eliminating the need for the transportation industry, the transporters of Star Trek can "beam" you from one place to another within seconds. To learn more about this idyllic technology, visit the sites below.

Antares Station: Federation Database: Transporters
www.antaresstation.freeserve.co.uk/database/technology/transporters.htm

Physics of Star Trek, The: Transporters
www.newscientist.com/nsplus/insight/startrek/transportation.html

Transporters, Replicators & Phasing FAQ
http://members.aa.net/~skeksis/Star_Trek/FAQs/transport-faq.html

Ultimate Star Trek Collection: Transporters
http://startrek.fns.net.fsn.net/a-z/33.html

Warp Drive

Without warp drive, the starships of Star Trek would not be able to traverse the galaxy. Want to know more about this powerful yet fictitious technology? If so, visit these sites:

Physics of Star Trek, The: Could Warp Drive Work?
www.newscientist.com/nsplus/insight/startrek/warp.html

Sector 0-0-1: Interactive Warp Speed Chart
http://members.aol.com/NCC2364/warp

Star Trek Frontier: Warp Speed Chart
www.geocities.com/Area51/Dimension/7551/warp.html

Star Trek Technology
gopher://wiretap.spies.com/00/Library/Media/Trek/trektech%09%09%2B

Ultimate Star Trek Collection: Warp Drive
http://startrek.fns.net.fsn.net/a-z/40.html

Warp & Subspace FAQ
http://members.aa.net/~skeksis/Star_Trek/FAQs/warp-faq.html

Warp Velocities FAQ
http://members.aa.net/~skeksis/Star_Trek/FAQs/warp_velocities-faq.html

Warp Velocity
www.surfshop.net/~majtown/Warp.htm

Warpspeed Mail (@warpseed.zzn.com)
http://warpspeed.zzn.com

STAR TREK
Aliens Online

From Andorians to Vulcans, Star Trek has established a menagerie of alien races over the years. Although the series and films have done a terrific job of embellishing the culture of these entirely fictitious species, many fans still want to know more. Use the sites in this chapter to assimilate your way into the Borg's collective culture, examine your honor in Klingon terms, and quiz yourself on Q.

Andorians

Did you ever wonder what those blue-skinned aliens with the antennae were called? Well, wonder no more -- they're Andorians. These sites will help you learn more about this highly visible yet rarely explored alien race.

A Grammatical Sketch & Dictionary of the Andorian Language
http://randyb.byu.edu/alioth/sketch.html

Andor Files, The
www.geocities.com/Area51/Station/1558/index.html

Blue Fleet
http://randyb.byu.edu/alioth/bf2.html

Rogues' Gallery of Andorians
www.magna.com.au/~lindsay/trek/Rogues.html

Summary of the Physiological Roots of Andorian Culture
www.geocities.com/Area51/Station/1558/Fish.html

Bajorans

The Bajorans, introduced in an episode of The Next Generation, are highly religious. Their religious side has become an intriguing part of the Star Trek mythos. Combined with the popularity of characters, such as Ro Laren and Kira Nerys, Bajorans have become the focus of many interesting web sites. Check out the ones listed here.

Bajor Mail (@bajor.zzn.com)
http://bajor.zzn.com

Bajoran Consulate
http://users.dx.com.au/wormhole/mainpage.html

Bajoran Encyclopedia
www.shakaar.demon.co.uk/archive/encyc/index.htm

Bajoran Newsgroup
alt.startrek.bajoran

Bajoran Picture Gallery
http://members.tripod.com/~ds9promenade/Bajoranindex.html

Bajoran Proverbs
http://www2.prestel.co.uk/majeed/sfdbase/databank/bproverb.htm

Bajoran Provisional Government
http://members.tripod.com/~Copper/provgov.html

Bajoran Web Page, The
http://members.tripod.com/~Copper/index.html

Internet Movie Database: Louise Fletcher (Vedek/Kai Winn)
http://us.imdb.com/Name?Fletcher,+Louise

My Adventure on Star Trek - Deep Space Nine
www.capital.net/~jorel/ds91.htm

Organizzazione Libera Bajor (Italian)
http://members.xoom.it/Bajor_it

Philip Anglim (Vedek Bareil) - Acting Naturally
www.angelfire.com/mo/gutterduck/ds9.html

Shakaar Society
www.shakaar.demon.co.uk/index.html

Star Trek Character Gallery: Ro Laren
http://members.easyspace.com/stcg/ro.html

Ultimate Star Trek Collection: Bajorans
http://startrek.fns.net.fsn.net/aliens/bajoran.html

Borg

"Resistance is futile." Not a part of the original series, the Borg are the most popular "new" alien race in the Star Trek universe. With their no holds barred attacks and powerful technology, the Borg have made themselves a formidable enemy of the Federation. Use the sites listed here to be assimilated into the "collective" love for the Borg found on the Internet.

AAA Star Trek: Borg Gallery
http://eonmagazine.com/startrek/borg%20gallery%20page%201.html

AAA Star Trek: The Borg
http://eonmagazine.com/startrek/borg%20page%202.html

All-Movie Guide: Alice Krige (Borg Queen)
http://allmovie.com/cg/x.dll?UID=10:51:20|PM&p=avg&sql=B39389

Assimilation Forum
http://disc.server.com/Indices/5634.html

Borg Collective, The
www.theborgcollective.com

Borg Collective, The: Collective Consciousness
http://theborgcollective.com/cgi-bin/miva?frames/com_area.mv

Borg Collective, The: Fan Fiction
www.theborgcollective.com/frames/fan_fiction.htm

Borg Collective, The: Star Trek Fan Art
www.theborgcollective.com/frames/fan_art.htm

Borg Collective, The: Who are the Borg?
www.theborgcollective.com/frames/borg_main.htm

Borg Cube, The
www.geocities.com/Area51/Vault/7900/BORGCUBE.htm

Borg Information Node
www.creadventures.com/borg

Borg Institute of Technology
http://grove.ufl.edu/~locutus/Bit/bit.html

Borg Newsgroup
alt.startrek.borg

Borg Tag Lines
http://www2.prestel.co.uk/majeed/sfdbase/databank/borgmtag.htm

Borgisms
http://www2.prestel.co.uk/majeed/sfdbase/databank/borgisms.htm

Crosis (German)
www.crosis.de

Dar's Borg Page
www.geocities.com/~darsplace/star_trek_vault/borg.html

Dave's Star Trek - Borg Page
www.geocities.com/Area51/Nebula/6309

Dave's Star Trek - Borg Page: Assimilated Species Pics
www.geocities.com/Area51/Nebula/6309/asspics.htm

Dave's Star Trek - Borg Page: Borg Encyclopedia
   www.geocities.com/Area51/Nebula/6309/RightFrame2.htm

Dave's Star Trek - Borg Page: Files (Audio, Pics & Backgrounds)
   www.geocities.com/Area51/Nebula/6309/borgfiles.htm

French Captain/Borg Newsgroup
   alt.french.captain.borg.borg.borg

Hugh Borg: Jonathan del Arco
   www.wlu.edu/~madams/3rd.of.5.html

Improvement of Human Technology by Borgification, The
   www.geocities.com/Area51/Chamber/8121

Locutus' Hang Webring
   www.geocities.com/Area51/Labyrinth/8852/webring.htm

Locutus' Hang: Borg Pictures
   www.geocities.com/Area51/Labyrinth/8852/pic6.htm

Sebius of Borg
   http://members.xoom.com/Sebius

Seven of Nine's Collective
   www.SevenofNineB.org

Star Trek Jokes: Borg
   http://www2.prestel.co.uk/majeed/sfdbase/databank/Jokesbor.htm

Starfleet Supply: History of the Borg
   www.geocities.com/Area51/Stargate/7952/borg.html

State of the Races: The Borg
   www.greatlink.org/stateraces/sotr-borg.html

The Borg Hive
   www.the-borg.org

The Borg vs. Microsoft Windows
   http://www2.prestel.co.uk/majeed/sfdbase/databank/borgwin.htm

Trek Worlds: The Borg Album
   www.geocities.com/Area51/Zone/3000/borgalbum.htm

Ultimate Star Trek Collection: Borg
http://startrek.fns.net.fsn.net/aliens/borg.html

Cardassians

The Cardassians were introduced during the run of Star Trek: The Next Generation. Characters like Gul Dukat (played by Marc Alaimo) and Elim Garak have made this race exceedingly popular. Visit these web pages to satisfy your need for a Kardassi fix.

Cardassia Forever Webring: Sites List
www.webring.org/cgi-bin/webring?ring=cardassians;list

Cardassia in Cahoots with the Dominion Web Site, The
www.geocities.com/Area51/Nebula/4349/frame.html

Cardassia Mail (@cardassia.zzn.com)
http://cardassia.zzn.com

Cardassian Newsgroup
alt.shared-reality.startrek.cardassian

Cardassians - Now We Like Them, Now We Don't
http://startrek.about.com/library/weekly/aa031799.htm?pid=2833&cob=home

Cardassians - The Unofficial Encyclopedia
http://members.aol.com/primeview/enctable.html

Dukat's Romantic Fanfiction
www.kardasi.com/gd/contents.htm

ElimGarak.Com
http://elimgarak.com

Federation Sound Archive: Aliens
www.domaindlx.com/timbo/aliens.html

Garek Gallery
www.geocities.com/Area51/Nebula/4349/g_garak.html

Gul Dukat
www.geocities.com/Area51/Labyrinth/8873/dukat.htm

Gul Dukat Gallery
www.geocities.com/Area51/Nebula/4349/g_dukat.html

Gul Dukat's Homepage
http://members.aol.com/malaimo/index.htm

Gul Maket's Cardassia Prime
http://members.tripod.com/Gul_Maket/index2.htm

Gul Traglor's Cardassian Fan Fiction
http://homestead.com/Cardassian/Cardie0.html

Kamar Sutra: Cardassian Symbols
http://elimgarak.com/art/symbols/cardsym.html

Lady Kardasi's Domain
www.kardasi.com

Official Cardassian Fan Web Page, The
http://members.aol.com/primeview/prime.html

Seventh Order, The: Art Gallery
www.7thorder.org/7art.htm

So, you want to be a Cardassian or just look like one?
http://members.aol.com/primeview/makeup.html

Star Trek Character Gallery: Dukat
http://members.easyspace.com/stcg/dukat.html

Star Trek Character Gallery: Garak
http://members.easyspace.com/stcg/garak.html

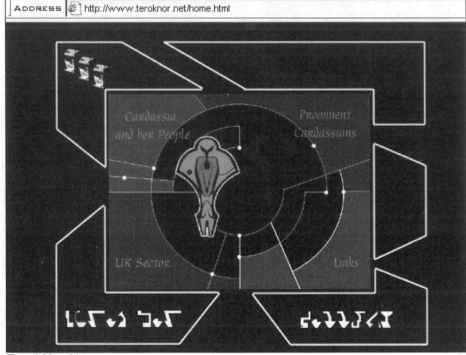

TerokNor.Net
www.teroknor.net/home.html

Ultimate Star Trek Collection: Cardassians
http://startrek.fns.net.fsn.net/aliens/cardassian.html

Dominion & Jem Hadar

Deep Space Nine introduced the Gamma Quadrant. And, along with this new territory, came new races. The Dominion and their "wardogs," the Jem Hadar, have posed a significant threat to the Federation. These sites will teach you more about these new, yet formidable, enemies.

Cardassia in Cahoots with the Dominion Web Site, The
www.geocities.com/Area51/Nebula/4349/frame.html

Cardassian Intelligence: Dominion War Summary
www.geocities.com/Hollywood/Academy/6325/dominion.html

Dominion Gallery
www.geocities.com/Area51/Nebula/4349/g_dominion.html

Dominion Mail (@dominion.zzn.com)
http://dominion.zzn.com

Dominion War Webring: Sites List
www.webring.org/cgi-bin/webring?ring=dominionwar&list

Jem' Hadar Webring: Sites List
www.webring.org/cgi-bin/webring?ring=jemhadar&list

Ultimate Star Trek Collection: Changelings or The Founders
http://startrek.fns.net.fsn.net/aliens/change.html

Ultimate Star Trek Collection: Jem'Hadar
http://startrek.fns.net.fsn.net/aliens/jemhadar.html

Ferengi

The Ferengi are consumed with a desire to make money, and although they did not appear until The Next Generation, they have become a prominent part of the Star Trek Universe. The sites listed here are your key to discovering more about the latinum-loving Ferengi.

Aron Eisenberg Fan Club
http://hometown.aol.com/SoupTime/Aron_Eisenberg-Nog_FanClub.htm

Dabok Emporium (Italian)
http://come.to/dabok

Ferengi Commerce Commission
http://belegost.mit.edu/steve/trek.html

Ferengi Cultural Hub, The
http://freenet.buffalo.edu/~bj803/ferengi.html

Internet Movie Database: Aron Eisenberg (Nog)
http://us.imdb.com/Name?Eisenberg,+Aron

Internet Movie Database: Max Grodenchik (Rom)
http://us.imdb.com/Name?Grod%E9nchik,+Max

Quark's Place: Gallery
www.orlinter.com/users/grandnag/cast.htm

Star Trek Character Gallery: Quark
http://members.easyspace.com/stcg/quark.html

Star Trek Frontier: Ferengi Rules of Acquisition
www.geocities.com/Area51/Dimension/7551/rules.html

Trek Worlds: Aliens Album 1
www.geocities.com/Area51/Zone/2200/aliensalbum1.htm

Worf's Star Trek Site: Ferengi Rules of Acquisition
www.bazza.com/sj/trek/ferengi.html

Klingons

The Klingons are perhaps the most widely known of the Star Trek races. With their darkly lit starships, their bumpy foreheads, and their staunch belief in honor, the Klingons have been a part of every single Star Trek series. The sites below focus on this warrior race. Use them to learn to speak Klingon, join a costuming group, and view the weaponry of this mighty race.

AAA Star Trek: Klingons
http://eonmagazine.com/startrek/klingon%20page2.html

Alien Battle Swords
www.deathstar.org/~sword/aliensword.html

An Introduction to Klingon Culture
www.sector001.com/qonos.htm

AURORA - Appreciation & Unity for the Robert O'Reilly Alliance
www.geocities.com/Area51/1908/aurora.htm

Authorized Klin Zha (Klingon Chess) Home Page
www.fyi.net/~kordite/klinzha.htm

Comitato d'azion Klingon (Italian)
www.geocities.com/Hollywood/5844

Dar's Klingon Page
www.geocities.com/~darsplace/star_trek_vault/klingon.html

Federation Sound Archive: Aliens
www.domaindlx.com/timbo/aliens.html

Gallery of Klingon Warriors
www.hotink.com/warriors

House of Kaos, The
http://members.tripod.com/~klingon_warrior/index.html

House of Martok - The Official JG Hertzler Fan Club
www.martok.org

House Trekkan
www.geocities.com/Area51/Lair/9261

House Veska
www.houseveska.org

Imperial Klingon Navy
www.geocities.com/Area51/Corridor/3440

Independent Klingon Line Registry, The
www.netvista.net/~mmaksel/iklr

Intergalaktik Klingon Empire
www.cyberramp.net/~klingon

Internet Movie Database: John Hertzler (General Martok)
http://us.imdb.com/Name?Hertzler,+John

Itibashi Klingon Museum
www.asahi-net.or.jp/~VZ4S-KUBC/tlhindex.html

K'Mel's Guide to Klingon Cyberspace
www.geocities.com/Area51/1908

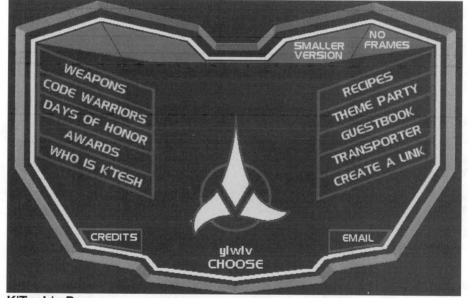

K'Tesh's Page
http://members.xoom.com/KTesh/index.htm

K'Tesh's Page: Klingon Recipes
http://members.xoom.com/KTesh/klingon_food.htm

Kang's Page: Costume Design
www.islandnet.com/~timespac/klingon/kampbell.html

KIDC: Klingon Rituals & Traditions
www.klingon.org/KIDC/pages/Rituals.html

Klin Zha Kinta (Klingon Chess)
www.geocities.com/Area51/Starship/3090/klinzhakinta.html

Klingon Assault Group (KAG) Domain, The
www.kag.org

Klingon Assault Group (KAG) of Australia
www.ozemail.com.au/~kagaus

Klingon Bitch Webring
www.geocities.com/SouthBeach/Cove/7072/KBwebring.html

Klingon Bitch Webrings: Sites List
www.webring.org/cgi-bin/webring?ring=klingonbitch;list

Klingon Costuming Message Board
www.egroups.com/group/klingon_costuming

Klingon Embassy (German)
www.klingon-embassy.de

Klingon Fan Clubs & Groups FAQ
www.khemorex-klinzhai.de/faqs/kli-faq.html

Klingon Imperial Diplomatic Corps
www.klingon.org/KIDC/pages/menu.html

Klingon Language Institute
www.kli.org

Klingon Language Webring
http://php.indiana.edu/~clipscom/

Klingon Newsgroup
alt.shared-reality.startrek.klingon

Klingon Newsgroup II
alt.startrek.klingon

Klingon Teddy Bears
http://members.tripod.com/~klingonbear/index.html

Klingon Vocabulary
gopher://wiretap.spies.com/00/Library/Media/Trek/klingon.doc%09
%09%2B

Klingon Warrior Society
www.auburn.edu/~bentoam/KWS

KlingonAcademy.Com
www.klingonacademy.com

Klingons Mail (@klingons.zzn.com)
http://klingons.zzn.com

Klingons With Honor (Picture Gallery)
http://members.tripod.com/~ds9promenade/klingons_with_honor.html

Official John Colicos Fan Club (Kor)
www.klingon.org/Colicos/pages

Oy, Klingons
www.geocities.com/Area51/Cavern/2395

Star Trek Character Gallery: Gowron
http://members.easyspace.com/stcg/gowron.html

Star Trek Continuum: Klingon Great Hall Chat
www.startrekcontinuum.com/kli/Quadrant.asp?ssector=greathall.asp

Star Trek Jokes: Klingon
http://www2.prestel.co.uk/majeed/sfdbase/databank/Jokeskli.htm

Star Trek: TNG: Cast Photographs: Suzie Plakson
www.daviestrek.com/trek/tng/suzieplakson.htm

Starfleet Headquarters: The Bird of Prey
http://home.earthlink.net/~cobarry/klingon.html

State of the Races: The Klingon Empire
www.greatlink.org/stateraces/klingons.html

Steve's Trek Page: Klingon Weapons Database
http://soli.inav.net/~nibblink/klingon.htm

Targ TV
http://members.aol.com/LaurThur/TARGTV.html

thIngn jev, the (Klingon Newsletter)
www.cyberramp.net/~klingon/jev/jev.htm

Trek Worlds: Aliens Album 2
www.geocities.com/Area51/Zone/2200/aliensalbum2.htm

Ultimate Star Trek Collection: Klingons
http://startrek.fns.net.fsn.net/aliens/klingon.html

WBS Klingon Webring
www.geocities.com/Hollywood/Hills/3786/klinweb.html

WBS Klingon Webring: Sites List
www.webring.org/cgi-bin/webring?ring=wbsklingon&list

Wolf359: Klingon 3D Stills
http://wolf359a.anet-stl.com/klingon.html

Wolf359: Klingon Ship Portraits
http://wolf359a.anet-stl.com/kport.html

Yahoo! Clubs: Klingon Costumes
http://clubs.yahoo.com/clubs/klingoncostumes

Other Aliens & General Alien Pages

Countless alien races have been invented within the mythos of Star Trek. Here are some pages devoted to other alien races and actors who've guest-starred as aliens.

AAA Star Trek: Species Database
http://eonmagazine.com/startrek/races.html

Alexander Enberg (Ensign Vorik) Fan Page
http://members.aol.com/BrentFemme/enberg.html

Aliens of Star Trek
http://members.tripod.com/~JeanetteY/Alien_Faces1.html

Andor Files, The
www.geocities.com/Area51/Station/1558/index.html

Andorian Home Page, The
http://izan.simplenet.com/andorian.htm

Authorized Klin Zha (Klingon Chess) Home Page
www.fyi.net/~kordite/klinzha.htm

Blue Fleet
http://randyb.byu.edu/alioth/bf2.html

Breen System, The
www.geocities.com/Area51/Zone/6151/trek-index.htm

Caitians (Feline species from the Animated Series)
www.geocities.com/Area51/Corridor/6496/caitian.html

Computer Core Dump: Alien Ships
www.ccdump.org/enemyship.html

Dave's Star Trek - Borg Page: Assimilated Species Pics
www.geocities.com/Area51/Nebula/6309/asspics.htm

Delta Quadrant Alien Database
www.geocities.com/Area51/Rampart/3448/aliens.html

Federation Sound Archive: Aliens
www.domaindlx.com/timbo/aliens.html

Gorn Home Page
http://izan.simplenet.com/gornpage.htm

Hirogen Holodeck, The
www.geocities.com/Hollywood/Boulevard/7855/index.html

Hirogen Hunters Webring
www.geocities.com/Hollywood/Boulevard/7855/hunters.html

Internet Movie Database: Aron Eisenberg (Nog)
http://us.imdb.com/Name?Eisenberg,+Aron

Internet Movie Database: John Hertzler (General Martok)
http://us.imdb.com/Name?Hertzler,+John

Internet Movie Database: Louise Fletcher (Vedek/Kai Winn)
http://us.imdb.com/Name?Fletcher,+Louise

Internet Movie Database: Max Grodenchik (Rom)
http://us.imdb.com/Name?Grod%E9nchik,+Max

Kazon Predator Class Starship
http://startrek.fns.net.fsn.net/ships/predator.html

Klin Zha Kinta (Klingon Chess)
www.geocities.com/Area51/Starship/3090/klinzhakinta.html

Krenim Home Page
www.geocities.com/Hollywood/Academy/9164

Lost Races of Star Trek: The Original Series
http://izan.simplenet.com/lostrace.htm

Major Species Appearances in the Next Generation
www.ugcs.caltech.edu/st-tng/trivia/species.html

Maquis Freedom Alliance
www.maquis.com/mfa

My Caitian World
www.concentric.net/~Psgibbs/index_.htm

Philip Anglim (Vedek Bareil) - Acting Naturally
www.angelfire.com/mo/gutterduck/ds9.html

Rogues' Gallery of Andorians
www.magna.com.au/~lindsay/trek/Rogues.html

Rogues' Gallery of Bolians
www.geocities.com/Area51/Station/1558/Bolians.html

Species 8472 Bioship
http://startrek.fns.net.fsn.net/ships/8472ship.html

Star Trek Millenium: Actors & Aliens Pictures
http://home.bip.net/s_t_m/aaapics.htm

Steve's Trek Page: Language Database
http://soli.inav.net/~nibblink/dictnary.htm

Summary of the Physiological Roots of Andorian Culture
www.geocities.com/Area51/Station/1558/Fish.html

ADDRESS 🐾 http://izan.simplenet.com/tellar.htm

Tellarites are basically humanoid, with a coarser skin texture and more facial and body hair than Humans. Their hair, covering all but the frontal face and the hands, is not as thick as animal fur, but is more reminiscent of an extremely hairy person.

Their home worlds have a thinner atmosphere than Terra, leading to their overdeveloped nasal openings, which have been unkindly (and sometimes insultingly) compared to the snouts of Terran swine.

They have a roll of abdominal fat that makes all Tellarites appears to be portly.

Tellarites are slightly stronger and more hardy than Humans, but their appearance and personality combine to give them a lower charisma.

Members of the Tellarite race are racially suspicious, argumentative and brash, at least by Human standards. Those who trust too much or give in too easily are consider weak fools in Tellarite society. Surprisingly, some Tellarites make good diplomats - they do not give in easily. Tellarites enjoy a good argument, and merchant's bazar on a Tellarite world is a very lively place, indeed!

Tellarites Home Page
http://izan.simplenet.com/tellar.htm

The Page that Turns You Into a Tribble
www.geocities.com/SoHo/6012/tribble.html

Threat Briefing: The Breen Confederacy
www.geocities.com/Hollywood/Academy/6325/tactical/threat-breen.html

Trill Newsgroup
alt.startrek.trill

Ultimate Star Trek Collection: Alien Races
http://startrek.fns.net.fsn.net/aliens/alien.html

Ultimate Star Trek Collection: Betazoids
http://startrek.fns.net.fsn.net/aliens/betazoid.html

Ultimate Star Trek Collection: Kazon
http://startrek.fns.net.fsn.net/aliens/kazon.html

Ultimate Star Trek Collection: Ocampa
http://startrek.fns.net.fsn.net/aliens/ocampa.html

Ultimate Star Trek Collection: Species 8472
http://startrek.fns.net.fsn.net/aliens/8472.html

Ultimate Star Trek Collection: Starships & Spacecraft
http://startrek.fns.net.fsn.net/ships/ships.html

Ultimate Star Trek Collection: Talaxians
http://startrek.fns.net.fsn.net/aliens/talaxian.html

Ultimate Star Trek Collection: Trill
http://startrek.fns.net.fsn.net/aliens/8472.html

Ultimate Star Trek Collection: Vidians
http://startrek.fns.net.fsn.net/aliens/vidiian.html

Q/John de Lancie

John de Lancie's character, Q, appeared in the first episode of Star Trek: The Next Generation and since then, he's been a well known part of the Trek universe. His quixotic behavior and quick-witted remarks have made him quite a fan favorite. The links below focus on Q, Q's race -- the Q Continuum, and John de Lancie himself.

Alien Voices (I)
http://alienvoices.com

Alien Voices (II)
http://members.tripod.com/~JohndeLancie/jdlav.html

Federation Sound Archive: Q Continuum
www.domaindlx.com/timbo/q.html

Hollywood Online - Movie People Database: John de Lancie
http://moviepeople.hollywood.com/people.asp?p_id=P|17807

Internet Movie Database: John DeLancie
http://us.imdb.com/Name?de+Lancie,+John

John de Lancie Tribute Page
http://members.tripod.com/~JohndeLancie/index.html

Q - Mad, Bad & Dangerous to Know: Q's Appearances
www.knownspace.demon.co.uk/q.htm

Q Continuum (I)
www.geocities.com/Area51/Zone/4431/frames1.htm

Q Continuum (I): Picture Section
www.geocities.com/Area51/Zone/4431/q-pics.html

Q Continuum (I): Q Movies
www.geocities.com/Area51/Zone/4431/q-movies.htm

Q Continuum (I): Q's Games
www.geocities.com/Area51/Zone/4431/games.htm

Q Continuum (I): Q's Live Chat
www.geocities.com/Area51/Zone/4431/chat.html

Q Continuum (I): Sound Clips
www.geocities.com/Area51/Zone/4431/frames2.htm

Q Continuum (II)
www.worc.u-net.com/alt.fan.q/index.html

Q Continuum (II): Q Humor
www.worc.u-net.com/alt.fan.q/humor.html

Q Fan Fiction Library
www.knownspace.demon.co.uk/qindex.htm

Q Mail (@q.zzn.com)
http://q.zzn.com

Q Newsgroup
alt.fan.q

Q's Star Trek Page
www.geocities.com/Area51/Corridor/9013

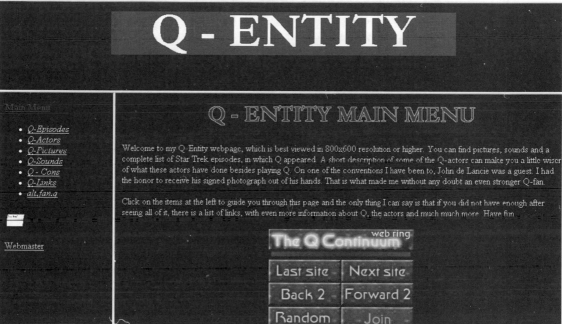

Q-Entity
www.geocities.com/Hollywood/Lot/4660/q.htm

Realm of Q
www.geocities.com/Area51/Corridor/9013

Star Trek at the Web Spot
www.eskimo.com/~bpentium/trek.html

Star Trek Character Gallery: Q
http://members.easyspace.com/stcg/q.html

Star Trek: TNG: Cast Photographs: John de Lancie
www.daviestrek.com/trek/tng/johndelancie.htm

Ultimate Star Trek Collection: Q Continuum
http://startrek.fns.net.fsn.net/aliens/qcontinuum.html

Vash's Q Chat Page
www.tedric.demon.co.uk/qchat.html

Whisper of Alien Voices (Interview with John de Lancie)
www.knownspace.demon.co.uk/alienv.htm

Romulans

The Romulans are the warlike equivalent of the Vulcans. With their pointy ears and cloaking devices, the Romulans have established the Romulan Star Empire. For more info on this long-time adversary of the Federation, visit the sites below.

AAA Star Trek: Romulans
http://eonmagazine.com/startrek/romulans%20page%201.html

An Introduction to Romulan Culture
www.sector001.com/romulus.htm

On Inventing a Romulan Language . . .
www.ibmpcug.co.uk/~owls/romlang.htm

Rihannsu Dictionary, The
www.geocities.com/Area51/Cavern/8717/contents.html

Romulan Ale Recipe
http://hbd.org/brewery/cm3/recs/12_06.html

Romulan Empire
www.geocities.com/Area51/Vault/5288

Romulan Invasions Squadron
http://cflmain.com/romulans

Romulan Newsgroup
alt.startrek.romulan

Romulan Star Empire International Inc
www.rsempire.org

Starfleet Headquarters: The Warbird
http://home.earthlink.net/~cobarry/romulan.html

State of the Races: The Romulan Star Empire
www.greatlink.org/stateraces/romulans.html

Trek Worlds: Aliens Album 2
www.geocities.com/Area51/Zone/2200/aliensalbum2.htm

Ultimate Star Trek Collection: Romulans
http://startrek.fns.net.fsn.net/aliens/romulan.html

Vorta

The Vorta are one of the most powerful races of the gamma quadrant. With their mental abilities, they've assisted the Founders in batttling the Federation. The sites below focus on the Vorta race.

Internet Movie Database: Jeffrey Combs (Wayoun)
http://us.imdb.com/Name?Combs,+Jeffrey

Ultimate Star Trek Collection: Vorta
http://startrek.fns.net.fsn.net/aliens/vorta.html

Vorta Gallery
www.geocities.com/Area51/Nebula/4349/g_vorta.html

Vorta Mail (@vorta.zzn.com)
http://vorta.zzn.com

Vorta Vortex
http://members.tripod.com/~vortavixen/vortex.htm

Vortaphiles
http://www0.delphi.com/Vortaphiles

Vulcans

Star Trek's most famous Vulcan, Spock, is really only half-Vulcan -- the other half is human. Nonetheless, there are many sites on the Web that examine various aspects of the Vulcan race. Surf long and prosper!

Federation Sound Archive: Aliens
www.domaindlx.com/timbo/aliens.html

Fondiazone Vulcaniana
www.geocities.com/Area51/4033/fondazione.html

Location of Vulcan: The Final Word
gopher://wiretap.spies.com/00/Library/Media/Trek/vulcan.loc%09%09%2B

Shi-Kahr
www.geocities.com/Hollywood/7646

Spock's Pages: The Vulcan Calendar
http://ourworld.compuserve.com/homepages/SpocksPages/vulcan/Calender.htm

Spock's Pages: The Vulcan Language
http://ourworld.compuserve.com/homepages/SpocksPages/vulcan/VulcLan1.htm

Spock's Pages: Vulcan & Her Solar System
http://ourworld.compuserve.com/homepages/SpocksPages/vulcan/SolarSys.htm

Star Trek: TNG: Cast Photographs: Mark Lenard
www.daviestrek.com/trek/tng/marklenard.htm

Ultimate Star Trek Collection: Vulcans
http://startrek.fns.net.fsn.net/aliens/vulcan.html

Vulcan Newsgroup
alt.startrek.vulcan

Vulcan Webring
http://users.erols.com/surel/ring/ring.htm

Vulcan Webring: Sites List
www.webring.org/cgi-bin/webring?ring=vulcan;index

STAR TREK
Site Profiles

Not sure where you want to start? Here you will find full descriptions of some of the web pages that appear in this book. Along with the description, you will see various icons that are designed to help you size up the sites before you visit them. For instance, sites that are considered "must see" material are marked with an 👁 icon. By browsing here before you go online, you can find out if these sites have content of any interest to you.

A History of the Ships Named Enterprise
www.cs.umanitoba.ca/~djc/startrek/SNE.html

> This site presents a detailed history of all ships named Enterprise, including those from as far back as 1705.

A Man I Call Friend - Patrick Stewart 🖼
http://members.tripod.com/~daisy1701dy/dyp.html

> The strength of this site is in that it offers some excellent black and white images of Patrick Stewart performing on stage.

🖼 IMAGES	🎬 VIDEO	📢 AUDIO
👁 MUST SEE!	$ SELLS STUFF	✉ ADULT CONTENT	🔍 SEARCHABLE
🗣 CHAT ROOMS	📥 MESSAGE BOARDS	📪 MAILING LISTS

AAA Star Trek 📪 ⬇ ♀

www.eonmagazine.com/startrek

AAA Star Trek is an enormous site. It offers pictures and information on just about every cast member and character. Each alien race is profiled, and there are a lot of images and animations throughout the site. You can even shop, join their mailing list, or post messages on their message boards.

Ad's Star Trek & MP3 Site 🖼 🔊

http://home.publishnet.nl/~admburgh

Listen to MIDIs while you view pictures, download sound files and more at Ad's Star Trek & MP3 Site.

Alien Voices (I) $🖼

http://alienvoices.com

Alternate URL: http://alienvoices.com/intro.html
This is the official site for the Alien Voices audio book series featuring the voices of both Leonard Nimoy and John de Lancie.

Alien Voices (II) 🖼

http://members.tripod.com/~JohndeLancie/jdlav.html

This page describes the audio book series "Alien Voices." The series features classic science fiction texts read by Leonard Nimoy and John de Lancie.

Andorian Home Page, The 🖼

http://izan.simplenet.com/andorian.htm

Ever wonder what race those aliens with blue skin and antennae belong to? Well, the answer is Andorians, and in cyberspace, even their race has a home page. Visit the Andorian Home Page to satisfy your curiosity about this oft-seen but rarely developed Trek alien race.

AURORA - Appreciation & Unity for the Robert O'Reilly Alliance

www.geocities.com/Area51/1908/aurora.htm

> AURORA offers news, images and appearance information for Robert O'Reilly, the actor who has played Chancellor Gowron on Star Trek: The Next Generation and Deep Space Nine.

Bad Guys of Star Trek, The

http://members.tripod.com/~Tvamp

> This site features a page for each Trek series (except Voyager) and its villains. Images and descriptions are included for each "bad guy."

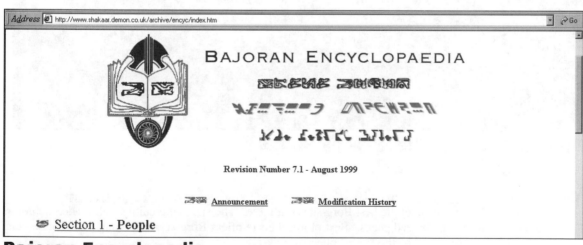

Bajoran Encyclopedia

www.shakaar.demon.co.uk/archive/encyc/index.htm

> Everything you could possibly want to know about Bajorans can be found here. Learn about Bajoran customs and beliefs as well as the flora and fauna of Bajor.

IMAGES   VIDEO   AUDIO

MUST SEE! $ SELLS STUFF   ADULT CONTENT   SEARCHABLE

CHAT ROOMS   MESSAGE BOARDS   MAILING LISTS

Big Bill's Star Trek Stuff
www.kruse.demon.co.uk/index.htm

Big Bill's Star Trek Stuff consists of a single page of questions and answers regarding episodes of Star Trek: The Next Generation. The top of the page offers links to the particular seasons of the series, and saving an HTML or text version of this page makes for fun reading offline.

BlazingKnight's ShipYards (Starship Creator)
www.geocities.com/starbase721

For users of the Star Trek: Starship Creator program, this site includes with ships, crews, and missions to download!

Borg Collective, The
www.theborgcollective.com

Alternate URL: www.theborgcollective.com/frames/central_node.htm
The Borg Collective is one of the best Borg sites out there. The site is incredibly well made, including Java animations and organized pages. Best of all, the site offers Borg-related media, information, and discussion. Be assimilated by the Borg Collective today!

BRING BACK KIRK!

Bring Back Kirk!

www.bringbackkirk.comwww.bringbackkirk.com

Alternate URL: www.bringbackkirk.com/main.shtml

The goal of Bring Back Kirk is exactly that -- resurrecting the captain of the original Enterprise. Read all about attempts to coerce Paramount into bringing back Kirk as well as send your own request all from this site.

Address 🔲 http://members.aol.com/primeview/enctable.html ▼

Cardassians

The Unofficial Encylopedia

by Tiffany L. Edenfield

Author's Notes	Introduction	Acknowledements
Just the Facts	Physiology	Character's TNG
Characters DSN	Collaborators	Technology

Cardassians - The Unofficial Encyclopedia

http://members.aol.com/primeview/enctable.html

Everything from Cardassian architecture to Cardassian technology is discussed in detail within this wonderful cyber-encyclopedia. If you're roleplaying as a Cardassian or merely enjoy reading about them, this site is for you!

🖼 IMAGES   🎬 VIDEO   📢 AUDIO

👁 MUST SEE! $ SELLS STUFF   📦 ADULT CONTENT   🔍 SEARCHABLE

🗣 CHAT ROOMS   ⬇ MESSAGE BOARDS   📪 MAILING LISTS

Casey Biggs
The Official Web Site

Casey Biggs: The Official Web Site (Damar) $ 🖼 🔊

http://members.aol.com/primeview/biggsclub.html

This site is dedicated to Casey Biggs, who has played Gul Damar in the Trek universe. The site includes images, audio, autographs for sale, a filmography, interviews, and reviews all dealing with Casey Biggs.

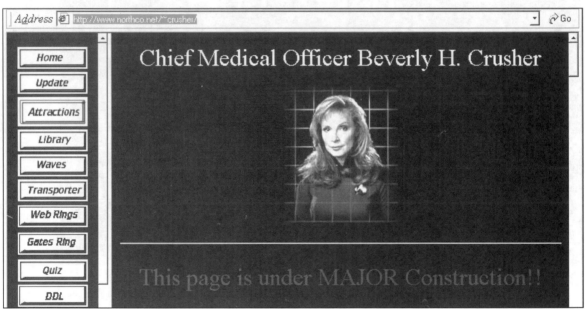

Chief Medical Officer Beverly H Crusher 🖼 🔊

www.northco.net/~crusher

This site includes .wav files, Windows theme files and appearance information for Gates McFadden, Star Trek: The Next Generation's Dr. Beverly Crusher.

CJ Tassilo Michelle Forbes Home Page

www.physik.uni-regensburg.de/~krt04517/Forbes

CJ Tassilo's Michelle Forbes Home Page is -- surprise, surprise -- devoted to everything and anything connected with Michelle Forbes. Read about her acting career, her life, and her interviews. Plus, you can view pictures and read song parodies of her Next Generation character, Ro Laren.

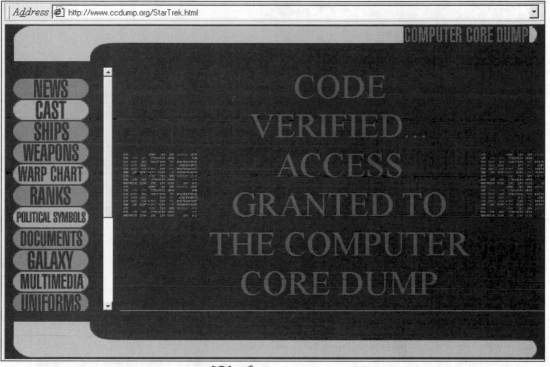

Computer Core Dump

www.ccdump.org

Looking for Trek fun? Access the Computer Core Dump! The Computer Core Dump has a lot of Star Trek information available in a LCARS format. You can read about the cast, the technology, and the universe itself at the Computer Core Dump. The cast section is particularly impressive with its extensive bios (with pictures) for almost every character.

Concise Star Trek Episode Guide, The

www.geocities.com/Area51/1125

Alternate URL: www.100acre.com/~hal

The Concise Star Trek Episode Guide is *more* than an episode guide. It includes reviews from the fans themselves as well as many other items of interest. The site includes all of the Star Trek series and films.

Core, The

www.stoga.force9.co.uk

> According to the site itself, The Core wants to be "the DEFINITIVE resource for Star Trek Webmasters." They want "to offer everything needed to set up your own Star Trek site, from background images to advice on HTML, from animated GIFs to the best free offers on the net."

Cosmic Dave's "The Star Trader" $👁

http://homes.acmecity.com/tv/thursday/324/stcards

> This site is an online Trek trading card database. You can buy and trade cards listed. Plus, every card is included so you can even use the site as a checklist for your collection.

Crossover Universe, The 👁

http://pages.prodigy.com/crossover

> The Crossover Universe is simply the best crossover site out there. Everything from Star Wars to Star Trek to Comic Books is mixed together in a wide range of articles and fan fiction. Discussion of who would beat who in a fight as well as "dream teams" are typical of the articles found on this site. The content is growing frequently and is very well organized.

Curt Danhauser's Guide to the Animated Star Trek 📇◀))👁

www.geocities.com/Area51/Stargate/3751/Main.html

> Curt Danhauser's Guide to the Animated Star Trek offers in-depth coverage of the only official animated Trek series ever produced. Everything from production information, reruns, videotapes, and characters are discussed on this site.

Address http://www.lustchip.com/dancingdoctor/

The Dancing Doctors Domain

"....its just that, that was a long time ago and I don't want to be known as the dancing doctor again!"

Welcome to the Dancing Doctor Domain, dedicated to the very talented actress of television, stage and screen, Gates McFadden, most recognised for her portrayal as Dr. Beverly Crusher in the tv series Star Trek: The Next Generation.

Dancing Doctor's Domain, The

www.lustchip.com/dancingdoctor

This page is devoted to Gates McFadden who played The Next Generation's Dr. Beverly Crusher. The Dancing Doctor's Domain includes a biography, and though under construction, the site promises to have images of McFadden in the future.

Das Star Trek Universum

http://aia.wu-wien.ac.at/Startrek/titelseite.html

Languages: German

This German site has a great deal of information on Star Trek. You can even read the Ferengi Rules of Acquisition in German (look for the word "Ferengi" in the links at the bottom of the page).

IMAGES   VIDEO   AUDIO

MUST SEE! $ SELLS STUFF   ADULT CONTENT   SEARCHABLE

CHAT ROOMS   MESSAGE BOARDS   MAILING LISTS

Database PADD 📫

http://lcars.simplenet.com/padd

Database PADD is an excellent online zine devoted to Star Trek. You can choose to "subscribe," which will send the latest in Trek news straight to your e-mailbox. You can also read the reviews and features articles on the site itself.

Delta Blues 👁

www.treknews.com/deltablues

Delta Blues is the most detailed episode summaries and reviews (20-40 pages on average) for Star Trek: Voyager available on the Internet. The next best thing to actually seeing the episode. Also includes the acclaimed Voy/DS9/TNG crossover fan novella, "Best of Both Girls."

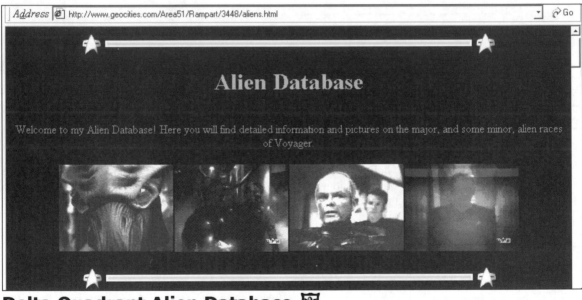

Delta Quadrant Alien Database 🖼

www.geocities.com/Area51/Rampart/3448/aliens.html

The Delta Quadrant Alien Database is your source for finding everything you want to know about the alien races that the starship Voyager has encountered during its journey home.

Desktop Starships ⬚🖼🔊👁
www.desktopstarships.com

Desktop Starships is your source for making your computer look and feel like a Trek starship. With themes, sounds, fonts and more, you can turn your computer into your very own "bridge." Plus, the site offers selections from many other sci-fi series as well! To begin, use the pop-up menu in the upper-lefthand corner of the main page to access the wallpaper selections.

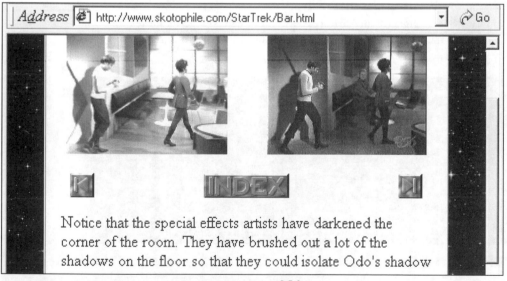

Double Trouble with Tribbles 🖼👁
www.skotophile.com/StarTrek/Tribbles.html

Double Trouble with Tribbles is an excellent essay that examines the technology involved in the making of the Deep Space Nine episode "Trials & Tribble-ations," which involved the use of footage from the original Star Trek series. Notably, the site features a scene by scene visual comparison between the original Tribbles episode and the modern one.

🖼 IMAGES   🎬 VIDEO   🔊 AUDIO

👁 MUST SEE! $ SELLS STUFF   ✦ ADULT CONTENT   🔍 SEARCHABLE

🗣 CHAT ROOMS   ⬇ MESSAGE BOARDS   ⬚ MAILING LISTS

Dukat's Romantic Fan Fiction 📬 🖼️ 🔊 👁️

www.kardasi.com/gd/contents.htm

This extremely well designed site features over fourteen image galleries of Dukat and fellow Cardassians. Not to mention, the site offers a tremendous amount of fan fiction.

ElimGarak.Com 🖼️ 🔊

http://elimgarak.com

Alternate URL: http://elimgarak.com/menu/menu.html
This site has just about everything a Garak fan could possibly want -- art, sounds, humor and more!

Eric's Excruciatingly Detailed Star Trek (TOS) Plot Summaries

www.treasure-troves.com/startrek

As its name implies, this site offers "excruciating" detail. Plus, the whole site is searchable making it stand out among most episode guides. Also, the episode summaries can be downloaded for viewing offline.

Fandom - Star Trek Central $ ⚲ 👁

www.fandom.com/star_trek

This site includes Star Trek articles, episode guides, interviews, virtual worlds, chat rooms, auctions, classifieds, online gaming and much much more.

IMAGES   VIDEO   AUDIO

MUST SEE! $ SELLS STUFF   ADULT CONTENT   SEARCHABLE

CHAT ROOMS   MESSAGE BOARDS   MAILING LISTS

FanFiction.Net: Other Star Trek Fiction 👁

www.fanfiction.net/text/browse-
listfiles.cfm?category=StarTrek%3A+Other

Over all, FanFiction.Net is an amazing site that offers easily organized fan fiction. Plus, many of the stories have been reviewed, and Internet users can rate them as well. This particular subpage of FanFiction.Net deals with Trek fan fiction that does not star any of the characters from the television and film series. Rather, these stories deal with new characters and new starships. After you've gotten to know these "new characters," be sure to explore the rest of FanFiction.Net!

Farpoint Station 🔊

www.farpointstation.org

Farpoint Station offers desktop themes, MP3s, MIDIs, screensavers, news and rumors.

Address   🖻   http://home.att.net/~fashion.voyager/   ▾   🔗 Go

Fashion Voyager

*Voyager Girl's analysis of fashion and style on **Star Trek: Voyager**.*
It's a dirty job, but somebody's got to do it

Delta Dish   **New Stuff**

Desirable Designs

Voyager Snippet of the Week: ▾

Fashion Faux Pas

IMHO: The Index   Sour Notes -- Clown costumes????? I don't think so!
(02/12)

The Quotable Q   Alien Fashions -- and we don't mean Janeway!

Fashion Voyager

http://home.att.net/~fashion.voyager

The fashion (or lack thereof) on Voyager is the subject of this site. Click on "Desirable Designs" to read positive fan commentary about the apparel seen on the latest episode of Voyager. If you're in the mood to hear the bad side of getting dressed in the Delta Quadrant, click on "Fashion Faux Pas."

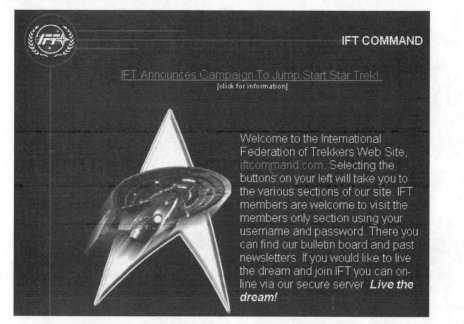

Federation CyberSpace - The Official Web Site fo the IFT

www.iftcommand.com

The International Federation of Trekkers is a tremendously active fan organization. One project of the IFT is the Excelsior Campaign -- an attempt to convince Paramount to produce a series that follows the adventures of the USS Excelsior and Captain Sulu. But the IFT is more than a Trek group. In fact, according to their site, the IFT is "concerned with environmental issues, the survival of all endangered species, and humanitarian needs. Our members around the world share these concerns and regularly take part in and submit articles on topics ranging from recycling programs to endangered species legislation. Our members really get involved with civic efforts like blood drives, tree planting campaigns, fund raising for civic and charitable activities, disaster relief, and much more."

Federation Intelligence -
International Star Trek Fan Organization

http://fedintel.net

The Federation's top secret Intelligence division. They're an International Star Trek Fan Organization with a dash of 007. The Men in Black and the CIA for the 24th Century. Are you ready to join the Elite today and become the Federation's next James Bond? Come on what are you waiting for? Membership is free!

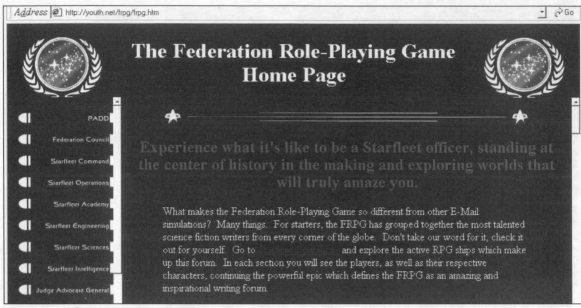

Federation RPG

http://youth.net/frpg/frpg.htm

> The Federation RPG is a play-by-e-mail role-playing game. According to the site, "The Federation RPG has two main purposes: to allow creative writers to express their talents in a Star Trek format and to promote writing skills in persons of all ages by providing a wholesome forum for their skills to develop and enhance. These two purposes, and goals to those in the administration, are accomplished using the technology available to us on the Internet, primarily Electronic Mail (E-Mail)."

FedNet: The UFP Network 📖 🔊

http://surf.to/FedNet

> FedNet offers sounds, images, fan fiction, episode guides, a timeline, and more!

Ferengi Cultural Hub, The 📖 👁

http://freenet.buffalo.edu/~bj803/ferengi.html

> Everything from the lifestyle to the religion to the physiology of the Ferengi is discussed in minute detail on this site. Read Ferengi jokes, see pictures of the Ferengi actors, and more -- it's the gold-pressed latinum of Ferengi sites!

Galactic Handbook for All Starfleet Cadets 📖 👁

http://welcome.to/galactic_handbook

> The Galactic Handbook for All Starfleet Cadets is fun! Everything from parody posters to detailed nitpicker guides, this site is an intergalactic party.

Gallery of Klingon Warriors 🏛 ◆

www.hotink.com/warriors

Nude Klingons? It's true! The Gallery of Klingon Warriors forgoes honor and exposes the Klingon race in its . . . ahem . . . full glory. These pictures are so well done that you don't have to squint to make them look real!

Garak's Star Trek Tailor Shop 🏛 🎬 🔊

www.geocities.com/Hollywood/Academy/6325/main.htm

As resourceful as the character the site is named after, Garak's Star Trek Tailor Shop has news, multimedia, and more. Its "Cardassian Intelligence" section is a great reference resource, and the "Holosuites" contain downloadable files. Check out the "Getting Around" link to learn more about what the site has to offer.

GNP/Crescendo Record Co Inc $ 👁

www.gnpcrescendo.com

Crescendo is THE online source for Star Trek music. They offer a great deal of fun and entertaining CDs of Star Trek audio as well as other sci-fi shows, including Lost in Space. Visit often to catch their specials!

IMAGES   VIDEO   AUDIO

👁 MUST SEE! $ SELLS STUFF   ADULT CONTENT   SEARCHABLE

CHAT ROOMS   MESSAGE BOARDS   MAILING LISTS

Grace Lee Whitney Official Fan Site
http://members.aol.com/starparty/glw_index.html

This is the official site for Grace Lee Whitney (AKA Yeoman Rand) information. You can read about her career and see pictures from her professional and private life. This site is a must see for any true Yeoman Rand fan!

THE GREAT LINK - THE HOME OF THE FOUNDERS

Great Link, The ☞
www.greatlink.org

Alternate URL: www.greatlink.org/DCIS/index.html
The Great Link is a UK-based site that offers up-to-the-minute Star Trek news, reviews, interviews and more. The interview section consists of many interesting texts featuring the cast and crew of the Star Trek franchise. If you want to keep up-to-stardate, bookmark this site.

Hielko's Star Trek Download Site 📬📠🎬🔊☞
http://come.to/hielko

Hielko's Star Trek Download Site has everything a Trekker into downloading could want -- audio, video, images, software and more. The site even offers a mailing list to keep you up-to-date on new additions to the site. Plus, the site is very well organized, making your visit fast and fun!

Ian's Star Trek Memories ☞
www.magna.com.au/~lindsay/trek/Trek.html

If you like Star Trek and homemade action figures, this site is an absolute must-visit. According the site's main page, "Ian has been creating his own Star Trek action figures from a pile of assorted heads, torsos and limbs." Have fun viewing Ian's well-made creations.

IBM Research: Quantum Teleportation
www.research.ibm.com/quantuminfo/teleportation

This IBM page discusses the real possibility of teleportation and the studies being undertaken to make it happen.

Illogical Spock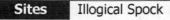

http://izan.simplenet.com/illspock.htm

This page uses a few pictures from the original series in an attempt to prove that Spock is indeed, illogical. You be the judge. Nonetheless, this site is worth visiting just to see a picture of Spock with a smile on his face.

Incredible Internet Guide for Trekkers ⬇

www.incredibleguides.com/trekkers

Visit the home page for this book, and you can post messages on our message board and even get your own free Klingons e-mail address. Plus, our web site offers the lowest price available online.

Incredible Internet Guide Series 📫🗣

www.incredibleguides.com

This is the home page for the Incredible Internet Guide Series. Find out what other titles are available in the series. Star Wars and Comic Books are just two of the other topics that are part of the Incredible Internet Guide Series.

Inside Voyager 👁

www.geocities.com/Area51/Stargate/7559/index.html

Inside Voyager is an extremely thorough site offering news about UPN's Star Trek: Voyager. This site is a must bookmark for any Voyager fan.

Insurrection Supplement

www.geocities.com/Area51/Dimension/9644/sti_addon.html

This text is meant to be a printable companion to the book called The Star Trek Encyclopedia. It covers new terms, characters, etc. from Star Trek: Insurrection.

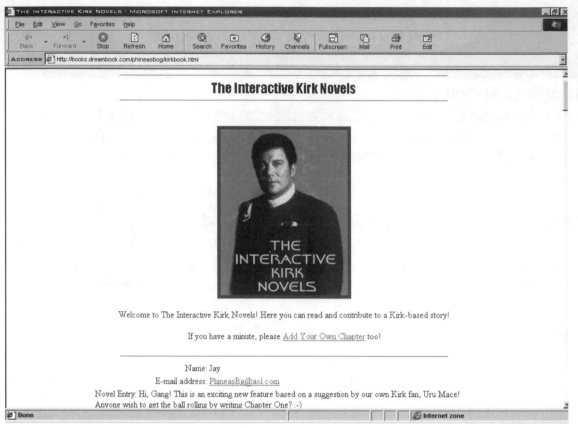

Interactive Kirk Novels, The

http://books.dreambook.com/phineasbog/kirkbook.html

The Interactive Kirk Novels site is essentially a guestbook that is being used as a medium for round robin storytelling featuring Captain Kirk. Visit this page to read the novel in progress or join in!

Jesse's Star Trek Crossover Page 👁

http://members.easyspace.com/trekxover

Jesse's Star Trek Crossover Page is a lot of fun. Here, you can read a great deal of fan fiction, most of which involves crossovers between the individual Trek series or with other Sci-Fi mythos. You can read stories featuring both the characters from Deep Space Nine AND Buffy the Vampire Slayer. Many other pairings await you at Jesse's Star Trek Crossover Page.

JK2 Costumers $

http://home.earthlink.net/~jk2costumers

JK2 Costumers specializes in made-to-order costumes. Everything from Star Trek to comic books to Battlestar Gallactica costumes is available.

Address http://www.geocities.com/~jupiterstation/ ▾ ⟳ Go

Welcome Speech

Greetings, and **welcome** to the JuPiter Station! **No**, this is not about the Jupiter Holographic Programming Station! (chuckle) As you can guess from the title image above, this site is dedicated to the Kathryn Janeway and Thomas Paris relationship! No, this site is **not** a campaign effort to get the two together in canon, but a place for Trek fans who enjoy J/P in fanfic stories, whether the stories show the pair as a romantic couple, close friends (platonic), or mentor/protege colleagues.

So, if you like to contribute your J/P stories to the J/P **Fanfic Archive**, you're **more** than welcome to come aboard! I want to make this site a place to find **all** J/P fanfic stories on the web for those seeking J/P under one friendly roof. Or I should say **orbiting** station. (grin) Also, stories involving J/P with a third person or more (example: J/C/P) are also welcome as long as the story involve J/P.

Besides fanfic stories, I'm also seeking photos or drawings (GIF or JPG) of the pair to place in the J/P **Picture Gallery**! As of now, the gallery have some photos, but I hope it'll grow as more photos and drawings are contributed or added in the future.

Also, I'm seeking WAV sounds of Janeway & Paris together for the J/P **Audio Records**! I have plenty of each alone, but only few of them together.

The Station has a **Narrative Challenges** section! Ideas are welcome to help spark story inspirations with fanfic authors! All one has to have is an imagination. <grin>

JuPiter Station (II)

www.geocities.com/~jupiterstation

> JuPiter station is dedicated to exploring the idea of a relationship between Voyager's Janeway and Paris. There is even a mailing list available -- simply click on "E-mail Listserve" to sign up.

K'Tesh's Page: Klingon Recipes 👁

http://members.xoom.com/KTesh/klingon_food.htm

> Learn culinary Klingon delights on this page. Visit this site for recipes to dazzle friends and Trek partygoers with authentic-looking 24th century alien food!

Kate Mulgrew Nexus, The

http://members.tripod.com/~SailorMoose/kmnexus/entrance.html

Alternate URL: http://members.tripod.com/~SailorMoose/kmnexus/nexus.html
> The Kate Mulgrew Nexus is pretty much a directory of Mulgrew/Janeway related sites. You can browse link lists of webrings, Janeway sites, Mulgrew sites, and even Chakotay/Janeway sites.

IMAGES   VIDEO   AUDIO
MUST SEE! $ SELLS STUFF   ADULT CONTENT   SEARCHABLE
CHAT ROOMS   MESSAGE BOARDS   MAILING LISTS

Klingon Language Institute 📭 $ 🔊

www.kli.org

According to the site itself, the purpose of the Klingon Language Institute is "to promote, foster, and develop the Klingon language, and . . . bring together Klingon language enthusiasts from around the world and provide them with a common forum for the discussion and the exchange of ideas." The Institute even offers a publication called HolQed. According to the site, "HolQeD is indexed by the Modern Language Association and is registered with the Library of Congress." The Institute is working on translating major works, such as the Bible and Shakespeare's plays into the Klingon language. One page (click on "Sounds" on the main page) includes audio of the Klingon alphabet. The site also offers Klingon merchandise, such as software and books.

Kret Rats P/T Home Page 📥 🖼

http://members.tripod.com/~Maihe

Kret Rats P/T Home Page is a tremendous site dedicated to Voyager's Paris and Torres (P/T). Fan fiction, pictures, message boards and more await you at this essential P/T page.

Kret Rats: Voyager Promo Pics 🖼 👁

http://members.tripod.com/~Maihe/promopics.html

This page from the Kret Rats has a lot of high quality and fascinating promotional pictures for the Voyager series. Want to see what the Voyager stars look like without alien make-up? If so, visit the URL above.

Kronos One ⬇️ 🖼️ 🎬 🔊 👁️

www.kronos.u-net.com/index.htm

Kronos One is a Star Trek fan club with an excellent web site. Their site is filled with multimedia, discussion, and links. An easy to use LCARS interface, makes this site a fun and efficient surfing stop. To access the multimedia of Kronos One, click on "Star Trek Database." For ease of download, many groups of files are zipped and available on the same page on which they appear individually. For more info on the club and the site itself, click on "Kronos 1 Database." Clicking on "Comms" will take you to the message board, guestbook and e-mail area of the site.

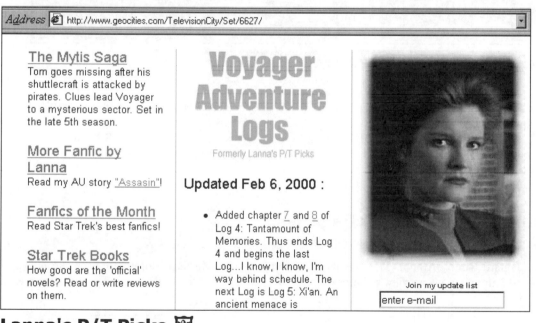

Lanna's P/T Picks 🖼️

www.geocities.com/TelevisionCity/Set/6627

Lanna's P/T Picks is home to Voyager Paris/Torres fan fiction as well as links.

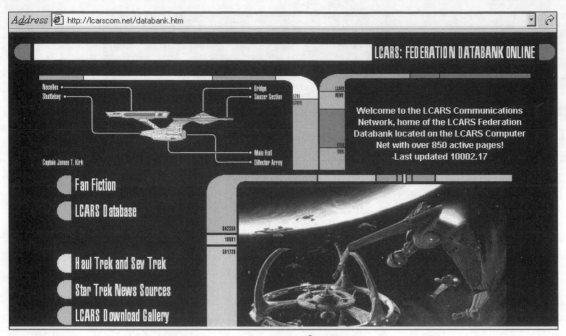

LCARS - Federation Databank 🗂 🗃 ◁ᵢᵢ 👁

http://LCARSCom.Net

This site contains over 800 active pages, all in LCARS format. It is the home of the LCARSComNet mailing list, where you can discuss all things Trek; the site also offers First Contact & Insurrection in Real Audio format, a great monthly contest with super prizes, over 100 LCARS-related WAVs for download, over 75 LCARS-related images to download, and a database so in-depth, you could spend days there and still not see it all.

Leonard Nimoy Albums Page 🗃 ◁ᵢᵢ

www.geocities.com/Hollywood/Set/1931/records.html

The Leonard Nimoy Albums Page, as its name implies, offers in-depth information on the music of Leonard Nimoy. You can view pictures of the album covers, read track listings and even listen to Real Audio clips.

Leonard Nimoy Club Online

www.nimoy.com

Leonard Nimoy Club Online's pages include a biography of the actor, news and a listing of upcoming convention appearances.

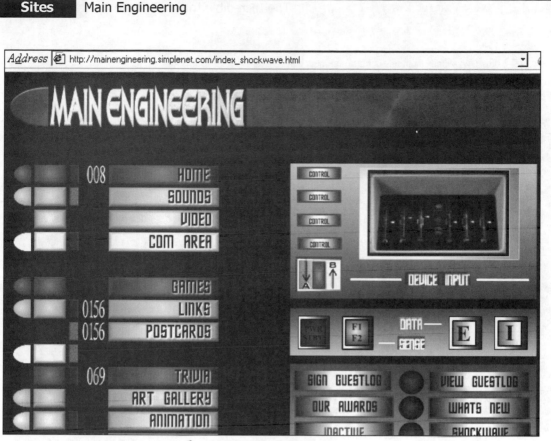

Address http://mainengineering.simplenet.com/index_shockwave.html

MAIN ENGINEERING

008 HOME
SOUNDS
VIDEO
COM AREA

GAMES
0156 LINKS
0156 POSTCARDS

069 TRIVIA
ART GALLERY
ANIMATION

CONTROL
CONTROL
CONTROL
CONTROL

B
A

DEVICE INPUT

PWR
LAT

F1
F2

DATA

SENSE

E I

SIGN GUESTLOG   VIEW GUESTLOG
OUR AWARDS   WHATS NEW
INACTIVE   SHOCKWAVE

Main Engineering

http://mainengineering.simplenet.com

Alternate URL: http://mainengineering.simplenet.com/index_shockwave.html
Main Engineering is a massive site. It has everything from software to sounds to fan art. Travel warp speed to this site!

Maquis Freedom Alliance

www.maquis.com/mfa

a small but growing organization dedicated to community service and charity work, and of course fun! They hold a Star Trek convention every October in Portage, Indiana, to raise money for charity.

Mark Harelik Fan Page, The (Inspector Kashyk - Voyager)

http://markharelik.com

Mark played "Inspector Kashyk" of the Devore Imperium in the Voyager episode "Counterpoint." The character has since been the topic of a deluge of fan fiction in the newsgroups! The site is dedicated to Mark's career in TV, movies, and on stage, with lots of photos and an extended section on the "Counterpoint" episode.

IMAGES   VIDEO   AUDIO

MUST SEE! $ SELLS STUFF   ADULT CONTENT   SEARCHABLE

CHAT ROOMS   MESSAGE BOARDS   MAILING LISTS

Maximum Defiant 📠 🎬 🔊 👁

www.maximumdefiant.com

> Maximum Defiant is a simple to use and fun to visit site. Devoted to the USS Defiant from Deep Space Nine, this site is extremely thorough in its coverage of the only Federation starship capable of cloaking. The site includes multimedia, behind the scenes information, and wallpaper. Unlike most Trek sites, it even offers a map of the site making navigation much easier. If you visit, be sure to check out the "Sketches & Diagrams" section of the Image Galleries -- there you'll find some incredible schematics of the Defiant.

Michelle Forbes Central 📠

www.jsp.umontreal.ca/~chabotma/Michelle.html

Languages: French
> This page composed mainly in French includes a gallery of Michelle Forbes (Ro Laren on Star Trek: The Next Generation) as well as a gallery of "pseudo-Michelles," actresses who resemble her. Plus, there are links and poetry devoted to Forbes.

Mikey's Star Trek Action Figure Page $📠

www.geocities.com/Area51/Vault/6934

> Mikey's Star Trek Action Figure Page is a great site for collectors and toy enthusiasts. Here, you can view images of figures, post free toy-related classifieds, as well as buy and trade action figures.

MJ's Star Trek Web Site

www.surfshop.net/~majtown/NoFrames1.html

> According to the site itself, MJ's Star Trek Web site "contains a good deal of information pertaining to the Star Trek universe, ranging from image libraries to technology, ranks, uniforms, humor, trivia and official documents of the United Federation of Planets and Starfleet Command."

My Adventure on Star Trek - Deep Space Nine

www.capital.net/~jorel/ds91.htm

> Read the adventures of two fans that got to be a Bajoran extras on the set of Deep Space Nine. Exclusive pictures are also available. Check it out!

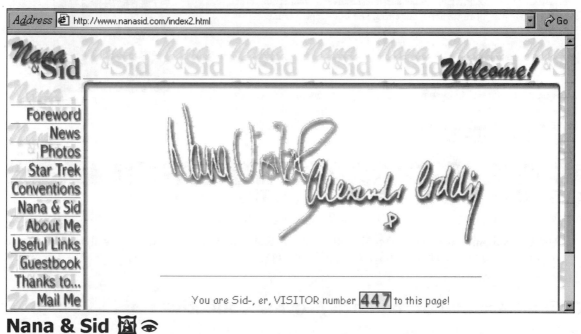

Nana & Sid

www.nanasid.com

> Nana & Sid is a fun site for fans of Siddig El Faddil and Nana Visitor. Great pictures of this real life couple and news of their upcoming projects make this site worth bookmarking. Check it out.

New Eye Studio: Star Trek Catalog $

www.neweyestudio.com/stsub.htm

> New Eye Studio is a great place to shop for new and rare Trek-related items. They offer everything from models to toys to compact discs.

New Eye Studio: Star Trek Uniforms $

www.neweyestudio.com/stc2u.htm

If you are going to have a Trek-themed party or attend a Star Trek convention, why not go in style? New Eye Studio offers pre-made Starfleet uniforms as well as patterns to do it yourself. Command the bridge of your pool party with Starfleet style!

Address http://members.aol.com/primeview/andysclub.html   ▾ ⟳ Go

events | charity | links | guest book | e-mail

Andy Robinson

While Andy is best known for his role as Elim Garak, the infamous tailor on Star Trek: Deep Space Nine, he has also guest starred in numerous screen, stage, and television productions, becoming one of the entertainment industry's rising repertory stage directors. He won the Los Angeles Drama Critics Circle's Directing Award in 1996 for "The Homecoming" and "Endgame."

Proving he can direct, Andy was granted the opportunity to direct his first television episode for Star Trek: Deep Space Nine. The episode's success has translated into directorial jobs on Star Trek: Voyager. To date, he has directed two Trek episodes.

home | fan club | about andy | articles | credits | pictures

Official Andy Robinson Web Site, The

http://members.aol.com/primeview/andysclub.html

The Official Andy Robinson Web Site offers many candid pictures of the actor as well as an extensive list of his credits and a fascinating biography of the actor.

Official Archive of the Paris/Torres Collective

www.geocities.com/~ptcarchive

Alternate URL: http://ljc.simplenet.com/ptcarchive
Archive of fan fiction centering on the characters of Tom Paris and B'Elanna Torres. Includes fan fiction by over 100 authors, message board, round robin board, beta reading board, fanfic FAQ, essays, links, exclusive interviews, Trek news, and more.

Official Armin Shimmerman Web Site, The 🖼

www.walrus.com/~quark/armin/index.html

Alternate URL: www.walrus.com/~quark/armin/home.html
The Official Armin Shimmerman Web Site features six pages of images of the actor. In addition, the site offers a biography and filmography for the actor.

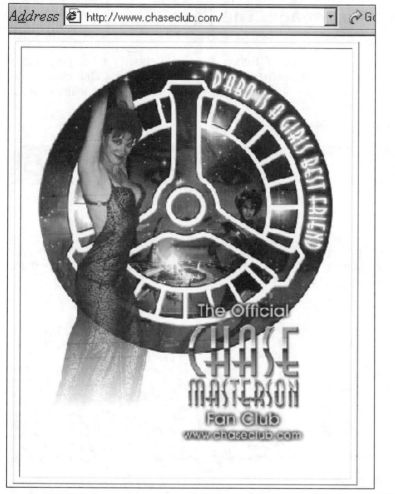

Address http://www.chaseclub.com/

Official Chase Masterson Fan Club, The 📷🔊

www.chaseclub.com

Alternate URL: www.chaseclub.com/index2.htm
The Official Chase Masterson Fan Club boasts a gallery of over 1000 images. It also features a detailed biography and news about the actress known for her portrayal of Leeta on Deep Space Nine.

Official Jeri Lynn Ryan Homepage, The 🗣📷🎬🔊👁

www.jerilynn.com

Alternate URL: www.jerilynn.com/index2.htm
The Official Jeri Lynn Ryan Homepage is enormous! It offers Real Video clips from Voyager and other television appearances. It includes sound clips of Ryan as well as over 1400 images! You can even chat with other fans about Ryan and her character, Voyager's Seven of Nine.

📷 IMAGES   🎬 VIDEO   🔊 AUDIO
👁 MUST SEE! $ SELLS STUFF   📦 ADULT CONTENT   🔍 SEARCHABLE
🗣 CHAT ROOMS   MESSAGE BOARDS   MAILING LISTS

Official Robert Picardo Homepage, The 🗿◄))👁

http://members.aol.com/rpicardo/index.html

> This page is extremely thorough in its coverage of Robert Picardo, famous for his portrayal as Voyager's holographic doctor. The site includes a biography, filmography, and fan club information. Furthermore, a section of the site known as "Con Reports" (click on the link of the same name) offers fan sightings of the actor.

Outpost 21 🗿🎬◄))

www.steve.simplenet.com

Alternate URL: www.steve.simplenet.com/index_nf.html
> Outpost 21 offers video clips, including trailers for some episodes. The site also includes a great deal of audio and impressive episode guides.

Patrick Stewart Online $🗿

www.tu-berlin.de/~stewart-page

> Patrick Stewart Online is a comprehensive resource for fans of the actor who played Star Trek: The Next Generation's Captain Jean-Luc Picard. The site includes a biography, a filmography, images and a listing of all of his theatrical performances. This site is a must-visit for any true Patrick Stewart fan!

Patrick Stewart Tribute Page 🗿

http://members.tripod.com/~PatrickStewart/index.html

Alternate URL: http://members.tripod.com/~PatrickStewart/pstewart.html
> The Patrick Stewart Tribute Page consists mainly of links to sites related to his film work. However, the site also does feature many Patrick Stewart animations, a list of his favorite things, and a biography.

Pedro's Shiporama 🖼 👁

www.shiporama.org

Pedro's Shiporama is an incredible resource for the model and starship fan alike. Quite comprehensive, this site has pictures of many starship classes, including a lot of rare images of production models.

Physics of Star Trek, The $

www.newscientist.com/nsplus/insight/startrek/startrek.html

The Physics of Star Trek is the home page for the book of the same name. Pictures of the author, the purpose behind the book, and ordering information are among the contents of this site.

Playtrek

www.playtrek.cjb.net

This site is the home page of Playtrek, a listserv group of Playmates' Trek figures collectors.

PM Productions International $

http2//www.pmprod.com

PM Productions International is a company that plans to offer a unique, Trek-inspired software product sometime after the year 2000. According to the site's main page, PM's software "uses Star Trek's Library Computer Access and Retrieval System (LCARS) and . . . functions as an independent [operating system] that runs on your [computer] and optimizes it radically. This also enables your system to sustain our LCARS apps. Find out more on this site."

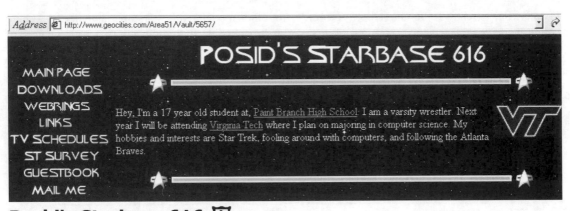

Posid's Starbase 616

www.geocities.com/Area51/Vault/5657

Posid's Starbase 616 has a Trek survey as well as few pictures and music files.

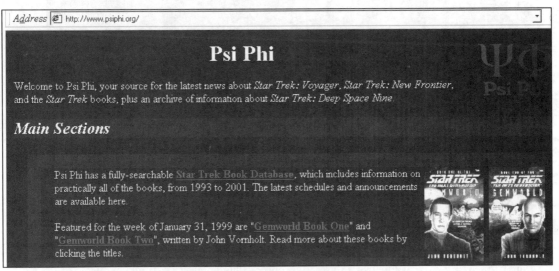

Psi Phi's Star Trek: Voyager Archive

www.psiphi.org/voy

In its usual fashion, Psi Phi.Org presents in-depth coverage of its topic. In this case, Star Trek: Voyager is profiled in extraordinary detail. You can read the Nielsen ratings history for the show, find transcripts of online chats with the cast, get the latest news, and discuss the show with other fans.

Q Continuum (I) 🗣❊ 🎬 📢

www.geocities.com/Area51/Zone/4431/frames1.htm

The Q Continuum (I) provides everything a fan of Q could possibly want: video clips, audio clips, images, links, chat, games and more!

Q Continuum (II) ❊ 📢

www.worc.u-net.com/alt.fan.q/index.html

The Q Continuum has pictures, sounds, links, and appearance information for fan-favorite omnipotent nuisance -- Q!

❊ IMAGES   🎬 VIDEO   📢 AUDIO

👁 MUST SEE! $ SELLS STUFF   ◈ ADULT CONTENT   🔍 SEARCHABLE

🗣 CHAT ROOMS   ⬇ MESSAGE BOARDS   📫 MAILING LISTS

Q Fan Fiction Library

www.knownspace.demon.co.uk/qindex.htm

You guessed it! All the stories offered at this fan fiction site feature the ever-popular Q!

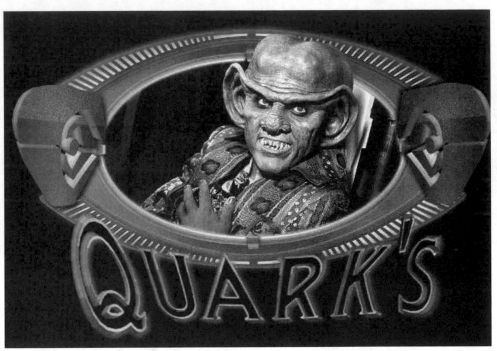

Quark's Place 🔳 ⬧

www.orlinter.com/users/grandnag/quarks.htm

Quark's Place is devoted to the only regular Ferengi character -- Quark. The site contains many images and animated GIFs as well as software.

Ressikan Flute, The: Composers

www.geocities.com/Area51/9140/composers.html

This portion of the Ressikan Flute site offers extensive information on the composers of the music used in the Star Trek series and films.

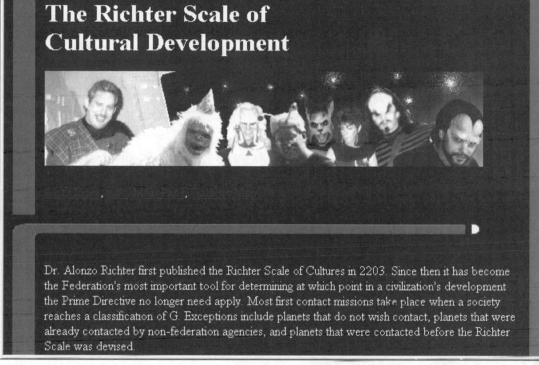

Address 🗕 http://members.aol.com/grewsomeco/richter.htm

The Richter Scale of Cultural Development

Dr. Alonzo Richter first published the Richter Scale of Cultures in 2203. Since then it has become the Federation's most important tool for determining at which point in a civilization's development the Prime Directive no longer need apply. Most first contact missions take place when a society reaches a classification of G. Exceptions include planets that do not wish contact, planets that were already contacted by non-federation agencies, and planets that were contacted before the Richter Scale was devised.

RIchter Scale of Cultural Development, The

http://members.aol.com/grewsomeco/richter.htm

This page details the classification system used to classify the alien cultures encountered by the Federation.

Roddenberry's Masterpiece

www.geocities.com/Area51/4396

Alternate URL: www.geocities.com/Area51/4396/main.html

Roddenberry's Masterpiece has links, reviews of Trek computer games and a page dedicated to Roddenberry himself.

🖼 IMAGES   🎬 VIDEO   📢 AUDIO

👁 MUST SEE! $ SELLS STUFF   ✉ ADULT CONTENT   🔍 SEARCHABLE

🗣 CHAT ROOMS   ⬇ MESSAGE BOARDS   📪 MAILING LISTS

Romulan Star Empire International Inc

www.rsempire.org

RSE International is devoted to Romulans and their fans. According to the group's site, "RSE International, Inc. is one of the largest Romulan-based Star Trek fan clubs in the world. Also known as the Romulan Star Empire, we are an organization whose purpose is to bring together fans of the Romulans across the galaxy. We meet new friends, hold chapter meetings, roleplay, attend conventions and help our community. Like the Romulans, the RSE International, Inc. believes in upholding honor through respect for oneself and others."

Rura's Star Trek Gallery

http://vision.simplenet.com/tomparis/trek.html

Rura's Star Trek Gallery offers many images of starships as well as a great deal of MIDI files. Episode guides are also available on this site, just click on "Episode Guides" on the main page.

Sci-Fi Channel Star Trek Episode Search

www.scifi.com/startrek/episodes

The Sci-Fi Channel's Star Trek episode search offers detailed profiles for every episode of the original Star Trek series. It includes pictures and trivia.

SciFiArt.Com

www.scifi-art.com

SciFiArt.Com is devoted to 3D rendering of starships. There is a gallery of creations (under the link "Shipyards"), but the best part of the site is its Discover Zone. According to the site itself, the "Discovery Zone is a collection of tutorials designed to both assist the beginning 3d modeler and provide the more experienced 3d artist with some new tricks. Here you'll find articles on modeling, texturing, animating, and special effects, as well as downloadable files to assist you in your modeling."

Scottfleet Command

www.geocities.com/Area51/Rampart/8103

By clicking on the "Transporter" button, you can read dossiers of many Trek characters. The site also features a unique interface that makes use of photographs of action figures.

Sector 0-0-1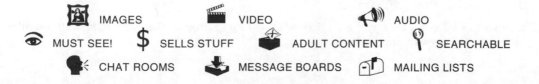

http://members.aol.com/NCC2364/index.html

Sector 0-0-1 contains a wide variety of fun Star Trek stuff. In addition, it is one of the most visually pleasing of the Trek sites on the Internet. By visiting Sector 0-0-1, you can view images of uniforms, characters, posters, and more. Plus, you can download icons and read episode guides.

Sector 001

www.powernet.net/~jcrafton

Alternate URL: www.powernet.net/~jcrafton/main.html
Sector 001's most impressive aspect is its index of the people involved in the creation of Star Trek.

You can view and print alphabetical lists of the actors, writers and directors who have been involved in

the series.

In addition, Sector 001 is full of information on just about every aspect of the Stark Trek fictional universe. Everything from starships to chemicals to biology is discussed in detail.

Sector 001: Academia

www.powernet.net/~jcrafton/academia.html

Sector 001's Academia page contains information on many references to academic institutions and programs made in the Trek series.

Sector 001: Alternate Timelines

www.powernet.net/~jcrafton/timealt.html

The Alternate Timelines page at Sector 001 details the many instances within the Star Trek universe wherein alternate realities were explored.

IMAGES   VIDEO   AUDIO
MUST SEE! $ SELLS STUFF   ADULT CONTENT   SEARCHABLE
CHAT ROOMS   MESSAGE BOARDS   MAILING LISTS

Sector 001: Assay Office

www.powernet.net/~jcrafton/assay.html

This page lists the minerals and elements created for the Star Trek series, and includes a brief description of each.

Sector 001: Units of Measurement

www.powernet.net/~jcrafton/units.html

This page lists the units of measurement used in the various Star Trek serious. Plus, it has an excellent chart detailing the ability of the Enterprise 1701-D to travel certain distances and the time required to do so.

Sector001.Com: Publications

www.sector001.com/filelib_pubs.htm

Here you will find back issues and subscription information for two Trek e-zines: PADD and Logbook.

Seska & Martha Hackett Fan Club 🖾$🖻🔊

www.marthahackett.com

If you are a fan of Martha Hackett's Seska, you must visit this site. In addition to the option to e-mail Hackett directly, the site includes Seska wallpaper, greeting cards, and a newsletter mailing list.

Sev Trek - A Cartoon Satire $🖻👁

www.sev.com.au/toonzone/sevtrek.htm

Sev Trek is a comic strip parody of Star Trek. There are strips devoted to each of the television series, and they are even translated into Klingon and Vulcan. Visit Sev Trek for a great way to relax and satisfy your craving for Star Trek.

Seventh Order, The

www.geocities.com/~ardeth

The Seventh Order is a play by e-mail (PBEM) roleplaying group. The site includes all the rules and information you need to start playing.

Shakaar Society 🖼👁

www.shakaar.demon.co.uk/index.html

The site's information page claims that the Shakaar Society "was founded in 1995 to serve as a society of friends and a forum to discuss the Bajoran race as seen in Star Trek : Deep Space Nine . . . . One of the major works of the society has been the Bajoran Encyclopaedia, which was the start of a series of works to document and expand on the Bajora." More than just a fan club, this site offers extensive data and fun for Bajoran fans.

Shatner.Com: The Official Worldwide Fan Club 💲🖼

www.shatner.com

Everything you ever wanted to know about William Shatner can be found at Shatner.Com. Find out when and where his next public appearance will be. Read about his career and buy Shatner-related merchandise. Some content is available to members only.

🖼 IMAGES   🎬 VIDEO   📢 AUDIO
👁 MUST SEE!   💲 SELLS STUFF   ◈ ADULT CONTENT   🔍 SEARCHABLE
🗣 CHAT ROOMS   ⬇ MESSAGE BOARDS   📪 MAILING LISTS

Ships of the Fleet
www.twguild.com/sotf

Ships of the Fleet bills itself as "THE Place for Original Trek Fiction!" This designation is accurate. Large amounts of fan fiction can be found on this site, making it a must-visit for all those interested in reading more Trek adventures!

Shuttle Bay 5
www.geocities.com/Area51/Corridor/8109/sb5.htm

Alternate URL:　　www.geocities.com/Area51/Corridor/8109
Shuttle Bay 5 offers a little bit of everything. Trek-themed electronic postcards, videos, sounds, chat rooms, cursors, and wallpaper are all available on this site.

Sid City -
The Official Web Site of Alexander Siddig/Siddig El Faddil
www.sidcity.com

Sid City includes a biography, filmography, images and links to all things Alexander Siddig.

Six Degrees of William Shatner!
www.geocities.com/Area51/Rampart/4537/6degree.html

Similar to the 'Kevin Bacon Game," his site poses the question "How does William Shatner connect to other famous celebrities?" Simply input another celebrity's name and see what happens. The site claims that if you try it, "you'll see that Bill is the TRUE Center of The Universe!"

THE SOUND SECTOR

Sound Sector, The
www.geocities.com//Hollywood/6275/index.html

The Sound Sector focuses solely on sounds. The site has sounds for every Trek series and films. The site even offers a mailing list so you can be informed each time the site is updated.

Spiner's Domain
www.spiner.org

Alternate URL:　　www.spiner.org/main/fmain.htm
Spiner's Domain has everything a Brent Spiner/Data fan could want -- pictures, audio, a message board, a chat room, a mailing list and more! Plus, the site is well-organized and easy-to-read.

Spock's Pages $◀))

http://ourworld.compuserve.com/homepages/SpocksPages

Spock's Pages are the home of the Official European Leonard Nimoy Fan Club. The site offers information on Leonard Nimoy and Star Trek fonts, cursors and more available for download.

Star Trash

http://members.xoom.com/startrash

Instead of "Live long and prosper," this site advises its visitors to "Die young and poor." Filled with parodies, pictures and more, Star Trash is a riot! In one of the spoofs, Kirk tells Scotty -- "I wouldn't put you on a landing party to the nearest john."

Star Trek - The Collection ▦ ◉

www.geocities.com/Hollywood/Set/6458

Star Trek - The Collection is an amazing resource for fans. The site's incredibly well-organized and up close pictures from conventions and other Trek events, make this site almost as good as being there. Lots of pictures from the Vegas attraction and the in-the-trenches fan point of view add up to a "must-see site!"

Star Trek - The Collective ⚓ 📢 ▦

www.geocities.com/Area51/Dimension/9644

Star Trek - The Collective is a superior web site. It has an easy to use interface and offers a wide variety of material. You can chat with fans, read supplementary text and more.

Star Trek Action Figure List (Variations, Oddities & Rarities) ▦

http://hometown.aol.com/strtrkker/INDEXe.HTM

This site offers an extremely thorough examination of the Playmates series of Trek action figures and their many variants.

Star Trek Actors' Other Roles FAQ

www.cris.com/~Carman

This FAQ site is very well-organized. It offers television ratings information and cast member credits as well as those of guest stars.

▦ IMAGES   🎬 VIDEO   📢 AUDIO
◉ MUST SEE! $ SELLS STUFF   ◆ ADULT CONTENT   ♀ SEARCHABLE
📢 CHAT ROOMS ⬇ MESSAGE BOARDS ▣ MAILING LISTS

Star Trek Animated GIF Archive 🖼 ⚲

www.staga.force9.co.uk

Alternate URL: www.staga.force9.co.uk/ie.htm
This site bills itself as "the biggest collection of Star Trek Animated GIFs" on the Intent. The GIFs themselves are divided into sections such as Starfleet Ships, Alien Ships, Insignia, and Exclusive GIFs. At the time of this writing, hundreds of animated GIFs were available.

Star Trek Animated GIFs & Other Pictures 🖼

www.televar.com/~jsquelch/animated.html

This site only has a few images, principally from the original series. However, most are of excellent quality.

Star Trek Art Gallery

www.cjnetworks.com/~tfrazier/stgalery.html

Many excellent CGI original images of Star Trek can be found on this page.

Star Trek Character Gallery 🖼 👁

http://members.easyspace.com/stcg

The Star Trek Character Gallery has a combination image gallery/link list/filmography for almost every regular cast member of the four Trek series. You can find out where to send fan mail, explore links devoted to that star, and view images of him or her.

Star Trek Continuum 🗣 🖼 👁

www.startrek.com

This is the official Paramount site for Star Trek. Here, you can chat with fellow fans, participate in Trek-oriented surveys, read cast bios, and more!

Star Trek Empire: 3D Chess 📬

http://www2.cybercities.com/s/startreke/games/index.htm

This page offers instructions on how to play Trek's 3D version of chess.

Star Trek Frontier 🖼

www.geocities.com/Area51/Dimension/7551

Star Trek Frontier offers pictures and info for each of the television series as well as humor, images and text.

Star Trek Frontier: Alien Ships 🖼

www.geocities.com/Area51/Dimension/7551/classalien.html

This page has pictures of the alien starships of Star Trek.

Star Trek Frontier: Federation Starships 🖼

www.geocities.com/Area51/Dimension/7551/class.html

This page offers detailed information on the history of the particular starships listed.

Star Trek Frontier: Starfleet's General Orders

www.geocities.com/Area51/Dimension/7551/generalorders.html

This site lists the "General Orders" of Starfleet. These may be read for a greater understanding of the Star Trek universe, or they may be used to expand roleplaying possibilities.

Star Trek in Sound & Vision 🖼 🔊

www.stinsv.com

Star Trek in Sound & Vision bills itself as "The DEFINITIVE source on the net for

Star Trek WAV sounds, Windows Wallpaper, Icons, Screensavers and other files for customizing the Windows operating system." It's one of the most beautifully designed sites on the Web!

Star Trek Mail (multiple @ domains) $

www.startrekmail.com

Star Trek Mail offers customized, Trek-related e-mail addresses. Some are free (such as yourname@startrekmail.com) , and some will cost you (options include: yourname@startrek.com and yourname@klingons.com).

Star Trek Millenium 🖼

http://home.bip.net/s_t_m

Star Trek Millenium offers galleries for each of the Trek series and each starship.

🖼 IMAGES	🎬 VIDEO	🔊 AUDIO
👁 MUST SEE!	$ SELLS STUFF	ADULT CONTENT	🔍 SEARCHABLE
🗨 CHAT ROOMS	⬇ MESSAGE BOARDS	📬 MAILING LISTS

Star Trek Names

www.infocom.com/~franklin/startrek/names/welcome.htm

> This site lists names used in the various incarnations of Star Trek and their inspiration. Find out where a particular alien got its name, and how they came up with the name for some of the ships.

Star Trek News

www.geocities.com/Hollywood/6952

> Star Trek News is a well-presented news source. Everything from reviews to headlines to transcripts of chats with the stars online can be found on this site. Updated frequently, Star Trek News is an excellent first stop when searching for the latest in Trek info.

Star Trek Nexus

http://members.aol.com/treknexus

> Star Trek Nexus is a massive site. It offers news, convention information, and a tremendous amount of links to Trek-related sites.

Star Trek Page

www.geocities.com/Hollywood/4401

Languages: Portuguese
> The Star Trek Page is entirely in Portuguese. One nice feature for Portuguese-speaking fans is that it offers a Star Trek mailing list written in Portuguese.

Star Trek Photo Gallery

http://clgray.simplenet.com/strtrk

> The Star Trek Photo Gallery is one of the most eye-catching and beautifully designed Trek sites on the Web. The name of the site does not do it justice. Beyond images, the Star Trek Photo Gallery offers sound files, games, Windows themes, screensavers, icons, fan fiction and more!

Star Trek Portal ⬇ 🗣 🖼

www.strek.com

Although this site requires registration (which is free), it is customizable. You can choose whether to receive news on all or some of the current Trek television programs. You can add links to your personalized page. The strength of the Star Trek Portal is its ability to connect you with other fans. The site offers chat rooms, message boards and member profiles.

Star Trek Relationshipper's Station

www.geocities.com/~teepee47

Star Trek Relationshipper's Station is THE place to discuss the myriad of actual and possible relationships between the characters of the various Trek series.

Star Trek Ship Registry

www.nemonet.com/users/rclow/html/paddship1.htm

This listing of starships is sorted by starship class and alien race.

Star Trek Ships Expanded 🖼 ♀

www.cs.umanitoba.ca/~djc/startrek/ships.expanded.html

Star Trek Ships expanded provides the names and specifics of ships for the following Trek groups and races: Bajoran, Borg, Cardassian, Dominion, Federation, Ferengi, Kazon, Klingon, and Romulan. Some excellent pictures are included.

🖼 IMAGES   🎬 VIDEO   📢 AUDIO

👁 MUST SEE! $ SELLS STUFF   ✉ ADULT CONTENT   ♀ SEARCHABLE

🗣 CHAT ROOMS   ⬇ MESSAGE BOARDS   📪 MAILING LISTS

Star Trek Singularity ⌐▯ 🖾 ◁ঐ👁

http://sts.alphalink.com.au

The Star Trek Singularity is a valuable Trek resource offering just about anything and everything a Trek fan could want. With episode guide, RPG, votes, downloads, newsletter and extensive news and information resources, the Star Trek Singularity is a truly excellent site.

Star Trek Store $

www.startrekstore.com

The Star Trek Store offers Trek merchandise of every kind. Everything from standees to tribbles in jars to videos are available authorized and online. Start or complete your collection by visiting the Star Trek store.

Star Trek Stuff 🖾 ◁ঐ

http://members.xoom.com/Neelix

Although this site is no longer being updated, it offers many excellent images, fonts, icons, cursors, and MIDI files. Plus, the site includes a substantial amount of Trek humor.

Star Trek Stuff @ Trekplanet.Com 👣🖾👁

www.trekplanet.com/startrek.html

Star Trek Stuff has it all: screensavers, character profiles, JAVA games, image galleries, articles and more.

Star Trek sur Dav's Clone

www.multimania.com/davclone/star.html

Languages: French
This site contains information on the airing of Star Trek in France.

Star Trek TNG List of Lists 👁

www.ugcs.caltech.edu/st-tng/trivia/list.html

This site is truly fascinating. You can read a large number of lists of facts about the Next Generation. The lists include: "TOS Crossovers in TNG," episodes in which the "Enterprise Exceeds Warp Limits," and episodes in which the "Crew is Taken Over."

Star Trek Uniforms

www.geocities.com/Area51/Keep/7522

Star Trek Uniforms contains tutorials on how to make your own Trek Costumes!

Star Trek Utopia 🖼️ 🎬 🔊 👁️
www.geocities.com/Area51/Dimension/8041

Star Trek Utopia is one of most visually stimulating sites on the Internet. Precise graphics have been used to represent most buttons and you can even choose your own interface design -- choose from Ferengi, Borg, Federation and more!

Star Trek Voyager - Lower Decks
http://ljc.simplenet.com/lowerdecks

Archive of fan fiction centering on the crew of the USS Voyager outside of the senior staff. Includes crew manifest with picture and actor credit where available, individual cast/character pages for popular guest stars and recurring characters, rank and insignia chart, fanfic FAQ, essays, links, webring, message board, and more.

Star Trek: Genesis Sim Group 🖼️ 👁️
http://members.aol.com/stgenesis/index.htm

Star Trek: Genesis is a sim game lover's dream come true. With exciting graphics and in-depth how-to articles, Star Trek: Genesis makes simming exactly what it should be -- fun!

Star Trek: The Animated Series 🗣️ 🖼️ 🔊 👁️
http://mainengineering.simplenet.com/tas_main.html

This site is THE site for information about the animated version of Star Trek. The site has tons of multimedia from the animated series as well as a chat room and games!

Star Trek: The Caption Generation 🖼️
www.twguild.com/captions

On this site, you can view many images from all of the Trek series along with humorous captions submitted by fans. You can even browse by a particular series and vote for your favorite captions.

Star Trek: The Experience 📫 🖼️
www.startrekexp.com

This is the official site for the Trek-themed Vegas attraction. You can take a "virtual tour" and read more about Star Trek's Vegas venture.

🖼️ IMAGES   🎬 VIDEO   🔊 AUDIO
👁️ MUST SEE! $ SELLS STUFF   ◈ ADULT CONTENT   🔍 SEARCHABLE
🗣️ CHAT ROOMS   ⬇️ MESSAGE BOARDS   📫 MAILING LISTS

Star Trek: The Experience - at the Las Vegas Hilton 📷

www.pcap.com/startrek.htm

> From this page, you can view many photos and read a thorough description of Las Vegas' Star Trek attraction.

Star Trek: The Sci-Fi Channel Special Edition ⚓🗣📷

www.scifi.com/startrek

> The Sci-Fi Channel owns exclusive rights to show the uncut versions of the original Star Trek series. Thus, they have created an excellent web site to help you determine the show times for your area. At the bottom of the main page is the Sci-Fi Channel program guide. All you need to do is use the pop-up window to choose your time zone. In addition, the site offers messages boards (click on "Board") and a chat channel (click on "Chat").

Starbase 28: The Holonovel

www.geocities.com/~jacobjou/holonove.html

> The Holonovel is more than just fan fiction -- it is a "Choose Your Own Adventure"-type story online. According to the site, "You are Ensign Miller aboard the USS Imperial, a refit Excelsior-class Starship. You get to decide how the story unfolds."

STARBASE 721 📷🔊

http://Travel.To/Starbase721

> A starbase like no other, with plenty of pictures to download, Sounds (MIDI & WAV), Postcards, Chat Rooms, your own Starbase721 E-mail account, the TrekLink Webring, and much MUCH MORE!

Starbase SDL (Starship Design Library)

http://beam.at/StarbaseSDL

> SDL is a starbase-style site that features a starship building program and shows fan made starship designs.

Starbase Vegas 📷

www.vegaslounge.com/startrek

> Starbase Vegas provides detailed coverage of the opening of Star Trek: The Experience in Las Vegas. The site includes several excellent photographs of the stars that showed up for the grand opening.

Starbase Vegas: FAQ

www.vegaslounge.com/startrek/questions.html

> This site offers a map to Las Vegas' Star Trek: The Experience and answers frequently asked questions about the Trek-themed attraction.

Starbase-1 $👁

www.starbase-1.com

The PLACE to get your Star Trek gourmet foods and coffee is Starbase-1. Check out their Raktajino -- it's the perfect drink for any Star Trek gathering!

Starchive, The

www.cs.umanitoba.ca/~djc/startrek

The Starchive presents many Trek-related Usenet documents in an easier to read format. The text has been cleaned up and fonts changed to make your reading of them much more pleasant.

STARFLEET - The International Star Trek Fan Association 👁

www.sfi.org

According to the site itself, "STARFLEET, founded by Star Trek enthusiasts in the year 1974, is an organization whose members (4000+) are united the world over in their appreciation of Star Trek: The Greatest Human Adventure. Hundreds of chapters worldwide link members into local fandom as well as the International organization."

Starfleet Collective Database 📬 ⬇

http://lcars.simplenet.com

Alternate URL: http://lcars.simplenet.com/index3.htm
The Starfleet Collective Database offers news, message boards and links to everything Star Trek. The links section is searchable, and the message boards are extensive.

Starfleet Database 📬 ⬇ 🗣 🖼 🔊

http://www2.prestel.co.uk/majeed

Alternate URL: http://ourworld.compuserve.com/homepages/Amjad_Majeed
The Starfleet Database offers online chat, mailing lists, message boards, downloads, news and more.

🖼 IMAGES	🎬 VIDEO	🔊 AUDIO
👁 MUST SEE!	$ SELLS STUFF	📦 ADULT CONTENT	🔍 SEARCHABLE
🗣 CHAT ROOMS	⬇ MESSAGE BOARDS	📬 MAILING LISTS

Starfleet Headquarters 🖼️ 🎞️ 🔊

http://home.earthlink.net/~cobarry

Alternate URL: http://home.earthlink.net/~cobarry/mainmenu.html
Starfleet Headquarters has a multitude of image, audio, video and software files that you can download.

Starfleet Missions II 🖼️ 👁️

www.amtc.net/users/~ziroc/sfm2p/index.htm

Starfleet Missions is a 3D rendered, fan written Trek comic book-like series. The graphics alone are incredible.

Starfleet Supply 🖼️

www.geocities.com/Area51/Stargate/7952

The Starfleet Supply site includes a page on the history of the Borg, a page dedicated to Jadzia Dax and a page of Trek humor.

Steve's Trek Page: Adopt a Trek Pet 🖼️

http://soli.inav.net/~nibblink/adptmain.htm

Adopt a Trek Pet gives you the opportunity to adopt a tribble, targ, or lematya. You get to name your pet and download an image of it. You can even put the image on your own web site!

Steve's Trek Page: Klingon Weapons Database 🖼️

http://soli.inav.net/~nibblink/klingon.htm

By visiting this page, you can examine the weapons used by the mighty Klingons. Choose between swords and disruptors to begin your studies. Detailed pictures make learning your Klingon weapons a virtual snap.

Steve's Trek Page: Language Database

http://soli.inav.net/~nibblink/dictnary.htm

This site is truly amazing. Have you ever wanted to learn how to say "love" in Bajoran? Ever want to know how the Klingon language is structured? If so, simply visit this site. You can view dictionaries (English to the alien language as well as the alien language to English). In addition, there are also lexicons available to instruct on the grammar of a particular alien language. Some of the languages discussed include: Borg, Cardassian, Ferengi and Trill.

Steve's Trek Page: Medical Database

http://soli.inav.net/~nibblink/medical.htm

This site offers information on the medical conditions experienced by the alien races of Star Trek. Entries include Bajoran, Borg, Cardassian, Founders, Ferengi, Jem'Hadar, Klingon, Romulans, Trill, Vorta and Vulcan diseases.

Style Ocampa: The Clothes & Times of Kes 🖼👁

www.geocities.com/Area51/Corridor/6466/Ocampa.html

Style Ocampa is an exceedingly in-depth look at every outfit worn by Kes during her character's stay on Voyager. Each outfit is illustrated and the number of episodes in which it appeared is mentioned.

Subspace Communications 📫📥🗣

http://subspace.virtualave.net

Alternate URL: http://subspace.virtualave.net/index.html
Subspace Communications is a great place to chat with others about Star Trek. They offer chat rooms, message boards, mailing lists and more.

Subspace Databank $

http://subspace.virtualave.net/databank/index.html

Subspace Databank offers Star Trek books, videos, CDs and DVDs for purchase.

SubSpaceMail.Com

www.subspacemail.com

Get your free @subspacemail.com e-mail address here!

T'Pring's Spock Page 🖼

http://members.tripod.com/~tpring

T'Pring's Spock Page offers a biography of Spock as well as a great deal of images.

🖼 IMAGES   🎬 VIDEO   📢 AUDIO

👁 MUST SEE! $ SELLS STUFF   📦 ADULT CONTENT   🔍 SEARCHABLE

🗣 CHAT ROOMS   📥 MESSAGE BOARDS   📫 MAILING LISTS

Targ TV

http://members.aol.com/LaurThur/TARGTV.html

Ever wonder what Klingon television might be like? WWF wrestling 24-hours a day (or however long it takes for the Klingon homeworld to orbit its star)? Well, check out this site for a fun portrait of what you might see on Klingon Television.

Ten Forward Lounge 📺 🎬 🔊

www.interlog.com/~pcarr/star_trek/home.html

The focus of Ten Forward Lounge is on the poker scenes in Star Trek: The Next Generation. On the site, you will find plenty of video clips and sound files from the poker games of the Enterprise-D.

The Chief Helmsman's Quarters 🔊

www.geocities.com/Area51/Capsule/1494/index.html

The Chief Helmsman's Quarters is dedicated to Star Trek Voyager, featuring Tom Paris and B'Elanna Torres. This site includes a fan fiction archive, pictures, biographies on the characters, fan art, links, web rings, a webmasters area, and sounds.

The World of EBE1 📺 🔊

www.geocities.com/Area51/Shadowlands/3306

Alternate URL: www.geocities.com/Area51/Shadowlands/3306/mainpage.html
This site is devoted to The X-Files, Star Trek: Voyager, and Madonna. What an anomaly! It has audio clips of Madonna's songs, and a gallery of X-Files images.

Thomas Models $

www.thomasmodels.com

According to the site's main page, Thomas Models is "your source for truly authentic resin and vacu-form Trek type model kits. Authenticity and ease of assembly is our primary goal . . . We hope that you will find our products of superior quality with special attention to detail and craftsmanship."

Tommy of Escondido's Alien Fonts Page

www.geocities.com/TimesSquare/4965

This site offers a wide array of downloadable fonts based on many popular science fiction series. In addition to Star Trek, the site provides fonts related to Star Wars and Babylon 5.

Total Eclipse Productions

http://thunderchild.simplenet.com

The Total Eclipse site is a lot of fun. Fans can find 3D Mesh Downloads as well as Operation Pathfinder II.

TrekArchive.Com

www.trekarchive.com

If you love video files, you'll love the TrekArchive.com. AVI, QuickTime, MPEG and Real Video files are all categorized by series and available for download.

IMAGES   VIDEO   AUDIO

MUST SEE! $ SELLS STUFF   ADULT CONTENT   SEARCHABLE

CHAT ROOMS   MESSAGE BOARDS   MAILING LISTS

Trek City

http://trekcity2.virtualave.net

Trek City 2 Web Services offers free CGI hosting for the Star Trek Community as well as many other web services.

Trek City Guestbooks

http://romulan.virtualave.net/services/gb

Are you the webmaster of a Trek-related web site? Interested in becoming one? If so, visit Trek City Guestbooks for a free, Trek-oriented guestbook.

Trek Files   Your Source For
                      Star Trek Files!

Trek Files 📷◀))) ⚲ 👁

http://trekfiles.strek.com

Trek Files is THE place to find Star Trek software! Everything from desktop themes to games to wallpaper is available from Trek Files. Always wanted your computer screen to look like the Bridge? Well, make it so with Trek Files!

Trek Galaxy: Star Trek 10

http://user.super.net.uk/~nikolas/startrek10.htm

Trek Galaxy's Star Trek 10 is an amazingly up-to-date, well-organized and informative site designed for anyone interested in the latest news regarding the tenth Trek film. If the news breaks, you'll probably find it here.

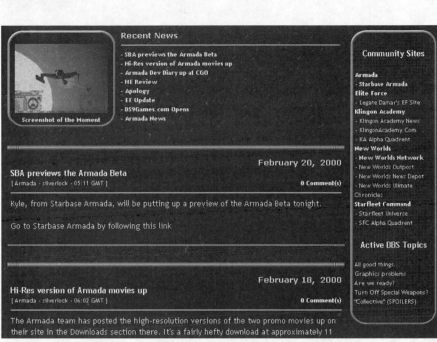

Trek Gaming Alliance ⬇ ⚲

www.trekgaming.com

The Trek Gaming Alliance is designed to be a resource for Trek-oriented gamers. The site offers message boards and news.

Trek Sites ⚲ 👁

www.treksites.com

Trek Sites is a subject directory devoted to Star Trek. Beautiful to view and smartly done, Trek Sites makes an excellent start page for your browser. With categories such as fan fiction, multimedia, and non-English sites, you can find even more Trek sites to visit as well as promote your own!

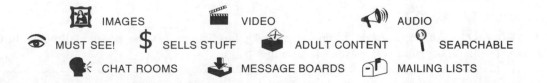

IMAGES   VIDEO   AUDIO

MUST SEE! $ SELLS STUFF   ADULT CONTENT   SEARCHABLE

CHAT ROOMS   MESSAGE BOARDS   MAILING LISTS

Trek Worlds 🖼️ 🔊

www.geocities.com/Area51/Zone/2200

Trek Worlds offers a wide array of images, including many excellent sources of wallpaper. It also provides software, links and more.

Trek Worlds: Odo's Security Font Files

www.geocities.com/Area51/Zone/3000/index_fonts.htm

This page has an amazing collection of fonts. Trill, Vulcan, Ferengi, Cardassian and even non-Trek sci-fi fonts are available.

Trek Writer's Guild ⬇️

www.twguild.com

The Trek Writer's Guild is filled with Trek-related stories and scripts written by fans for fans. The site even gives descriptions of the words and honors the best stories with "outstanding achievement" awards.

TrekExpress.Com 🗣️ 🔍

www.trekexpress.com

TrekExpress.Com offers Star Trek forums, chat, links, fan fiction, surveys, gossip and more! In the future, TrekExpress plans to offer Trek site hosting.

Address http://www.angelfire.com/nc/TrekkerOne/index.html

Navigation

Home Page

Pictures

Sounds

Chat

Humor

My Collection

Trekker One

www.angelfire.com/nc/TrekkerOne/index.html

Trekker One is a fun site that includes the latest info on upcoming conventions, a nice gallery, chat rooms and more!

Trekker One: Trekker Five: Star Trek Humor

www.angelfire.com/nc/TrekkerFive/index.html

Trekker One's Trek humor page offers pictures, lists, bloopers and sound files all with a humorous bent to them.

Trekker One: Trekker Three: Star Trek Sounds

www.angelfire.com/nc/TrekkerThree/index.html

Trekker One's sounds page includes WAV files of some of Trek's special effects and clips from the shows themselves. The page also offers MIDI files of Star Trek music.

Trekkie Register

www.datania.com/trek-reg/trekreg_frm.htm

The Trekkie Register is an attempt to list the name and e-mail address of every Star Trek fan. You can register yourself as well as find other fans to correspond with simply by visiting this site.

IMAGES   VIDEO   AUDIO

MUST SEE! $ SELLS STUFF   ADULT CONTENT   SEARCHABLE

CHAT ROOMS   MESSAGE BOARDS   MAILING LISTS

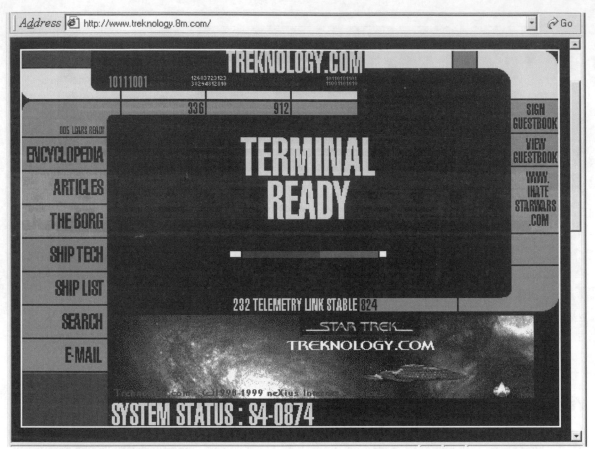

Treknology.Com

www.treknology.8m.com

Treknology.Com's focus is, as its name implies, on the technology of Star Trek. Visit this site to read in-depth essays on everything "treknological," including warp engines, planets and more.

TrekToday.Com 👁

www.trektoday.com

TrekToday.Com bills itself as "The first and only daily updated guide to all things Trek." From the looks of it, TrekToday.Com is updated on a daily basis, and the news is presented in a easy-to-read format. Bookmark this page to stay on top of Trek news.

TrekWeb.com ⬇$🗣🔖

www.trekweb.com

TrekWeb.com is an excellent site for Star Trek news. The site also sells Star Trek books.

Tuvok Secret Agent Man

www.geocities.com/Area51/Lair/4979/disguise.html

Mr. Potatoehead and the Colorforms attack the starship Voyager! Well, not the ship, but they certainly seem to get hold of the chief of security -- Mr. Tuvok. See Tuvok morph into Michael Jackson, a pirate of the Caribbean, and more on this wacky site.

UCESS - United Coalition of Earthwide Starfleet Simulations

$ 🗣 🎬 📢

www.geocities.com/Area51/Rampart/4776/ucess.html

Alternate URL: www.geocities.com/Area51/Rampart/4776/index2.html

The webmasters of UCESS describe it as a "union of independent Star Trek simulations. Each ship sims with us by choice, realizing the mutual benefits to both the ship and organization, by utilizing this web site. For the ship's crews, the UCESS hosts a variety of ways to sim, instructional lessons and pages for new recruits, an easy and quick way to read/post logs, multimedia access, ship's homepages, technical information, and so much more." Plus, non-roleplayers can read the site's crew logs, because those who play are required to record their adventures.

Uhura.Com $ 🖼

www.uhura.com

Alternate URL: www.uhura.com/nf/greetings.htm

This is the official site for Nichelle Nichols' character, Uhura. The site includes writings by Nichols as well as images of the star. Uhura.com also gives you the opportunity to purchase autographs, fashions and music from Nichelle Nichols.

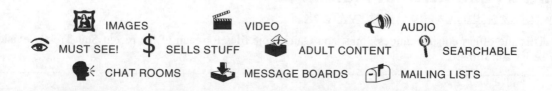

🖼 IMAGES	🎬 VIDEO	🔊 AUDIO	
👁 MUST SEE!	$ SELLS STUFF	📦 ADULT CONTENT	🔍 SEARCHABLE
🗣 CHAT ROOMS	📥 MESSAGE BOARDS	📪 MAILING LISTS	

UK's Star Trek Stories, Artwork, Links & More! 🖼

www.geocities.com/SoHo/Atrium/2560

As its name implies, this site offers a great deal of fan-generated Trek material. Excellent fan fiction and artwork awaits all those who visit. To read the stories, scroll in the left-hand frame until you reach the "Stories" section.

Ultimate Star Trek Collection 🖼 ⚲ 👁

http://startrek.fns.net.fsn.net

The Ultimate Star Trek Collection is massive. Everything from Star Trek humor to images to WinAmp skins can be found on this well-organized site. The starship and uniform sections are infinitely enjoyable.

Ultimate Star Trek Graphic Gallery, The 🔊

www.geocities.com/Area51/Corridor/4914/index1.html

This site has an incredible gallery. It even includes pictures of cast members without make-up side-by-side with their pictures in full alien attire. The Ultimate Star Trek Graphic Gallery also has images of cast autographs as well as pictures from Deep Space Nine and Voyager.

United Federation of Kids 👁

www.ufk.org

The United Federation for Kids is, as the site states, "the first and largest kids Star Trek fan club."

United Federation of Phoenix 👁

www.U-F-P.org

The United Federation of Phoenix is arguably the third oldest continuously active Star Trek club in the country (Behind the Boston Star Trek Association and Starfleet Intl). They are a Phoenix, Arizona, independent Star Trek and general SciFi fan club that meets 2 weeks, usually on Saturdays.

United Federation of Planets 🎬

www.gh.cs.su.oz.au/~matty/Trek

This site offers episode guides, links, and QuickTime files for each of the recent Star Trek television series and films.

Untitled Star Trek (I)

http://aia.wu-wien.ac.at/Startrek/Archiv/autogrammadressen.html

This German site presents addresses to which you may write the stars of the Trek series to request an autograph.

USS Aurora

www.geocities.com/TimesSquare/4818/trek.htm

The USS Aurora lists the airdates of upcoming Star Trek episodes. It also has essays on Trek and a list of technobabble terms.

USS Concordant

http://goliat.eik.bme.hu/~wraith

This site includes detailed information about all three of the recent Star Trek television series.

USS Dreadnought ▨

http://welcome.to/dreadnought

Alternate URL: http://members.xoom.com/_XOOM/Dreadnought/index.html
By clicking on "General Overview," you can see images and specs for the USS Dreadnought, a fan-created starship.

USS Enterprise 1701-G ▨

www.geocities.com/Area51/Vault/5990

The USS Enterprise 1701-G has photos from both Star Trek: The Next Generation and Star Trek: First Contact.

▨ IMAGES   🎬 VIDEO   🔊 AUDIO

👁 MUST SEE! $ SELLS STUFF   ⬥ ADULT CONTENT   💡 SEARCHABLE

🗣 CHAT ROOMS   ⬇ MESSAGE BOARDS   📫 MAILING LISTS

USS Enterprise Memorial ⬚

www.geocities.com/Area51/Rampart/4777

Alternate URL: www.geocities.com/Area51/Rampart/4777
Languages: English, Portuguese
    The USS Enterprise Memorial is a beautiful site. The graphics are excellent, and the site is well-organized. Each version of the Enterprise (1701 through 1701-E) is given its own page of images. Plus, the site includes some incredible images of alien ships.

USS Hope 👁

www.uss-hope.freeserve.co.uk/index.html

    The USS Hope is perhaps one of the best play-by-email sites. Its design is beautiful and joining the game is easy, simply click on "Join" and type in your e-mail address.

USS Hornet NCC-1714: Stellar Cartography ⬚

www.geocities.com/SiliconValley/Way/3761/stellarcartography.html

    Stellar Cartography's focus is on maps and animations of celestial objects related to Star Trek. Many excellent images can be found here making this site well worth a visit.

USS Jaguar ⬚

www.worldkids.net/jaguar

Alternate URL: www.worldkids.net/jaguar/turbolift.html
    This site dubs itself a "starship for kids." True to its word, the site is run by a teenager, and in order to join the ships crew you must be under 18.

USS Missouri ⚓ 🖼

`http://members.tripod.com/~stidham/missouri.htm`

The USS Missouri presents fan fiction written about the crew of a starship of the same name. Click on "Mission Logs" to read the adventures, and see how each "episode" is given its own stylized logo and poster!

USS Prometheus ⚓ 🖼 👁

`www.geocities.com/Area51/Rampart/3448/index.html`

The USS Prometheus is a truly fun site to visit. There are many original pages, including trivia quizzes, essays, tributes, surveys, reviews and more. The majority of the site is devoted to Voyager, but there is some Deep Space Nine and Next Generation content as well.

USS Quetzalcoatl 👁

`http://members.xoom.com/Tona_Q/NCC-20942`

Languages: Spanish, English
The USS Quetzalcoatl covers every Star Trek series, including the animated version and feature films. Plus, it offers technological commentary and essays.

USS Quetzalcoatl: Star Trek Universe 🖼

`http://members.xoom.com/_XOOM/Tona_Q/NCC-20942/trek-e.htm`

USS Quetzalcoatl's guide to the Star Trek Universe is an excellent primer for those who confused by the massive amount of Trek media that exists. The site discusses what is considered canon and gives information on the series' creators.

USS Repulse NCC-2544

`http://uss-repulse.starfleet.com/home.html`

Alternate URL: `http://uss-repulse.starfleet.com/Repulse/bridge.html`
The USS Repulse is truly a unique Star Trek site. It doesn't really have much Star Trek content. Rather it is a subject directory of useful Internet sites. However, the site's entire interface is Star Trek-based. Therefore, you can navigate the Web as though you were pressing the buttons on a Starfleet starship.

USS Roo 🖼️🔊

www.geocities.com/Area51/4948

The USS Roo is a basically an interactive starship. You can even adjust the controls.

USS Victory NCC-67019 🖼️

www.angelfire.com/al/alphafleet

USS Victory presents many detailed images of the set for Star Trek: Voyager.

USS Voyager Crew Manifest
A joint effort of
Steve's Trek Page &
Star Trek the Collective

Original Crew Complement: 141
Additional Maquis Crew Members: 19 (13)
Additional Delta Quadrant Crew Members: 10 (-3)
Total Known Deceased: 21
Current Crew Complement: (as of "Equinox") 132 (16)
How many we've got so far: 107

Name and Rank	Maquis?	Department	Species	Status	Seen in
Regular Crew Members					
Captain Kathryn Janeway	SF	Command	Human	-	Caretaker - present
Commander Chakotay	MQ	Command	Human	-	Caretaker - present
Lieutenant Commander Tuvok	SF	Security	Vulcan (14)	Promoted	Caretaker - present
Ensign Harry Kim	SF	Operations	Human	-	Caretaker - present
Ensign Tom Paris	SF (Captured Maquis)	Helm & Medical	Human	Demoted	Caretaker - present
Lieutenant B'Elanna Torres	MQ	Engineering	Human + Klingon hybrid	-	Caretaker - present
Neelix	-	Civilian	Various	Talaxian	Caretaker - present
Emergency Medical Hologram (EMH)	SF	Medical	Computer generated hologram	Program fixed for long-term use, can travel freely	Caretaker - present

USS Voyager Crew Log

http://soli.inav.net/~nibblink/pages/voycrew.html

The USS Voyager Crew Log presents an incredibly detailed list of the crew of Voyager. Given that the ship is too far from earth to receive reinforcements, keeping track of the finite crew is fascinating.

Utopia Planitia Starship Database 🖼️

http://utopia.solareclipse.net

The Utopia Planitia Starship Database is a must-see for all die-hard Star Trek fans. It lists the names of all the starships mentioned or seen within the Star Trek realm. The list includes the class of starship as well as its status. For those who are into Star Trek roleplaying, this site is an invaluable resource. Major classes, such as the Intrepid, Galaxy and Excelsior classes are given their own page with full specs and history.

Address 🔘 http://www.sttc.co.uk/feat-jny.html

Voyager Journey Guide

Voyager is a lot closer to home than you'd think. Here's the journey breakdown:

Episode	Comments	Distance Left to Earth
"Caretaker"	Pilot episode - Voyager is thrown 70,000 light years into the Delta Quadrant.	**70,000 LY**
Seasons 1-3	If it will take them 70 years to get home, that's an average 1,000 light years travelling each year.	- 1,000LY * 3... **67,000 LY**
"The Gift" (Episode 4-02)	Kes throws Voyager beyond Borg space.	-10,000 LY... **57,000 LY**
"Year of Hell, Part 1" (Episode 4-08)	The new Astrometrics Lab helps Seven plot a new course for Voyager, shaving 5,000 LY off their journey.	-5,000 LY... **52,000 LY**
Season 4	An extra year of travel	-1,000 LY... **51,000 LY**
"Hope and Fear" (Episode 4-26)	Voyager uses quantum slipstream drive from the *Dauntless* to hop an extra 300 LY before the drive conks out.	-300 LY **50,700 LY**
"Night" (Episode 5-01)	The ship uses a wormhole to get themselves out of the void.	-2,500 LY... **48,200 LY**
"Timeless"	Kim's efforts to use the slipstream again make Voyager crash at first but later they get a little success. I'm not sure of the figure...	-10,000 LY... **38,200 LY**
"Dark Frontier"	Janeway steals a transwarp drive from you-know-who, and makes their most successful jump yet.	-15,000 LY... **22,200 LY**
Season 5	Now finished in the States, so that's another 1000LY.	-1000 LY... **21,200 LY**

At 21,200 LY to go, really Voyager is now well out of the Delta Quadrant and is just passing or exiting the galactic core. They still have quite a way to go to the Romulans and the Federation (the Federation spans 8000 LY, so it's roughly 4000 from the edge to the centre which is around Earth).

Voyager Journey Guide

www.sttc.co.uk/feat-jny.html

The Voyager Journey Guide plots the course of the off-course Voyager. It details instances wherein the ship has managed to shave light years off of its journey toward Federation space. Plus, it lists the current distance between Voyager and Earth.

Wally's Weird Star Trek Tribute 🔊

www.wallys.com/startrek/startrek.htm

Wally's Weird Star Trek Tribute has many funny Star Trek WAV sounds you can download for use on your PC.

WarpMail

http://warpmail.enterwarp.com

Visit WarpMail to get your own @warpmail.zzn.com e-mail address.

Webtrekker 🗣🔊

www.geocities.com/Area51/Rampart/8138/webtreker.html

Alternate URL: www.geocities.com/Area51/Rampart/8138/webtreker.html
    Webtrekker offers Star Trek chat, blooper videos, sounds and more. The site also includes animation.

🅰 IMAGES		🎬 VIDEO		🔊 AUDIO	
👁 MUST SEE!	$ SELLS STUFF		🔷 ADULT CONTENT		🔍 SEARCHABLE
🗣 CHAT ROOMS		📥 MESSAGE BOARDS		📬 MAILING LISTS	

WilliamShatner.Com $

www.williamshatner.com

WilliamShatner.Com has very little to do with the actor mentioned in its domain name. Rather, the purpose of this site is to sell pre-paid phone cards decorated with Trek images.

Wolf359 🎴 👁

http://members.aol.com/wolfpak359

Wolf359's pages are filled with Star Trek, Babylon 5 and Star Wars 3D graphics. The images are incredibly realistic and well-worth viewing.

Wonderful World of Star Trek, The 🎴 🔊

www.geocities.com/Area51/Corridor/4584

The Wonderful World of Star Trek has several pictures and some sounds of the Next Generation cast. The sounds include some from Worf, the computer, and Q.

Worf's Star Trek Page

Worf's Star Trek Site

www.bazza.com/sj/trek

This site offers a tremendous amount of links to FAQs, newsgroups, and web sites. It also has a lot of Star Trek humor (including "Your captain might be a redneck if . . ."). Plus, the site has a large collection of quotes from all of the television series and films. To access the quotes, click on Quotes on the main page.

Worf's Star Trek Site: Ferengi Rules of Acquisition

www.bazza.com/sj/trek/ferengi.html

On this page you can read the Ferengi Rules of Acquisition.

Worf's Star Trek Site: Ode to Spot

www.bazza.com/sj/trek/ode.html

This page presents the full text of Data's poem, "Ode to Spot."

World-Wide Collectors Digest: Star Trek Conventions

www.wwcd.com/shows/trek-home.html

This site lists all you need to know about upcoming Trek conventions. The information listed includes dates, locations, ticket costs, guest star appearances, and a phone number for more information.

Yahoo! . . . Star Trek

http://dir.yahoo.com/News_and_Media/Television/Genres/Science_Fiction__Fantasy__and_Horror/Star_Trek

Yahoo! has compiled a list of Star Trek sites. The sites are organized by the particular show as well as categories such as Episode Guides, Scripts and Soundtracks.

Yahoo! Internet Life: The Star Trek Universe Online

www.zdnet.com/yil/content/mag/9812/trek.html

Yahoo!'s Internet Life section on Star Trek is impressive. There are interviews with the cast of Star Trek: Insurrection. There is also a segment on the Best Star Trek Love Scenes.

Yahoo! Internet Life: Star Trek Special: Spiner Speaks

www.zdnet.com/yil/content/mag/startrek/spiner9612a.html

In this interview with Yahoo! Internet Life, Brent Spiner discusses the Internet and sites devoted to him.

You Can't Do That on Star Trek!

http://washington.xtn.net/~philipb/youcant.htm

You Can't Do That on Star Trek is a unique gallery site, offering images of Star Trek characters mixed with characters from other sci-fi series and more! The site has received a lot of awards, including Yahoo's Red Sunglasses, and was mentioned by William Shatner in his book, Get a Life.

IMAGES   VIDEO   AUDIO   MUST SEE! $ SELLS STUFF   ADULT CONTENT   SEARCHABLE   CHAT ROOMS   MESSAGE BOARDS   MAILING LISTS

YSK's Star Trek Page

www.geocities.com/Area51/Corridor/3546

The software section of YSK's Star Trek Page (accessed by clicking the "Downlo." link), includes a calendar program and an English to Klingon translator. The site also includes information on Star Trek in Israel. The site focuses primarily on the Next Generation series, but it does include some info about the other shows as well.

STAR TREK
Stardate
Listing

"Captain's log, stardate . . ." should be familiar words to any trekker. Yet, these dates are not simply random numbers. The producers and writers of Star Trek in all of its various incarnations have used stardates as a frame of reference for the characters and the fans.

For the collector and those interested in a chronology of the Star Trek universe, stardates are crucial. However, most stardate lists in existence only include one or two incarnations of Star Trek (i.e. just the stardates for the television episodes, etc.). The existing lists are not very useful for someone trying to read and watch his or her entire Star Trek collection in chronological order. As such, as a special bonus for Trekkers, this section offers something you won't find online -- a list of stardates from all five television series (including the animated version), the films, the comic books, and the novels.

A few things to keep in mind . . .

Not every episode, comic book, novel, etc. was given a stardate. Therefore, most of those that were not given a stardate have been left out of this list.

Others (designated with an M after the stardate) were given made-up stardates relative to their position in the history of the Star Trek universe.

This list is not complete, so please, if you have any additions or corrections, send them to `Trek_Changes@klingons.zzn.com`, so that we may include them in the next edition.

About the comic book series . . .

Several companies have had the license to produce Trek-based comics, and as such, keeping up with these titles can be confusing. For example, "Early Voyages" was the title of a series of comic books produced by Marvel. The stories of these comics take place during Christopher Pike's tenure as captain of the USS Enterprise. Use the series, company and number columns of the Stardate Listing to determine which issue is listed. For instance, the first line of the table refers to the first issue of Marvel's Early Voyages series.

About the novels . . .

Two companies have produced Trek fiction -- Pocket Books and Bantam. Most of the books have been published by Pocket Books. Use the company column to determine which publisher published the book listed. Keep in mind there are some books that have only been released in hardcover format.

About the series & films . . .

The number in the number column refers to the production number for the episode or the order in which it takes place in the film (for example, Wrath of Kahn has 002 in the number column because it was the second Trek film). Also, the company column is blank for all film and series list entries. Paramount is the company responsible for all the films and series. The absence of data in the company column makes it easier to spot which list entries are viewable and which are textual (Textual items -- comic books and novels -- have data in the company column).

Stardate	Series	Story Title	Company	Number
00225.2340	Early Voyages	*Flesh of My Flesh*	Marvel	001
00237.81	Early Voyages	*The Fires of Pharos*	Marvel	002
00238.57	Early Voyages	*Our Dearest Blood*	Marvel	003
00238.61M	Original Series	*The Cage*		001
00238.63M	Early Voyages	*Nor Iron Bars a Cage*	Marvel	004
00239.45M	Early Voyages	*Cloak & Dagger, Part I*	Marvel	005
00239.66	Early Voyages	*Cloak & Dagger, Part II*	Marvel	006
00259.9	Early Voyages	*The Flat, Gold Forever*	Marvel	007
00360.3	Early Voyages	*Immortal Wounds*	Marvel	008
00361.6	Early Voyages	*One of a Kind*	Marvel	009
00371.2	Early Voyages	*The Fallen, Part I*	Marvel	010
00371.7	Early Voyages	*The Fallen, Part II*	Marvel	011
00389.4	Early Voyages	*Futures, Part I*	Marvel	012
01245.4	Animated Series	*The Magicks of Megas-Tu*		009
01312.4	Original Series	*Where No Man Has Gone Before*		002
01329.8	Original Series	*Mudd's Women*		004
01512.2	Original Series	*The Corbomite Maneuver*		003
01513.1	Original Serles	*The Man Trap*		006
01533.6	Original Series	*Charlie X*		008
01672.1	Original Series	*The Enemy Within*		005
01704.2	Original Series	*The Nake Time*		007
01709.2	Original Series	*Balance of Terror*		009

Stardate	Series	Story Title	Company	Number
01927.4	Original Series	*The Psychocrystals*	Whitman	
02124.5	Original Series	*The Squire of Gothos*		018
02213.5	Original Series	*Rules of Engagement*	Pocket	048
02712.4	Original Series	*What Are Little Girls Made Of?*		010
02713.5	Original Series	*Miri*		012
02715.1	Original Series	*Dagger of the Mind*		011
02817.6	Original Series	*The Conscience of the King*		013
02821.5	Original Series	*The Galileo Seven*		014
02947.3	Original Series	*Court Martial*		015
03005.1	Original Series	*No Compromise, Part II*	DC (Vol. 2)	059
03012.4	Original Series	*The Menagerie, Part I*		016
03013.1	Original Series	*The Menagerie, Part II*		016
03018.2	Original Series	*Catspaw*		030
03025.3	Original Series	*Shore Leave*		017
03045.6	Original Series	*Arena*		019
03087.6	Original Series	*The Alternative Factor*		020
03113.2	Original Series	*Tomorrow Is Yesterday*		021
03125.3	Original Series	*Web of the Romulans*	Pocket	010
03127.1	Original Series	*The Tears of the Singers*	Pocket	019
03141.9	Original Series	*Space Seed*		024
03156.2	Original Series	*The Return of the Archons*		022

A - Comic Book Annual   **FB** - Flashback in Comic Book   **M** - Made-up Stardate

Stardate	Series	Story Title	Company	Number
03183.3	Animated Series	*Practical Joker*		021
03192.1	Original Series	*A Taster of Armageddon*		023
03196.1	Original Series	*The Devil in the Dark*		026
03198.4	Original Series	*Errand of Mercy*		027
03211.7	Original Series	*The Gamesters of Triskelion*		046
03219.8	Original Series	*Metamorphosis*		031
03287.2	Original Series	*Operation: Annihilate!*		029
03372.7	Original Series	*Amok Time*		034
03417.3	Original Series	*This Side of Paradise*		025
03451.9	Original Series	*The Changeling*		037
03468.1	Original Series	*Who Mourns for Adonais?*		033
03471.4	Original Series	*Retrospect (Flashback)*	DC (Vol. 1)	A3-FB
03478.2	Original Series	*The Deadly years*		040
03497.2	Original Series	*Friday's Child*		032
03614.9	Original Series	*Wolf in the Fold*		036
03619.2	Original Series	*Obsession*		047
03715.3	Original Series	*The Apple*		038
03842.3	Original Series	*Journey to Babel*		044
03948.6	Original Series	*Faces of Fire*	Pocket	058
04040.7	Original Series	*Bread and Circuses*		043
04187.3	Animated Series	*Slaver Weapon*		011
04211.4	Original Series	*A Private Little War*		045

Stardate	Series	Story Title	Company	Number
04307.1	Original Series	*The Immunity Syndrome*		048
04372.5	Original Series	*Elaan of Troyius*		057
04385.3	Original Series	*Spectre of the Gun*		056
04496.1	Original Series	*The Galactic Whirlpool*	Bantam	
04513.3	Original Series	*I, Mudd*		041
04523.3	Original Series	*The Trouble with Tribbles*		042
04657.5	Original Series	*By Any Other Name*		050
04720.1	Original Series	*Klingon Gambit*	Pocket	003
04729.4	Original Series	*The Ultimate Computer*		053
04740.5	Star Trek/X-Men	*Star Trek/X-Men*	Marvel	
04768.3	Original Series	*Return to Tomorrow*		051
04769.1	Original Series	*Mutiny on the Enterprise*	Pocket	012
04842.6	Original Series	*Paradise Syndrome*		058
04925.2	Original Series	*Double, Double*	Pocket	045
04978.5	Animated Series	*Mudd's Passion*		008
04997.54	Original Series	*Cornoa*	Pocket	015
05027.3	Original Series	*Enterprise Incident*		059
05029.5	Original Series	*And the Children Shall Lead*		060
05049.2	Original Series	*The Unforgiven*	DC (Vol. 2)	A3
05064.4	Original Series	*Abode of Life*	Pocket	006
05121.5	Original Series	*The Empath*		063

A - Comic Book Annual   **FB** - Flashback in Comic Book   **M** - Made-up Stardate

Stardate	Series	Story Title	Company	Number
05143.3	Animated Series	*The Survivor*		005
05258.7	Original Series	*Legacy*	Pocket	056
05267.2	Animated Series	*The Time Trap*		010
05268.1	Original Series	*The Dreamwalkers*	DC (Vol. 2)	A5
05275.6	Animated Series	*Albatross*		019
05371.3	Animated Series	*One of Our Planets Is Missing*		007
05373.4	Animated Series	*Yesteryear*		003
05392.4	Animated Series	*More Tribbles, More Troubles*		001
05419.4	Original Series	*Windows on a Lost World*	Pocket	065
05423.4	Original Series	*The Mark of Gideon*		072
05431.4	Original Series	*Spock's Brain*		061
05459.4	OS: New Voyages	*The Patient Parasites*	Bantam	002
05476.3	Original Series	*For the World is Hollow & I Have Touched the Sky*		065
05483.7	Animated Series	*The Lorelei Signal*		006
05499.9	Animated Series	*The Ambergris Element*		014
05501.2	Animated Series	*The Eye of the Beholder*		017
05521.3	Animated Series	*Beyond the Farthest Star*		004
05554.4	Animated Series	*The Infinite Vulcan*		002
05577.3	Animated Series	*The Terratin Incident*		016
05591.2	Animated Series	*Once Upon a Planet*		015
05630.7	Original Series	*Is There In Truth No Beauty?*		062

Stardate	Series	Story Title	Company	Number
05683.1	Animated Series	*The Jihad*		012
05693.2	Original Series	*Tholian Web*		064
05710.5	Original Series	*Wink of an Eye*		068
05718.3	Original Series	*Whom Gods Destroy*		071
05725.3	Original Series	*The Lights of Zetar*		073
05730.2	Original Series	*Let That Be Your Last Battlefield*		070
05784.2	Original Series	*Plato's Stepchildren*		067
05818.4	Original Series	*The Cloud Minders*		074
05832.3	Original Series	*The Way to Eden*		075
05843.7	Original Series	*Requiem for Methuselah*		076
05906.4	Original Series	*The Savage Curtain*		077
05928.5	Original Series	*Turnabout Intruder*		079
05943.7	Original Series	*All Our Yesterdays*		078
05960.2	Original Series	*Pawns & Symbols*	Pocket	026
05992.4	Original Series	*The Alone, Part I*	DC (Vol. 2)	062
05993.6M	Original Series	*The Alone, Part II*	DC (Vol. 2)	063
05996.5	Original Series	*The Final Voyage*	DC (Vol. 1)	A2
06063.4	Animated Series	*How Sharper Than a Serpent's Tooth*		022
06118.9	Original Series	*The Cry of the Onlies*	Pocket	046
06121.8	Original Series	*Deadlock*	DC (Vol. 2)	077
06132.8	Original Series	*Planet of Judgment*	Bantam	

A - Comic Book Annual   FB - Flashback in Comic Book   M - Made-up Stardate

Stardate	Series	Story Title	Company	Number
06188.4	Original Series	*Treck to Madworld*	Bantam	
06218.9	Original Series	*The Chosen, Part I*	DC (Vol. 2)	078
06221.4	Original Series	*The Chosen, Part II*	DC (Vol. 2)	079
06228.5	Original Series	*The Chosen, Part III*	DC (Vol. 2)	080
06276.6	Original Series	*Mudd's Angels*	Bantam	
06334.1	Animated Series	*The Pirates of Orion*		020
06451.3	Original Series	*Vulcan!*	Bantam	
06527.5	Original Series	*The Starless World*	Bantam	
06720.8	Original Series	*Spock, Messiah!*	Bantam	
06770.3	Animated Series	*The Counter-Clock Incident*		023
06827.3	Original Series	*Perry's Planet*	Bantam	
06834.5	OS: New Voyages	*Ni Var*	Bantam	001
06987.31	Original Series	*The Lost Years*	Pocket	
07006.4	Original Series	*Mindshadow*	Pocket	027
07403.6	Animated Series	*BEM*		018
07412.6	Feature Films	*The Motion Picture*		001
07502.9	Original Series	*World Without End*	Bantam	
07513.5	Original Series	*Crisis on Centaurus*	Pocket	028
07521.4	Untold Voyages	*Worlds Collide*	Marvel	002
07521.6	Original Series	*The Trellisane Confrontation*	Pocket	014
07685.3	Untold Voyages	*Past Imperfect*	Marvel	003
07815.3	Original Series	*Covenant of the Crown*	Pocket	004

Stardate	Series	Story Title	Company	Number
07823.6	Original Series	*Deep Domain*	Pocket	033
08036.2	Original Series	*Enemy unseen*	Pocket	051
08130.3	Feature Films	*Wrath of Khan*		002
08140.1	Original Series	*Retrospect*	DC (Vol. 1)	A3
08163.5	Original Series	*Mortal Gods*	DC (Vol. 1)	005
08201.3	Feature Films	*Search for Spock*		003
08261.1	Original Series	*Blaise of Glory*	DC Special	001
08263.5	Original Series	*The D'Artagnan Three*	DC (Vol. 1)	017
08390.0	Feature Films	*Voyage Home*		004
08454.1	Feature Films	*Final Frontier*		005
08475.3	Original Series	*Probe*	Pocket	
08490.7	Original Series	*...Gone*	DC (Vol. 2)	009
08495.6	Original Series	*The First Thing We Do...*	DC (Vol. 2)	010
08496.9M	Original Series	*Let's Kill All the Lawyers*	DC (Vol. 2)	011
08498.1	Original Series	*Trial & Error*	DC (Vol. 2)	012
08526.8	Original Series	*Time Crime, Part IV*	DC (Vol. 2)	056
08538.2	Original Series	*Target: Mudd!*	DC (Vol. 2)	024
08588.3	Original Series	*Veritas*	DC (Vol. 2)	030
08620.3	Original Series	*A Little Man-To-Man Talk*	DC (Vol. 2)	045
08668.2	Original Series	*Bait . . . And Switch*	DC (Vol. 2)	065
08673.9	Original Series	*Rivals, Part I*	DC (Vol. 2)	066

A - Comic Book Annual   FB - Flashback in Comic Book   M - Made-up Stardate

Stardate	Series	Story Title	Company	Number
08674.8	Original Series	*Rivals, Part II*	DC (Vol. 2)	067
08678.3	Original Series	*Rivals, Part III*	DC (Vol. 2)	068
08684.2	Original Series	*Door in the Cage*	DC (Vol. 2)	061
08685.1	Original Series	*A Wolf . . . In Cheap Clothing, Part I*	DC (Vol. 2)	069
08688.8	Original Series	*A Wolf . . . In Cheap Clothing, Part II*	DC (Vol. 2)	070
08690.3	Original Series	*A Wolf . . . In Cheap Clothing, Part III*	DC (Vol. 2)	071
08691.2	Original Series	*A Wolf . . . In Cheap Clothing, Part IV*	DC (Vol. 2)	072
08748.4	Original Series	*Renegade*	DC (Vol. 2)	051
08826.2	Original Series	*Epilogue: The Alone, Part II*	DC (Vol. 2)	063EP
08889.2M	Original Series	*Double Bind, Part I*	DC (Vol. 1)	024
08890.1	Original Series	*Double Bind, Part II*	DC (Vol. 1)	025
08914.6	Original Series	*A Little Adventure*	DC (Vol. 2)	042
09521.6	Feature Films	*Undiscovered Country*		006
09521.9	Early Voyages	*Futures, Part III*	Marvel	014
09522.0	Early Voyages	*Now and Then*	Marvel	015
09625.1	Original Series	*The Fearful Summons*	Pocket	074
41153.7	Next Generation	*Encounter at Farpoint*		101/102
41187.5	Next Generation	*Where No One Has Gone Before*	DC (Mini-Series)	001
41190.3	Next Generation	*Spirit in the Sky*	DC (Mini-Series)	002
41195.7	Next Generation	*Q Factor*	DC (Mini-Series)	003
41198.3	Next Generation	*Q's Day*	DC (Mini-Series)	004
41198.7	Next Generation	*Q Affects*	DC (Mini-Series)	005

Stardate	Series	Story Title	Company	Number
41199.3	Next Generation	*Here Today*	DC (Mini-Series)	006
41209.2	Next Generation	*The Naked Now*		103
41235.25	Next Generation	*Code of Honor*		104
41242.4	Next Generation	*Datalore*		114
41249.3	Next Generation	*Lonely Among Us*		108
41255.6	Next Generation	*Justice*		109
41263.1	Next Generation	*Where None Have Gone Before*		106
41294.5	Next Generation	*Haven*		105
41309.5	Next Generation	*Too Short a Season*		112
41365.9	Next Generation	*11001001*		116
41386.4	Next Generation	*The Last Outpost*		107
41416.2	Next Generation	*Coming of Age*		119
41463.9	Next Generation	*Home Soil*		117
41503.7	Next Generation	*Heart of Glory*		120
41506.6M	Next Generation	*Ghost Ship*	Pocket	001
41509.1	Next Generation	*When the Bough Breaks*		118
41554.4M	Next Generation	*The Peacekeepers*	Pocket	002
41590.5	Next Generation	*Hide and Q*		111
41594.2M	Next Generation	*Survivors*	Pocket	004
41597.3M	Next Generation	*Symbiosis*		123
41601.3	Next Generation	*Skin of Evil*		122

A - Comic Book Annual   **FB** - Flashback in Comic Book   **M** - Made-up Stardate

Stardate	Series	Story Title	Company	Number
41636.9	Next Generation	*Angel One*		115
41697.9	Next Generation	*We'll Always Have Paris*		124
41723.9	Next Generation	*The Battle*		110
41775.5	Next Generation	*Conspiracy*		125
41798.2	Next Generation	*Arsenal of Freedom*		121
41877.6M	Next Generation	*The Children of Hamlin*	Pocket	003
41986.0	Next Generation	*The Neutral Zone*		126
41997.7	Next Generation	*The Big Goodbye*		113
42073.1	Next Generation	*The Child*		127
42102.5	Next Generation	*Lifesigns*	DC	051
42142.3M	Next Generation	*Captain's Honor*	Pocket	008
42193.6	Next Generation	*Where Silence Has Lease*		128
42286.3	Next Generation	*Elementary, Dear Data*		129
42305.7	Next Generation	*Return to Raimon*	DC	001
42307.2	Next Generation	*Murder Most Foul*	DC	002
42360.0	Next Generation	*The Derelict*	DC	003
42361.8	Next Generation	*The Hero Factor*	DC	004
42372.5	Next Generation	*Imzadi*	Pocket Hardcover	002
42402.7	Next Generation	*The Outrageous Okona*		130
42411.3M	Next Generation	*Power Hungry*	Pocket	005
42422.5	Next Generation	*Power ⬚Hungry*	Pocket	006

Stardate	Series	Story Title	Company	Number
42437.5	Next Generation	*The Schizoid Man*		131
42477.2	Next Generation	*Loud as a Whisper*		132
42494.8	Next Generation	*Unnatural Selection*		133
42499.3M	Next Generation	*Strike Zone*	Pocket	005
42506.5	Next Generation	*A Matter of Honor*		134
42523.7	Next Generation	*The Measure of a Man*		135
42546.3M	Next Generation	*Metamorphosis*	Pocket Giant	001
42568.8	Next Generation	*The Dauphin*		136
42581.4M	Next Generation	*Masks*	Pocket	005
42609.1	Next Generation	*Contagion*		137
42625.4	Next Generation	*The Royale*		138
42679.2	Next Generation	*Time Squared*		139
42686.4	Next Generation	*The Icarus Factor*		140
42695.3	Next Generation	*Pen Pals*		141
42761.3	Next Generation	*Q Who?*		142
42779.1	Next Generation	*Samaritan Snare*		143
42823.2	Next Generation	*Up the Long Ladder*		144
42859.2	Next Generation	*Manhunt*		145
42901.3	Next Generation	*The Emissary*		146
42908.6	Next Generation	*A Call to Darkness*	Pocket	007
42923.4	Next Generation	*Peak Performance*		147

A - Comic Book Annual   FB - Flashback in Comic Book   M - Made-up Stardate

Stardate	Series	Story Title	Company	Number
42976.1	Next Generation	*Shades of Grey*		148
43009.4M	Next Generation	*Gulliver's Fugitives*	Pocket	011
43026.7M	Next Generation	*Ensigns of Command*		149
43068.7M	Next Generation	*A Rock and a Hard Place*	Pocket	010
43125.8	Next Generation	*Evolution*		150
43131.4	Next Generation	*Forbidden Fruit*	DC	018
43152.4	Next Generation	*The Survivors*		151
43173.5	Next Generation	*Who Watches the Watchers?*		152
43197.5	Next Generation	*Doomsday World*	Pocket	012
43198.7	Next Generation	*The Bonding*		153
43201.8	Next Generation	*Serafin's Survivors*	DC	005
43202.6	Next Generation	*Shadows in the Garden*	DC	006
43205.6	Next Generation	*Booby Trap*		154
43265.4	Next Generation	*The Pilot*	DC	007
43266.7	Next Generation	*The Battle Within*	DC	008
43268.1	Next Generation	*The Payoff*	DC	009
43269.1	Next Generation	*The Noise of Justice*	DC	010
43269.3	Next Generation	*The Imposter*	DC	011
43270.4	Next Generation	*Whoever Fights Monsters*	DC	012
43349.2	Next Generation	*The Enemy*		155
43385.6	Next Generation	*The Price*		156
43421.9	Next Generation	*The Vengeance Factor*		157

Stardate	Series	Story Title	Company	Number
43423.6	Next Generation	*The Hand of the Assassin*	DC	013
43429.1	Next Generation	*Exiles*	Pocket	014
43462.5	Next Generation	*The Defector*		158
43489.2	Next Generation	*The Hunted*		159
43510.7	Next Generation	*The High Ground*		160
43539.1	Next Generation	*Deja Q*		161
43610.4	Next Generation	*A Matter of Perspective*		162
43625.2	Next Generation	*Yesterday's Enterprise*		163
43657.0	Next Generation	*The Offspring*		164
43673.4M	Next Generation	*Fortune's Light*	Pocket	015
43685.2	Next Generation	*Sins of the Father*		165
43700.4M	Next Generation	*Reunion*	Pocket Hardcover	001
43714.1	Next Generation	*Allegiance*		166
43738.8	Next Generation	*The Gift*	DC Annual	001
43741.6M	Next Generation	*Eyes of the Beholders*	Pocket	013
43745.2	Next Generation	*Captain's Holiday*		167
43747.3	Next Generation	*Boogeymen*	Pocket	017
43779.3	Next Generation	*Tin Man*		168
43807.4	Next Generation	*Hollow Pursuits*		169
43810.7	Next Generation	*Holiday on Ice*	DC	014

A - Comic Book Annual   **FB** - Flashback in Comic Book   **M** - Made-up Stardate

Stardate	Series	Story Title	Company	Number
43811.1	Next Generation	*Prisoners of the Ferengi*	DC	015
43843.5M	Next Generation	*Q in Law*	Pocket	018
43872.2	Next Generation	*The Most Toys*		170
43878.1	Next Generation	*I Have Heard the Mermaids Singing*	DC	016
43887.2M	Next Generation	*The Weapon*	DC	017
43902.8M	Next Generation	*Honorbound*	DC	029
43917.4	Next Generation	*Sarek*		171
43920.6	Next Generation	*Federation*	Pocket Hardcover	
43925.4M	Next Generation	*Spartacus*	Pocket	020
43930.7	Next Generation	*Menage a Troi*		172
43957.2	Next Generation	*Transfigurations*		173
43989.1	Next Generation	*The Best of Both Worlds, Part I*		174
44001.4	Next Generation	*The Best of Both Worlds, Part II*		175
44012.3	Next Generation	*Family*		178
44085.7	Next Generation	*Brothers*		177
44143.7	Next Generation	*Suddenly Human*		176
44161.2	Next Generation	*Remember Me*		179
44215.2	Next Generation	*Legacy*		180
44246.3	Next Generation	*Reunion*		181
44261.6	Next Generation	*Contamination*	Pocket	016
44272.5M	Next Generation	*The Lesson*	DC	019

Stardate	Series	Story Title	Company	Number
44286.5	Next Generation	*Future Imperfect*		182
44290.4	Next Generation	*The Flight of the Albert Einstein*	DC	020
44295.6	Next Generation	*Mourning Star*	DC	021
44296.2	Next Generation	*Trapped!*	DC	022
44297.3M	Next Generation	*The Barrier*	DC	023
44298.2	Next Generation	*Homecoming*	DC	024
44307.3	Next Generation	*Final Mission*		183
44356.9	Next Generation	*The Loss*		184
44390.1	Next Generation	*Data's Day*		185
44395.7	TNG: Modala Imperative	*In Memory Yet Green...*	DC (Mini-Series)	001
44396.0	TNG: Modala Imperative	*Lies and Legends!*	DC (Mini-Series)	002
44397.7	TNG: Modala Imperative	*Prior Claim*	DC (Mini-Series)	003
44398.7	TNG: Modala Imperative	*Game, Set and Match*	DC (Mini-Series)	004
44429.6	Next Generation	*The Wounded*		186
44474.5	Next Generation	*Devil's Due*		187
44491.3M	Next Generation	*Vendetta*	Pocket Giant	002
44502.7	Next Generation	*Clues*		188
44562.9M	Next Generation	*Dark Mirror*	Pocket Hardcover	
44614.6	Next Generation	*Galaxy's Child*		190

A - Comic Book Annual   **FB** - Flashback in Comic Book   **M** - Made-up Stardate

Stardate	Series	Story Title	Company	Number
44624.3	Next Generation	*Thin Ice*	DC	A2
44628.7M	Next Generation	*First Contact*		189
44631.2	Next Generation	*Night Terrors*		191
44664.5	Next Generation	*Identity Crisis*		192
44685.2M	Next Generation	*Debtor's Planet*	Pocket	030
44704.2	Next Generation	*The Nth Degree*		193
44741.9	Next Generation	*QPid*		194
44769.2	Next Generation	*The Drumhead*		195
44805.3	Next Generation	*Half a Life*		196
44821.3	Next Generation	*The Host*		197
44839.2	Next Generation	*Imbalance*	Pocket	022
44885.5	Next Generation	*The Mind's Eye*		198
44932.3	Next Generation	*In Theory*		199
44995.3	Next Generation	*Redemption, Part I*		200
45020.4	Next Generation	*Redemption, Part II*		201
45047.2	Next Generation	*Darmok*		202
45076.3	Next Generation	*Ensign Ro*		203
45122.3	Next Generation	*Silicon Avatar*		204
45156.1	Next Generation	*Disaster*		205
45175.8M	Next Generation	*Sins of Commission*	Pocket	029
45195.7	Next Generation	*Perchance to Dream*	Pocket	019
45208.2	Next Generation	*The Game*		206

Stardate	Series	Story Title	Company	Number
45223.4	Next Generation	*Grounded*	Pocket	025
45233.1	Next Generation	*Unification, Part I*		208
45245.8	Next Generation	*Unification, Part II*		207
45265.3	Next Generation	*Wayward Son*	DC	025
45265.7	Next Generation	*Strangers in Strange Lands*	DC	026
45265.9	Next Generation	*City Life*	DC	027
45267.2M	Next Generation	*The Remembered One*	DC	028
45349.1	Next Generation	*A Matter of Time*		209
45376.3	Next Generation	*New Ground*		210
45397.3	Next Generation	*Hero Worship*		211
45429.3	Next Generation	*Violations*		212
45452.9M	Next Generation	*Chains of Command*	Pocket	021
45470.1	Next Generation	*The Masterpiece Society*		213
45482.6	Next Generation	*The Rift*	DC	030
45482.9	Next Generation	*Kingdom of the Damned*	DC	031
45494.2	Next Generation	*Conundrum*		214
45532.1M	Next Generation	*War Drums*	Pocket	023
45571.2	Next Generation	*Power Play*		215
45582.4M	Next Generation	*Wet Behind the Ears*	DC	032
45587.3	Next Generation	*Ethics*		216
45614.6	Next Generation	*The Outcast*		217

A - Comic Book Annual   FB - Flashback in Comic Book   M - Made-up Stardate

Stardate	Series	Story Title	Company	Number
45652.1	Next Generation	*Cause and Effect*		218
45703.9	Next Generation	*The First Duty*		219
45733.6	Next Generation	*Cost of Living*		220
45741.9	Next Generation	*Guises of the Mind*	Pocket	027
45761.3	Next Generation	*The Perfect Mate*		221
45838.4	Next Generation	*Shore Leave in Shanzibar*	DC	036
45843.2	Deep Space Nine	*Destiny*		461
45852.1	Next Generation	*Imaginary Friend*		222
45854.2	Next Generation	*I, Borg*		223
45873.3	Next Generation	*The Devil's Heart*	Pocket Hardcover	
45892.4	Next Generation	*The Next Phase*		224
45944.1	Next Generation	*The Inner Light*		225
45948.8	Next Generation	*The Broken Moon*	DC	A3
45959.1	Next Generation	*Time's Arrow, Part I*		226
46001.3	Next Generation	*Time's Arrow, Part II*		227
46041.1	Next Generation	*Realm of Fear*		228
46071.6	Next Generation	*Man of the People*		229
46125.3	Next Generation	*Relics*		230
46154.2	Next Generation	*Schisms*		231
46192.3	Next Generation	*True-Q*		232
46235.7	Next Generation	*Rascals*		233

Stardate	Series	Story Title	Company	Number
46253.3	Next Generation	*Bridges*	DC	039
46254.4	Next Generation	*Bone of Contention*	DC	040
46257.8	Deep Space Nine	*Stowaway*	Malibu	001
46271.5	Next Generation	*A Fistful of Datas*		234
46301.8	Next Generation	*Childish Things*	DC	045
46307.2	Next Generation	*The Quality of Life*		235
46318.6	Next Generation	*The Maze*	DC	046
46357.4	Next Generation	*Chain of Command, Part I*		236
46360.8	Next Generation	*Chain of Command, Part II*		237
46379.1	Deep Space Nine	*Emissary*		401/402
46421.5	Deep Space Nine	*A Man Alone*		403
46423.7	Deep Space Nine	*Babel*		405
46424.1	Next Generation	*Ship in a Bottle*		238
46461.3	Next Generation	*Aquiel*		239
46479.3	TNG: Shadowheart	*The Lion and the Lamb*	DC Mini-Series	001
46481.2M	TNG: Shadowheart	*Dealers in Darkness*	DC Mini-Series	002
46483.5M	TNG: Shadowheart	*My Brother's Keeper*	DC Mini-Series	003
46485.7M	TNG: Shadowheart	*The Prince of Madness*	DC Mini-Series	004
46519.1	Next Generation	*Face of the Enemy*		240
46531.2	Deep Space Nine	*Q-Less*		407

A - Comic Book Annual   FB - Flashback in Comic Book   M - Made-up Stardate

Stardate	Series	Story Title	Company	Number
46578.4	Next Generation	*Birthright, Part I*		242
46682.4	Next Generation	*Starship Mine*		244
46693.1	Next Generation	*Lessons*		245
46729.1	Deep Space Nine	*The Storyteller*		414
46731.5	Next Generation	*The Chase*		246
46759.2	Next Generation	*Birthright, Part II*		243
46759.5	Next Generation	*A House Divided*	DC	A4
46778.1	Next Generation	*Frame of Mind*		247
46830.1	Next Generation	*Suspicions*		248
46844.3	Deep Space Nine	*Progress*		415
46852.2	Next Generation	*Rightful Heir*		249
46853.2	Deep Space Nine	*If Wishes Were Horses*		416
46892.6	Next Generation	*The Romulan Strategem*	Pocket	035
46910.1	Deep Space Nine	*Dax*		408
46915.2	Next Generation	*Second Chances*		250
46922.3	Deep Space Nine	*Dramatis Personae*		418
46925.1	Deep Space Nine	*The Forsaken*		417
46944.2	Next Generation	*Timescape*		251
46982.1	Next Generation	*Descent, Part I*		252
47025.4	Next Generation	*Descent, Part II*		253
47135.2	Next Generation	*Gambit, Part I*		256
47146.2	Next Generation	*Dragon's Honor*	Pocket	038

Stardate	Series	Story Title	Company	Number
47160.1	Next Generation	*Gambit, Part II*		257
47177.2	Deep Space Nine	*Cardassians*		425
47182.1	Deep Space Nine	*Invasive Procedures*		424
47215.5	Next Generation	*Interface*		255
47225.7	Next Generation	*Phantasms*		258
47229.1	Deep Space Nine	*Melora*		426
47254.1	Next Generation	*Dark Page*		259
47268.4	Next Generation/ Deep Space Nine	*TNG/DS9*	DC Mini-Series	001
47269.1	Deep Space Nine/ Next Generation	*DS9/TNG*	Malibu Mini	001
47270.9	Deep Space Nine/ Next Generation	*DS9/TNG*	Malibu Mini	002
47272.1M	Next Generation/ Deep Space Nine	*TNG/DS9*	DC Mini-Series	002
47282.5	Deep Space Nine	*Necessary Evil*		428
47304.2	Next Generation	*Attached*		260
47310.2	Next Generation	*Force of Nature*		261
47329.4	Deep Space Nine	*Second Sight*		429
47391.2	Next Generation	*Parallels*		263
47391.7	Deep Space Nine	*The Alternate*		432
47410.2	Next Generation	*Inheritance*		262
47423.9	Next Generation	*Homeward*		265
47457.1	Next Generation	*The Pegasus*		264

A - Comic Book Annual   FB - Flashback in Comic Book   M - Made-up Stardate

Stardate	Series	Story Title	Company	Number
47511.3	Next Generation	*Foreign Foes*	Pocket	031
47566.7	Next Generation	*Lower Decks*		267
47573.1	Deep Space Nine	*Paradise*		435
47581.2	Deep Space Nine	*Whispers*		434
47603.3	Deep Space Nine	*Shadowplay*		436
47611.2	Next Generation	*Thine Own Self*		268
47615.2	Next Generation	*Masks*		269
47623.2	Next Generation	*Eye of the Beholder*		270
47653.2	Next Generation	*Genesis*		271
47751.2	Next Generation	*Journey's End*		272
47779.4	Next Generation	*Firstborn*		273
47821.2	Next Generation	*Requiem*	Pocket	032
47829.1	Next Generation	*Bloodlines*		274
47869.2	Next Generation	*Emergence*		275
47941.7	Next Generation	*Preemptive Strike*		276
47944.2	Deep Space Nine	*The Tribunal*		445
47961.2	TNG: Ill Wind		DC Mini-Series	002
47962.1	TNG: Ill Wind		DC Mini-Series	003
47962.6	TNG: Ill Wind		DC Mini-Series	003
47988.1	Next Generation	*All Good Things...*		277/278
48015.1	Next Generation	*Convergence, Part II*	DC	A6
48212.4	Deep Space Nine	*The Search, Part I*		447

Stardate	Series	Story Title	Company	Number
48213.6M	Deep Space Nine	*The Search, Part II*		448
48252.6	Next Generation	*War and Madness, Part II*	DC	072
48315.6	Voyager	*Caretaker*		101/102
48319.4	Next Generation	*Suspect*	DC	076
48423.2	Deep Space Nine	*Meridian*		454
48439.7	Voyager	*Parallax*		103
48467.3	Deep Space Nine	*Defiant*		455
48481.2	Deep Space Nine	*Past Tense, Part I*		457
48482.6M	Deep Space Nine	*Past Tense, Part II*		458
48498.4	Deep Space Nine	*Life Support*		459
48521.5	Deep Space Nine	*Heart of Stone*		460
48532.4	Voyager	*Phage*		105
48546.2	Voyager	*The Cloud*		106
48573.3	DS9: Maquis	*Soldier of Piece, Part I*	Malibu Mini	001
48575.6M	DS9: Maquis	*Soldier of Piece, Part II*	Malibu Mini	002
48577.4M	DS9: Maquis	*Soldier of Piece, Part III*	Malibu Mini	003
48579.4	Voyager	*Eye of the Needle*		107
48623.5	Voyager	*Emanations*		109
48632.4	Feature Films	*Generations*		007
48642.5	Voyager	*Prime Factors*		110
48658.2	Voyager	*State of Flux*		111

A - Comic Book Annual   **FB** - Flashback in Comic Book   **M** - Made-up Stardate

Stardate	Series	Story Title	Company	Number
48693.2	Voyager	*Heroes and Demons*		112
48734.2	Voyager	*Cathexis*		113
48784.2	Voyager	*Faces*		114
48832.1	Voyager	*Jetrel*		115
48846.5	Voyager	*Learning Curve*		116
48892.1	Voyager	*Projections*		117
48921.3	Voyager	*Elogium*		118
48959.1	Deep Space Nine	*The Adversary*		472
48975.1	Voyager	*The 37's*		120
48979.1	DS9: Maquis	*Soldier of Piece, Part III*	Malibu Mini	004
49005.3	Voyager	*Initiations*		121
49011.0	Voyager	*Non Sequitur*		122
49011.4	Deep Space Nine	*The Way of the Warrior*		473/474
49066.5	Deep Space Nine	*Hippocratic Oath*		475
49195.5	Deep Space Nine	*Rejoined*		478
49208.5	Voyager	*Maneuvers*		127
49263.5	Deep Space Nine	*Starship Down*		479
49301.2	Voyager	*Death Wish*		130
49337.4	Voyager	*Alliances*		131
49373.4	Voyager	*Threshold*		132
49447.0	Voyager	*Dreadnought*		134
49485.2	Voyager	*Investigations*		135

Stardate	Series	Story Title	Company	Number
49504.3	Voyager	*Lifesigns*		136
49548.7	Voyager	*Deadlock*		137
49556.2	Deep Space Nine	*Sons of Mogh*		487
49641.6	Voyager	*Homeostasis, The Conclusion*	Marvel	005
49655.2	Voyager	*Tuvix*		140
49665.3	Deep Space Nine	*Rules of Engagement*		490
49690.1	Voyager	*Resolutions*		141
49904.2	Deep Space Nine	*To the Death*		496
49924.6	Deep Space Nine	*Risk, Part I*	DC	006
49962.4	Deep Space Nine	*Broken Link*		498
50032.7	Voyager	*Basics, Part II*		146
50049.3	Deep Space Nine	*The Ship*		500
50063.2	Voyager	*Sacred Ground*		143
50074.3	Voyager	*False Profits*		144
50126.4	Voyager	*Flashback*		145
50156.2	Voyager	*The Chute*		147
50203.1	Voyager	*Remember*		148
50252.3	Voyager	*The Swarm*		149
50312.5	Voyager	*Future's End, Part II*		151
50348.1	Voyager	*Warlord*		152
50384.2	Voyager	*The Q and the Grey*		153

A - Comic Book Annual   **FB** - Flashback in Comic Book   **M** - Made-up Stardate

Stardate	Series	Story Title	Company	Number
50416.2	Deep Space Nine	*The Darkness and the Light*		509
50425.1	Voyager	*Macrocosm*		154
50444.1	Deep Space Nine	*Public Enemies, Private Lives Conclusion*	Marvel	009
50460.3	Voyager	*Alter Ego*		155
50485.2	Deep Space Nine	*For the Uniform*		511
50518.6	Voyager	*Coda*		158
50537.2	Voyager	*Blood Fever*		157
50564.2	Deep Space Nine	*By Inferno's Light*		513
50614.2	Voyager	*Unity*		159
50693.2	Voyager	*The Darkling*		161
50712.5	Deep Space Nine	*Ties of Blood and Water*		517
50732.4	Voyager	*Favorite Son*		162
50796.5	Voyager	*Cloud Walkers*	Marvel	013
50814.2	Deep Space Nine	*Children of Time*		520
50836.2	Voyager	*Real Life*		164
50893.5	Feature Films	*First Contact*		008
50912.4	Voyager	*Displaced*		166
50923.1	New Frontier	*Book One*	Pocket	002
50929.4	Deep Space Nine	*In the Cards*		523
50953.4	Voyager	*Worst Case Scenario*		167
50975.2	Deep Space Nine	*Call to Arms*		524
50984.3	Voyager	*Scorpion, Part I*		168

Stardate	Series	Story Title	Company	Number
51003.7	Voyager	*Scorpion, Part II*		169
51019.3	Voyager	*Survival of the Fittest, Part I*	Marvel	014
51019.6	Voyager	*Survival of the Fittest, Part II*	Marvel	015
51082.4	Voyager	*Nemesis*		171
51145.3	Deep Space Nine	*Behind the Lines*		528
51244.3	Voyager	*Scientific Method*		175
51247.5	Deep Space Nine	*You're Cordially Invited...*		531
51268.4	Voyager	*Year of Hell, Part I*		176
51367.2	Voyager	*Random Thoughts*		178
51386.4	Voyager	*Concerning Flight*		179
51408.6	Deep Space Nine	*Waltz*		535
51425.4	Voyager	*Year of Hell, Part II*		177
51449.2	Voyager	*Mortal Coil*		180
51474.2	Deep Space Nine	*One Little Ship*		537
51501.4	Voyager	*Hunters*		183
51597.2	Deep Space Nine	*Change of Heart*		540
51652.3	Voyager	*Prey*		184
51679.4	Voyager	*Retrospect*		184
51715.2	Voyager	*The Killing Game, Part II*		185
51721.3	Deep Space Nine	*In the Pale Moonlight*		543
51762.4	Voyager	*Vis a Vis*		188

A - Comic Book Annual　　　　**FB** - Flashback in Comic Book　　　　**M** - Made-up Stardate

Stardate	Series	Story Title	Company	Number
51781.2	Voyager	*The Omega Directive*		189
51813.4	Voyager	*Unforgettable*		190
51825.4	Deep Space Nine	*Valiant*		546
51929.3	Voyager	*One*		193
51948.3	Deep Space Nine	*The Sound of Her Voice*		549
51978.2	Voyager	*Hope and Fear*		194
52081.2	Voyager	*Night*		195
52136.4	Voyager	*In the Flesh*		198
52143.6	Voyager	*Timeless*		201
52152.6	Deep Space Nine	*Shadows and Symbols*		552
52179.4	Voyager	*Thirty Days*		202
52188.7	Voyager	*Infinite Regress*		203
52542.3	Voyager	*Bliss*		209
52576.2	Deep Space Nine	*Penumbra*		567
52586.3	Voyager	*Course: Oblivion*		213
52619.2	Voyager	*Dark Frontier*		211/212
52647.0	Voyager	*Someone to Watch Over Me*		216
52861.3	Deep Space Nine	*The Dogs of War*		574
53049.2	Voyager	*Survival Instinct*		222
53167.9	Voyager	*Dragon's Teeth*		227
53263.2	Voyager	*Riddles*		226
53292.7	Voyager	*One Small Step*		228

Stardate	Series	Story Title	Company	Number
53556.4	Voyager	*Virtuoso*		234

Have a Site You Think We Should Add?

Spotted a Change?

For review, e-mail details about the site (including its name and URL) to

`Trek_Changes@klingons.zzn.com`

Want to Find Out About
Other Titles in the
Incredible Internet Guide Series?

Visit us on the Web at

`www.brbpub.com/iig`